HERMENEUTIC COMMUNISM

INSURRECTIONS: *Critical Studies in Religion, Politics, and Culture*

INSURRECTIONS: *Critical Studies in Religion, Politics, and Culture*

Slavoj Žižek, Clayton Crockett, Creston Davis, Jeffrey W. Robbins, Editors

THE INTERSECTION OF RELIGION, POLITICS, AND CULTURE IS ONE OF THE MOST DISCUSSED AREAS IN THEORY TODAY. IT ALSO HAS THE DEEPEST AND MOST WIDE-RANGING IMPACT ON THE WORLD. INSURRECTIONS: CRITICAL STUDIES IN RELIGION, POLITICS, AND CULTURE WILL BRING THE TOOLS OF PHILOSOPHY AND CRITICAL THEORY TO THE POLITICAL IMPLICATIONS OF THE RELIGIOUS TURN. THE SERIES WILL ADDRESS A RANGE OF RELIGIOUS TRADITIONS AND POLITICAL VIEWPOINTS IN THE UNITED STATES, EUROPE, AND OTHER PARTS OF THE WORLD. WITHOUT ADVOCATING ANY SPECIFIC RELIGIOUS OR THEOLOGICAL STANCE, THE SERIES AIMS NONETHELESS TO BE FAITHFUL TO THE RADICAL EMANCIPATORY POTENTIAL OF RELIGION.

After the Death of God, John D. Caputo and Gianni Vattimo, edited by Jeffrey W. Robbins

The Politics of Postsecular Religion: Mourning Secular Futures, Ananda Abeysekara

Nietzsche and Levinas: "After the Death of a Certain God," edited by Jill Stauffer and Bettina Bergo

Strange Wonder: The Closure of Metaphysics and the Opening of Awe, Mary-Jane Rubenstein

Religion and the Specter of the West: Sikhism, India, Postcoloniality, and the Politics of Translation, Arvind Mandair

Plasticity at the Dusk of Writing: Dialectic, Destruction, Deconstruction, Catherine Malabou

Anatheism: Returning to God After God, Richard Kearney

Rage and Time: A Psychopolitical Investigation, Peter Sloterdijk

Radical Political Theology: Religion and Politics After Liberalism, Clayton Crockett

Radical Democracy and Political Theology, Jeffrey W. Robbins

Hegel and the Infinite: Religion, Politics, and Dialectic, edited by Slavoj Žižek, Clayton Crockett, and Creston Davis

What Does a Jew Want? On Binationalism and Other Specters, Udi Aloni

HERMENEUTIC COMMUNISM

FROM HEIDEGGER TO MARX

GIANNI VATTIMO ★ SANTIAGO ZABALA

Columbia University Press   NEW YORK

COLUMBIA UNIVERSITY PRESS

PUBLISHERS SINCE 1893

NEW YORK · CHICHESTER, WEST SUSSEX

Copyright © 2011 Columbia University Press

All rights reserved

Paperback edition, 2014

Library of Congress Cataloging-in-Publication Data

Vattimo, Gianni, 1936–

Hermeneutic communism : from Heidegger to Marx / Gianni Vattimo and Santiago Zabala.

p. cm. — (Insurrections)

Includes bibliographical references (p. 199) and index.

ISBN 978-0-231-15802-2 (cloth : alk. paper)—ISBN 978-0-231-15803-9 (pbk. : alk. paper)—

ISBN 978-0-231-52807-8 (e-book)

1. Communism—Philosophy.   2. Philosophy, Marxist.   3. Hermeneutics.   I. Zabala, Santiago,

1975–   II. Title.   III. Series.

HX73.V385 2011

335.401—dc22

2011008349

Columbia University Press books are printed on permanent and durable acid-free paper.

Printed in the United States of America

c 10 9 8 7 6 5 4 3 2 1

p10 9 8 7 6 5 4 3 2 1

Cover design: Change Jae Lee

Cover images: (top) Hwa Duck Hun, Neo-Spo Apartment Exterior, 180cm x 230 cm, 2008, C-print,
South Korea; (bottom) Marcus Bleasdale/VII/VII/Corbis, 2008, Caracas, Venezuela

References to Internet Web sites (URLs) were accurate at the time of writing. Neither the author nor
Columbia University Press is responsible for URLs that may have expired or changed since the
manuscript was prepared.

CONTENTS

ACKNOWLEDGMENTS

WE WORKED ON THIS BOOK BETWEEN THE REELECTION of President George W. Bush in 2004 and President Obama's decision to increase the soldiers deployed in Afghanistan in 2010. Although the material published here has never been released before, there are two books that have determined the production of this text: Gianni's *Ecce Comu: Come si diventa ciò che si era* (2007) and Santiago's *The Remains of Being: Hermeneutic Ontology After Metaphysics* (2009). In the former, Vattimo emphasized the political necessity of reevaluating communism; in the latter, Zabala insisted on the progressive nature of hermeneutics. *Hermeneutic Communism* can be considered a radical development of both.

This book would not have been written without the constant interest of our editor at Columbia University Press, Wendy Lochner. She has not only promoted the publication of the book but actually stimulated and supported our research over the past years. We are very fortunate to have her as editor and hope to continue to work with her in the future.

We are also very grateful to Michael Haskell for going through the whole manuscript and suggesting several corrections that improved the text. His help was crucial.

Finally, but not least, we are grateful to Pablo Cardoso, Manuel Cruz, Franca D'Agostini, Carmelo Dotolo, William Egginton, Robert Fellman, Daniel Gamper, Jean Grondin, Philip Larrey, Michael Marder, Ana Messuti, Richard Palmer, Mauro Piola, Richard Polt, Jeffrey W. Robbins, Robert Valgenti, and Ugo Ugazio for having helped us in different ways.

This book is dedicated to Castro, Chávez, Lula, and Morales.

HERMENEUTIC COMMUNISM

INTRODUCTION

FOR, MEANWHILE, IT HAS ALSO BEEN DEMANDED OF PHILOSOPHY THAT IT NO
LONGER BE SATISFIED WITH INTERPRETING THE WORLD AND ROVING ABOUT IN
ABSTRACT SPECULATIONS, BUT RATHER THAT WHAT REALLY MATTERS IS CHANGING
THE WORLD PRACTICALLY. BUT CHANGING THE WORLD IN THE MANNER INTENDED
REQUIRES BEFOREHAND THAT THINKING BE CHANGED, JUST AS A CHANGE OF
THINKING ALREADY UNDERLIES THE DEMAND WE HAVE MENTIONED. (CF. [275]
KARL MARX, *THE GERMAN IDEOLOGY*: "A. THESES ON FEUERBACH AD FEUERBACH, II":
"THE PHILOSOPHERS HAVE ONLY INTERPRETED THE WORLD IN VARIOUS WAYS; THE
POINT IS TO *CHANGE IT*.") BUT IN WHAT WAY IS THINKING SUPPOSED TO CHANGE
IF IT DOES NOT TAKE THE PATH INTO THAT WHICH IS WORTHY OF THOUGHT? NOW,
THE FACT THAT BEING PRESENTS ITSELF AS THAT WHICH IS WORTHY OF THOUGHT
IS NEITHER AN OPTIONAL PRESUPPOSITION NOR AN ARBITRARY INVENTION. IT
IS THE VERDICT OF A TRADITION THAT STILL GOVERNS US TODAY, AND THIS FAR
MORE DECISIVELY THAN ONE MIGHT CARE TO ADMIT.
—MARTIN HEIDEGGER, *KANT'S THESIS ABOUT BEING*, 1944

IF MARXIST PHILOSOPHERS UNTIL NOW HAVE FAILED
to change the world, it isn't because their political approach was wrong
but rather because it was framed within the metaphysical tradition.
Contrary to other thinkers of the twentieth century, Heidegger did not
propose a new philosophy capable of correcting metaphysics but instead indicated the difficulty of such pretentiousness. Only once we recognize how metaphysics cannot be overcome in the sense of *überwun-
den*, defeating and leaving at large, but only in the sense of *verwindung*,
that is, incorporating, twisting, or weakening, does it become possible
to change the world: "Overcoming is worthy only when we think about
incorporation."[1] This is why by weakening our objectivistic *forma mentis*
(which has always belonged to those in power), a productive postmetaphysical philosophy will not only surpass metaphysics but also favor its

1

discharge, that is, the weak who have become the vast majority of the population throughout the world. After all, no weak individual, group, or nation has ever believed that the world is in order the way it is or that there is a form of objective rationality that must be cherished, followed, and applied. While metaphysics or, which is the same, the politics of descriptions is the philosophy of the winners who wish to conserve the world as it is, the weak thought of hermeneutics becomes the thought of the weak in search of alternatives.

In this book, we do not claim that communism can be translated into a particular philosophical stance or hermeneutics into a political position but that both draw our attention to a current lack of emergency, that is, the increasing homologizing of the political, economic, and social structures of power. As the political alternative to the impositions of neoliberal capitalism and the philosophy of the interpretative nature of truth, communism and hermeneutics, more than revolutionary positions at the service of power, have become alternative responses for the losers of history, that is, the weak. The fact that communism is often presented as tyrannical and hermeneutics is reduced to pure nihilism by their critics is not an indication of their dangers but rather of their ineffectiveness for today's bearers of power. While the winners of history want the conservation of the world as it is, the losers demand a different interpretation, that is, hermeneutic communism. Contrary to many interpreters of Marx, who present themselves as "scientific socialists," this is a book by two "hermeneutic communists," that is, those who believe that politics cannot be founded on scientific and rational grounds but only on interpretation, history, and event. This is why, together with Richard Rorty, we also consider it a flaw that "the main thing contemporary academic Marxists inherit from Marx and Engels is the conviction that the quest for the cooperative commonwealth should be scientific rather than utopian, knowing rather than romantic."[2]

As we will show, hermeneutics contains all the utopian and romantic features that Rorty refers to because, contrary to the knowledge of science, it does not claim modern universality but rather postmodern particularism. But what brings together communism and hermeneutics? The answer: the dissolution of metaphysics, that is, the deconstruction of the objective claims of *truth, Being, and logocentrism, which* Nietzsche, Heidegger, and Derrida circumscribed in their philosophies. But if communism today represents an alternative to capitalism, it is not only because of its weakness as a political force in contemporary governments but also because of its theoretical weakness. With the triumph of capitalism, communism lost both effective power and all those metaphysical claims that characterized its original Marxist formulation as the *ideal of development, which inevitably also draws toward a logic of war. Today, it's just these ideals and logics that characterize and guide not only conservative governments but also those* reformist governments that are losing the support they had after the fall of the Berlin wall.

Communism and hermeneutics or, better, "hermeneutic communism" leaves aside both the *ideal of development* and also the general call for revolution. Unlike Alain Badiou, Antonio Negri, and other contemporary Marxist theorists, we do not believe that the twenty-first century calls for revolution because the forces of the politics of descriptions are too powerful, violent, and oppressive to be overcome through a parallel insurrection: only such a weak thought as hermeneutics can avoid violent ideological revolts and therefore defend the weak.[3] In our postmetaphysical condition, the defeated of history are left, as Slavoj Žižek critically noticed, only with "weak thought . . . a thought attentive to the rhizomatic texture of reality; we should no longer aim at all explaining systems and global emancipatory projects; the violent imposition of grand solutions should leave room for norms of specific resistance and intervention."[4] While communism motivates the resistance to capitalism's inequalities, hermeneutics intervenes, indicating the interpretative nature of truth.

Although the versions of "communism" and "hermeneutics" we will refer to go further than Marx and Heidegger intended, both can be found in the thought of each because of the project of emancipation from metaphysics they share. For example, that Heidegger commented on Marx's passage on interpretation, reproduced in this introduction's epigraph, shows both the possibility of a theory of interpretation in Marx's philosophy and also Heidegger's interest in allowing such a theory to find its place in Marx's thought. The adjective *hermeneutisch* (hermeneutic) appeared only once in Marx's works, the noun *hermeneutic* (hermeneutics) never appeared,[5] and in his *Theses on Feuerbach* he remarked, "the philosophers have only *interpreted* the world in various ways; the point is to *change* it." This does not mean, however, that Marx had no theory of interpretation. Contrary to the majority of Marx's classical interpreters, we do not believe he was discrediting hermeneutics with this statement but only evoking how, for interpretation to work, a change must occur. Unlike in description, for which reality must be imposed, interpretation instead must make a new contribution to reality. And what about the presence of communism in Heidegger's thought? He discredited communism, along with capitalism and democracy, not because of his early sympathies for Nazism but rather because of his need to overcome metaphysics. After all, Heidegger wrote during the period in which Soviet communism was enmeshed in the *ideal of development, that is, in its metaphysical realization against Western capitalist democracies and German National Socialism. The "other" thought and, therefore, politics that he evoked was not another metaphysical organization of beings but rather the thought of Being, that is, where Being's event becomes philosophy's groundless realm. If Marx emphasized the significance of keeping our feet anchored to the earth, it is Heidegger who indicated through the thought of Being how such earth is constantly moving and changing, constantly in conflict.* The task of philosophy today is not to describe such movement but rather to learn to interpret it productively. Perhaps the time has come, after the deconstruction of metaphysics, to rephrase Marx's statement in order to emphasize how "the philosophers have only *described* the world in various ways; the moment now has arrived to *interpret* it."

Although communism has often been applied to all the domains of society and hermeneutics has been restricted to a simple technique of interpretation, we will invert this account, restricting communism to its social function and emphasizing the philosophical essence of hermeneutics, which, as we said above, shares the same project of emancipation from metaphysics. This is why in this book we will not refer to historical Soviet communism nor to the contemporary Chinese model but rather to the present South American (democratically elected) communist governments, which are determined to defend the interests of their weakest citizens. We believe this is the region of the world that best represents the communism of the twenty-first century,[6] which, as Eric Hobsbawm said, must first and foremost be a

> critique of capitalism, critique of an unjust society that is developing its own contradictions; the ideal of a society with more equality, freedom, and fraternity; the passion of political action, the recognition of the necessity for common actions; the defense of the causes of the poorest and oppressed. This does not mean

anymore a social order such as the Soviet one, an economic order of total organization and collectivity: I believe this experiment failed. Communism as motivation is still valid, but not as
program.[7]

As we will see, the governments of Hugo Chávez in Venezuela, Evo Morales in Bolivia, and other Latin American politicians represent an alternative to capitalism and an effective defense of the weakest that no capitalist state can match.

Just as we will not refer to Soviet communism, neither will we refer
to hermeneutics as the traditional technique of interpretation that has
been applied to the discovery of the hidden meanings of biblical, juridical, or literary texts. Instead, we will treat hermeneutics as the whole
existence of the human being. This ontological essence of hermeneutics
was fully acknowledged at the beginning of the twentieth century by
Nietzsche, Heidegger, and Gadamer and has now become the common
language in contemporary philosophy, where not only has truth dissolved into its own interpretations but so too has philosophy.[8] While
descriptive impositions desire to acquire power by pretending to become identical with the object of knowledge, hermeneutics instead
struggles for conflicts of interpretations, that is, against the conservation of natural laws, values, and principles. Hermeneutics is not a conservative political position, as it has been presented until now, but a
progressive one, opposed to the objective state of affairs. This is why
Rorty, who, together with Jacques Derrida, has inspired this book,
could affirm that the "hermeneutical . . . attitude is in the intellectual
world what democracy is in the political world,"[9] in sum, the respect of
minorities, differences, and the weak. But who are the "weak"?

The weak are the discharge of capitalism, that is, of metaphysical realism, and they are what Heidegger called "Being"; Derrida, the "margins of philosophy"; and Walter Benjamin, "the tradition of the oppressed." These concepts reflect not only those disciplines that refuse to submit to science's rational development but also all the underdeveloped states, useless shareholders, and slums that represent more than three-quarters of the world population. The opponents of the weak are not the strong but the powerful, that is, the winners of history, whose philosophical voice speaks through people like John Searle, Francis Fukuyama, and Robert Kagan, for whom politics has become the completion of science's liberal ideal of objectivity. These winners consider themselves the bearers not only of "true" knowledge but also of "just" democratic procedures, economic systems, and humanitarian wars,[10] which are actually wars against the weak. We will confront this metaphysical realism philosophically (in chapter 1) and through its political and economic impositions (in chapter 2), which have been criticized by, among others, Naomi Klein, Ellen Meiksins Wood, and Joseph Stiglitz, whose investigations we refer to throughout the book. The alternative to the systems of framed democracies will be explored in the second part, where we will investigate the progressive political project of hermeneutics and the "weakened communism"[11] that is guiding South America.

In sum, what called us to write this book is the lack of emergency that reigns over the world now. The terrorist attacks of 9/11 and the 2008 economic crisis have led not to massive change but to an intensification of the politics that created these events in the first place. The fact that President Obama and his allies have strengthened the military and neoliberal agendas after these events calls for all thinkers not only to recognize this condition of lack of emergency but also, and most of all, to favor philosophical or political emergency, that is, to favor alternatives. As effective examples of emergency, alternative, and change, it should not be a surprise that South American communism and philosophical hermeneutics are constantly presented as perilous by the political and philosophical establishment: while neoliberal capitalism conserves its financial markets throughout the world for its convenience, metaphysical realism reigns over the academic philosophers, who submit philosophy to science. If change is really the goal of our Western antiglobalization protesters, there are political and philosophical alternatives that we hope this book will invite them to follow.

PART I

FRAMED DEMOCRACY

1. IMPOSING DESCRIPTIONS

THE TASK OF THE PHILOSOPHER IS TO GET THE PROBLEM INTO A PRECISE
ENOUGH FORM, TO STATE THE PROBLEM CAREFULLY ENOUGH, SO THAT IT ADMITS
OF A SCIENTIFIC RESOLUTION.

—JOHN SEARLE, *FREEDOM AND NEUROBIOLOGY* (2007)

ON WEDNESDAY, NOVEMBER 17, 2004, PRESIDENT GEORGE W.
Bush awarded the National Humanities Medal to, among others, John
Searle. In this beautiful ceremony at the White House, Searle was hon-
ored for his "efforts to deepen understanding of the human mind, for
using his writings to shape modern thought, defend reason and objectivity, and define debate about the nature of artificial intelligence."[1]
What is most interesting about the awarding of this prize is not that
Searle accepted it but rather what sort of philosophy is endorsed by a
president who had both just invaded a country contrary to the desires
of the majority of the world's population and restricted the fundamental civil rights of his own citizens. While Searle's justifications for accepting a prize from such a source might run from a need for national
recognition to a feeling of personal accomplishment, the prize itself is

appropriate to his philosophical position, which represents a politics of descriptions as the latest development at the service of power.

A politics of descriptions does not impose power in order to dominate as a philosophy; rather, it is functional for the continued existence of a society of dominion, which pursues truth in the form of imposition (violence), conservation (realism), and triumph (history). These metaphysically framed political systems hold that society must direct itself according to truth (the existing paradigm), that is, in favor of the strong against the weak. Only the strong determine truth, because they are the only ones that have the tools to know, practice, and impose it. Philosophers like Searle, just as Plato, Hegel, or Tarski, for example, do not want their philosophies to dominate, but in fact they help maintain a society in which they find themselves at ease—that is, in which they have become more or less conscious servants of the dominant political class. But what is most significant is not that philosophers have been serving the dominant political powers but that the need for dominion often results in metaphysical thought. Metaphysics is an aspect and a consequence of dominion, not its cause.

Although legislators, politicians, and ownership classes need all members of a society to follow their imposed paradigm, such paradigms cannot be sustained without the support of the intellectual community. If, among all the disciplines, the empirical sciences have maintained a central role within the structures of power, it is not because they manage to obtain better results but because they represent the greatest fulfillment of the essence of metaphysics. This essence consists in revealing the ultimate truthful context of the subject matter under analysis, which can vary from the intrinsically materialist nature of physical reality to the theological meaning of divine commands. Regardless of the subject matter, the search for objective truth came to condition not only these philosophers but also those different sectors of culture whose progress should not be measured objectively. Richard Rorty (who for the past thirty years fought against this objectivist tradition) indicated how the "Newtonian physical scientist," since the Enlightenment, became the "model of the intellectual" from whom social reforms were requested. But the problem with this intellectual is that he centered these reforms only around "objective knowledge of what humans beings are like—not knowledge of what Greeks or Frenchmen or Chinese are like, but of humanity as such."[2] As we can see, the search for universal truth became an imposition on individual differences and identities.

Derrida, following Nietzsche and Heidegger, indicates how this metaphysical nature of philosophy has not only structured knowledge in terms of established polarities (presence vs. absence, truth vs. error, mind vs. matter, good vs. evil, man vs. woman) but also produced a hierarchical order in a way that always favors the first term over the second. In sum, by determining Being as presence, Western philosophy has become a simple set of descriptions of the present state of affairs and automatically privileges terms of temporal, spatial, and unified presentness over their opposites. This is why Heidegger explained that "insofar as the *pure relationship* of the *I-think-unity* (basically a tautology) becomes the unconditioned relationship, the *present that is present to itself* becomes the measure for all beingness."[3] Although these sets of measurable descriptions took very different approaches throughout the history of philosophy (from the Platonic realm of pure forms, to Kant's transcendental conditions of experience, to Marx's inevitable movement of history), the philosopher was committed to considering Being always as a motionless, nonhistorical, and geometric object, operating just like the European sciences (which Husserl declared to be in crisis). In order to assure its progress within society, philosophy, through its metaphysical obsession with truth, dissolved into the sciences, that is, into the global organization of all beings within a predictable structure of causes and effects.

As we can see, especially since the Enlightenment, when the empirical sciences were given priority because of their access to Nature, philosophy became a scientific enterprise, leaving aside the wider realms from which philosophic problems arise. For this reason, prominent philosophers such as W. V. O. Quine can declare that "philosophy of science is philosophy enough,"[4] and now Searle, with other contemporary metaphysical philosophers, tries to submit philosophy to scientific methods or, as Rorty indicated, to "the secure path of science."[5] But by submitting thought to the secure path of science (or to truth in general), contemporary analytic and continental philosophies have fallen back into "realism," that is, into the simple analysis and conservation of facts in order to help scientific disciplines develop, which was already the main concern of the Enlightenment. However, in doing so, philosophy evades what has been one of its most important tasks: suggesting alternative, different, or innovative possibilities. *Philosophy is not a disengaged, contemplative, or neutral reception of objects but rather the practice of an interested, projected, and active possibility.* In this return to "reality," through the complete neutralization of differences, philosophy becomes not only conservative but also a servant of the strongest political power (in this case the American-style neoliberally framed democracies), which in turn maintains philosophy. It must have been for these reasons that Heidegger noticed, already in the early 1930s, how it did not take long for "'science' to realize that its 'liberal' essence and its 'ideal of objectivity' are not only compatible with the political-national 'orientation' but also indispensable to it. . . . The national 'organization' of science moves along the same lines as the 'American' " organization of science.[6]

Although many philosophers believe this critique (of the bond between the objectivist goals of the sciences and the prevailing political power or, which is the same, the foundation of politics on truth) only began with Heidegger, Kuhn, and Derrida, already at the beginning of the twentieth century Spengler, Popper, and others were sounding the alarm about the dangers that came from spreading Enlightenment-style scientific objectivism to all the disciplines. Classic texts such as Spengler's *The Decline of the West* (1918–1922), Popper's *The Open Society and Its Enemies* (1945), and even Arendt's *The Origins of Totalitarianism* (1951) were concerned with the rationalization of the world, a rationalization that we are witnessing today at a much more profound level. Although all these texts did accuse the Enlightenment, it was Adorno and Horkheimer, in their *Dialectic of Enlightenment* (1947), who explicitly stated that the "enlightenment is totalitarian" in order to indicate how the disastrous world wars of the twentieth century were rooted in its development.[7] But the most important feature of these classic alarms over the politics of descriptions is not a belief that objectivism is erroneous, fallible, or untrue but rather that it is unjust, in other words, a murderous attack on ethics, freedom, and democracy. The "total subordination of reason to metaphysical reality," declared Herbert Marcuse, "prepares the way for racist ideology."[8] It is not an accident that all these classic texts appeared at the same time that Claude Lévi-Strauss was producing his anthropological studies, that is, when encounters with different cultures provided a starting point for the theoretical decentralization of European civilization.

The goal of this first chapter is to remind the realistic strain of contemporary philosophy that Popper's, Adorno's, and Benjamin's alarms against scientific objectivism and realism were also directed against future metaphysical inclinations. We also seek to indicate the authoritarian political meaning of this realism into which philosophers such as Searle have fallen. Heidegger, who can be considered the first to demand an explicit return to the ontological nature of philosophy against scientific or phenomenological inquiries, was not only criticizing the oppressive objective impositions of truth seeking but also indicating what metaphysics left out: the forgotten Being. Against the majority of Heidegger's interpreters, we believe that this did not demand a deeper scientific search for the "object" of Being but rather a recollection of the oppressed history of metaphysics, what Derrida called "the margins of philosophy" and Benjamin "the tradition of the oppressed." It is in this forgotten, defeated, and different history that one can find the victims of the politics of descriptions—and probably also an emancipation from it. Also, it should not be considered an accident that most of these antiobjectivist authors (Popper, Benjamin, and Adorno) wrote these texts against Western rationality in exile, in other words, in a condition of exclusion and foreignness. But why are we able today to expose the history, reasons, and politics of the weak? Certainly not because we have found the appropriate representation of truth. Rather, after the deconstruction of metaphysics performed mainly by Heidegger and Derrida, it is no longer possible to impose truth without violence, that is, to force the rational results obtained by the dominating civilization.

The paradigmatic example of these politics of descriptions is represented not only by centuries of oppressive colonialism but also by the recent failure of the American capitalist system all over the world. While the economic and military consequences of metaphysically framed democracy will be examined in the second chapter,[9] we will now venture into three essential theoretical features of the politics of descriptions: the violence of truth, the conservative nature of realism, and the winner's history.

TRUTH'S VIOLENCE

In a discussion with the distinguished French analytical philosopher Pascal Engel on the uses of truth, Rorty showed how contemporary philosophy is divided not only between realist and antirealist conceptions of truth but most of all between those who argue over truth's realism or antirealism and those who try to avoid this metaphysical quarrel altogether.[10] While Engel was only interested in justifying his "minimal realism" theory of truth at all costs, Rorty tried to indicate that while both realist and antirealist theorists belong to the politics of descriptions (because even the antirealist imposes his description of truth's nonexistence), those who overcome such dualism belong to a post-metaphysical culture, that is, to a politics of interpretation (which we will study in chapter 3). But Rorty's most significant implications concern not the democratic opportunities that philosophy might gain from leaving aside the realist-versus-antirealist quarrel but rather the violent political consequences of the politics of descriptions. It must be for these reasons that Rorty, in a famous essay of 1985 entitled "Solidarity or Objectivity?" emphasized the centrality of truth in our philosophical tradition:

> The tradition in Western culture which centers around the notion of the search for Truth, a tradition which runs from the Greek philosophers through the Enlightenment, is the clearest example of the attempt to find a sense in one's existence by turning away from

solidarity to objectivity. The idea of Truth as something to be pursued for its own sake, not because it will be good for oneself, or for one's real or imaginary community, is the central theme of this tradition.[11]

While most philosophers would agree with Rorty that truth is the central theme of our tradition, not all of them will believe it is responsible for a turn away from solidarity. The origin of this dispute lies in the essence of truth, that is, in its pragmatic nature, without which it also loses its meaning. Truth is not only "violent," in that it turns away from solidarity, but it is "violence," because it can easily become an imposition on our own existence. Being "violent" might imply that it can also be peaceful, but truth instead often implies an imposed description whose acceptance is assumed. Violence is the political meaning of truth, because truth always implies a concluding constriction that varies from its definition in the Gospels ("The truth will make you free"), in Hegel ("Truth is the whole"), or more recently in Baudrillard ("The simulacrum is true"). Although these definitions of truth probably have our well-being at heart, they also pretend to impose themselves regardless of our different religious, existential, or social Being. Like the metaphysical philosophies mentioned earlier, these definitions of truth want to maintain the social order that they find themselves comfortable in, and they also claim to justify it.

Although truth, as the reflection of a given objective order, has always inspired ethical and moral ideals of life, these same ideals depended on truth's unity, that is, the unity of opinions in the true. While this unity has effectively become reality today because of the establishment of a global political system (which we call framed democracy), truth does not therefore cease being violent, because *claims of truth are also claims of political power.* But how does this violence take place in our global political culture? Principally through the use of dialogue as the "moralization of politics," that is, as the apparently peaceful exchange of opinions—but, as we all know, even Plato's exemplary dialogues aimed to conduct one of the two interlocutors (often the slave) to recognize the truth that the other already knew from the beginning. If truth claims are also always claims of political power, that is, violence, and if this same violence is nothing else than the "silencing" of other interlocutor through an apparent dialogue, truth and violence become interchangeable. Only the recognition of truth's violence will allow one to consider the implicit danger of those politics that claim to have an ultimate foundation, that is, politics founded on truth. As we will see, the foundation of truth through dialogue fixes thought within framed democracy: a conservative moralized order where the democratic is only what legally enters the order established by metaphysics.

The most successful definitions of truth within contemporary analytic and continental philosophy continue to belong to Husserl's phenomenological theory and Alfred Tarski's philosophy of language (in 1933, Tarski developed Aristotle's "correspondence theory of truth," expressed in medieval philosophy as *veritas est adaequatio rei et intellectus*). While many historians will have us believe that there is a substantial difference between the two theories from a semantic point of view, few have discussed the metaphysical implication that both theories share. Contrary to the majority of Tarski's interpreters, we believe that the quotation marks in his principle (" 'p' is True if and only if p")[12] are essential, because they indicate its pragmatic essence, in other words, for "whom" truth is significant. In sum: the position of *P* outside the quotation marks is always expressed, affirmed, and sustained by someone who needs it to be outside, hence, who is interested in imposing *P*.

Metaphysical philosophers would respond that this imposition, and therefore the exclusion of the quotation marks from the second P, is necessary in order for our "affirmations, actions, and thoughts" to distinguish themselves from *other* affirmations, actions, and thoughts. Without this opposition (between "P" and P), our opinions would be useless, they say, and therefore we need Tarski's principle to share our common experiences. But do we really need the opposition between "P" and P to share our common experiences? Can't there be a group satisfied with "P" without any interest in the apparent real P?

This opposition or difference has become evident thanks to Heidegger's analysis of truth, starting with *Being and Time*, where he distinguished Husserl's metaphysical approach from a different hermeneutic one. Truth for Husserl depends on the difference between the mere "intention" of the phenomenological Being and the matter "itself"—in other words, between the manner in which something appears and the manner in which it is "itself." This difference, just like Tarski's opposition between "P" and P, consists in identifying an entity or order precisely as it is in itself; that is, a proposition would be true only if it "refers" to things in a way that permits them to be seen as they are in themselves. But this "reference" is not very different from the pragmatic "imposition" we mention above, because its purpose is still to explain how something reveals itself (truth) in opposition to its concealing (false).

Against this metaphysical interpretation, Heidegger noticed how every statement, whether true or false, valid or invalid, good or evil, is always a derivative one, since the "apophantic as" is only possible within the "hermeneutic as." In other words, there is no "presuppositionless" apprehension of something presented to us that could be "objectified" by means of subjective predicative modalities. Prior to the predicative knowledge, which can also be expressed in Tarski sentences, humans beings already have a "preontological" or "pretheoretical" understanding of the Being of things that does not require a derivative one, as proposed by Husserl's or Tarski's theories. This is why in *Being and Time* Heidegger explained:

> The statement is not the primary "locus" of truth but the *other way around*: the statement as a mode of appropriation of discoveredness and as a way of being-in-the-world is based in discovering, or in the *disclosedness* of Dasein. The most primordial "truth" is the "locus" of the statement and the ontological condition of the possibility that statements can be true or false (discovering or covering over).[13]

While we will analyze Heidegger's specific ontological structure of human Being (Dasein) in chapter 3,[14] it is important to understand here how the truth of statements is not derivative because erroneous but rather because its roots refer back to the disclosedness of understanding that determines every linguistic or prelinguistic adequacy. It is a question not only of thematizing prelinguistic phenomena but of emphasizing the priority of thought over knowledge, Being over beings, and the "hermeneutic as" over the "apophantic as." While the "apophantic as" allows both truth and error, at the level of the "hermeneutic as" there is neither, since the "proposition is not the place of truth; truth is the place of the proposition."[15] As we can see, Heidegger did not expose this metaphysical understanding of truth because it is wrong; he exposed it for its superficiality, that is, against the metaphysical attempt to reduce the philosopher's task to attesting "how we experience truth" or that "there is actually truth" when in fact we find ourselves inevitably presupposing it. Puzzling over the correspondence between subject and object, we lose sight both of the world within which all things are given and of our own engagement as beings.

Truth, whether in Aristotle's, Tarski's, or Husserl's terms, shares the metaphysical structure that is at the origin of all Western logic, where Being is interpreted only as the presence of something present, that is, objectively. In this distinction, the subject and predicate—in other words, the relation between two terms where one refers to the other—not only represent the logical and verbal structure but also the imposition of this same structure. Heidegger named the difference between our relation to beings (truth) and our understanding of Being (disclosure) the "ontological difference," which allows us to recognize how within our metaphysical tradition "Being and truth 'are' equiprimordially."[16] As we can see, Heidegger's analysis of truth (like Popper's, Arendt's, and Adorno's alarms against scientific objective realism that we mentioned earlier) was meant to emphasize its violence, because truth is nothing other than the justification of Being, which, as we said, has always been understood as objective presence. It is also for this reason that Heidegger later declared that "to raise the question of *aletheia*, of unconcealment as such, is not the same as raising the question of truth,"[17] where distinctions can be imposed (presence of Being) and justified (truth as correspondence). This is why Ernst Tugendhat (and other distinguished interpreters of Heidegger such as Habermas and Apel) pointed out that Heidegger's conception of truth as *aletheia*, that is, the "event of unconcealment," renounces the distinction not only between true and false assertions "but also between good and evil actions."[18] What they pointed out is correct and also a confirmation of Heidegger's opposition to truth as violent imposition, which, as we said, justifies its descriptions. This is why within our "scientific global organization," "neutral world," or, which is the same, framed democracy any proposition, interpretation, or ethics that is not framed within the realm of truth (or its opposite, falsehood) is wrong, an alteration and disruption of the established order that must therefore be silenced. The philosophical disruption of the established order's philosophical hermeneutics (as we will see in chapter 3) is continually accused of relativism, nihilism, and even political anarchism, because instead of relying on truth descriptions, it is involved in interpretative "events of unconcealment." Only such a nontheoretical way of thinking as hermeneutics (the modern version of which began as a defense of the extramethodical truth of the human sciences against the natural sciences)[19] can do justice to these events that resist those claims of absolute truth able to guarantee "peaceful" coexistence, that is, framed democracies.

In sum, to distance ourselves from the "peaceful" neutrality of metaphysics, we must leave, discard, or cancel truth: *the end of truth is the beginning of democracy*.[20] If this were not the case, then the objective laws of economics or the outcomes of political dialogues would prevent the constant crises that are part of our lives. But as we well know, economic and political crises are not only constant but often also supported by these same laws and dialogues, since they depend on the metaphysical justification of objective descriptions, that is, of truth. It is here that dialogue becomes the best way to moralize politics, that is, to conserve framed democracy's interests, condition, and immunity. In order to demonstrate how these claims of truth are also claims of political power, it is necessary to look into Plato's dialogues, which still today represent the paradigmatic example of political morality.

The slaves in Plato's allegory of the cave could today be represented by the weak, that is, by those oppressed cultures, citizens, and states that are constantly called on to join Western civilization (also named the "Washington consensus," IMF, or United Nations). Just like Plato, the West believes that it holds truth, that is, the appropriate knowledge capable guiding the interest of all the other states. Although Plato probably thought his dialogues were in the slaves' best interest, the fact that he would also consider it necessary to "drag the slave away by force into the light of the sun" if he was not convinced (through the dialogue) implies that Plato himself was serving other interests. But which interests? The interests of truth, which belong to those who understand, know, and probably even created it in order to justify their objective presences. This is why in most of Plato's dialogues truth is not an outcome but is always presupposed by those who opportunely interrogate the others.

Although the slave in Plato's *Meno* might discover the geometric truth, he will not have "understood" it until he also submits to Plato's interrogation. Just as philosophy, in the epigraph from at the beginning of this chapter, must "[admit] of a scientific resolution,"[21] so must the slave "submit to Plato's truth." Both are examples of oppressive impositions of metaphysics, which demand a correspondence without which the dialogue or philosophy cannot take place. As we can see, Plato's dialogues, just like science, are the prelude to submission to truth or, which is the same, violence, because Plato, by assisting his interlocutors on their journey ("from the darkened cave to the divine light of the Good"), is still serving the existence of a society of dominion maintained by these same dialogues. Apart from the violence that truth imposes on the slave, another significant feature of Plato's allegory are the dangerous consequences that will come from knowing the truth. As Plato narrates, upon the slave's return from the journey the others not only mock him because he can no longer see in the darkness but also want to kill him for requesting that they follow him. They are afraid of the journey, that is, of truth, because it implies a certain violence that might not be worth it. As we can see, truth becomes violence not only for all those who do not accept leaving the cave but also for those who return (and have in the meantime become philosophers according to Plato's "philosopher-king" model) and now feel compelled to lead:

> Once [the philosophers] have seen the Good itself, using this as a pattern, each in his turn must order [*kosmein*] city, private men, and themselves for the rest of their lives. Now for the most part they spend their time in philosophy, but when a person's turn comes, he labors in politics and rules for the sake of the city, not as though he were doing what is fine, but that which is necessary.
>
> (*Rep.* 540a–b)

As we can see, the philosopher, according to Plato, must sustain the establishment. He cannot "work out Being for itself"[22] again for a different paradigm or propose other possibilities to the established organization but instead "must order," that is, impose, what "is necessary." As the promoter of dialogues, Plato does not want the established order to be disrupted, altered, or shocked by either those artists that he banned from the Republic or by the philosopher, who could also act this way. Banning mimetic art because it is a copy that does not have limitations and can therefore bewitch us is not very different from circumscribing philosophy to what is necessary. Such "necessity" is nothing other than the silencing of the other through dialogue, that is, an act of violence for the sake of conserving truth. This points at the difference between dialogues and conversations. Conversations, just like Heidegger's "event of unconcealment," represent the disruption of the order that dialogues protect, because in the conversational exchange truth is not presupposed but rather discarded from the beginning. If a conversation is never what we wanted to conduct but rather a situation in which we become involved as it develops, it represents the greatest enemy of the dialogue's order: an unannounced event.[23] While the concepts of "conversation" and "event" will be analyzed in chapter 3, its difference from the concept of dialogue should be kept in mind, as it indicates a possible shift from dialogue (that is, from the politics of descriptions or, which is the same, framed democracy) to "hermeneutic communism." While the inevitable conflict that takes place in a conversation refers to a latent anarchism, relativism, and weakness of thought, dialogue's impositions instead require a realism capable of conserving political order.

THE CONSERVATIVE NATURE OF REALISM

As we have seen, Plato and most of the philosophical tradition that followed him demanded that philosophy not only find truth but also conserve it. Dialogues, which once served as the moralization of politics, have also become the establishment's main concern during any crisis, alteration, or shock that might appear. Contemporary disputes over true and false assertions (whether philosophical, theological, or scientific) are the symptom of a politically conservative philosophical culture prepared to impose its order through violence. This, after all, is why Karl Popper in *The Open Society and Its Enemies* accused Plato, Hegel, and Marx of totalitarianism. This classic text was meant to demonstrate how the enemies of the open and democratic society are those philosophers who pretend to found politics on truth either through the "light outside the cave" (Plato), the "end of history" (Hegel), or the "emancipative consequences of the revolution" (Marx). Popper's text was severely attacked by Platonists, Hegelians, and Marxists to the point of becoming the least-studied text in the German master's enormous bibliography.

If political thought today for the most part still ignores this text, it is because of its attack on the notion of truth in politics. But what is most interesting is that this attack is not very different from Heidegger's, as we saw above; after all, both Popper's "open society" and Heidegger's "event of unconcealment" were directed against dialogue's implicit order, that is, against any attempt to found politics on truth. Although together with Popper there were several other "counter-Enlightenment" philosophers who warned against scientific-objective realism, as we said above, there seems to be a return in some sectors of contemporary philosophy (phenomenology and so-called analytical ontology) to a more radical realism. The most interesting feature of this return to realism is not only its expression of fear (and therefore its demand for security) but also the conservative nature it exposes through its desire for global unification.

Among the various causes of this return, the completion of metaphysics seems to us as the most plausible explanation, because it indicates how the dissolution of philosophy into the objective sciences has further submitted it to the service of the dominant political powers.[24] But if realism is simply the conservation of objective data that philosophy must recognize, politics submit to, and faith cherish, it can only triumph within a framed democracy, that is, where transformation and change are almost impossible. Dialogues exclude the very possibility of transformation, because they impose truth on any form of dissent from the prevailing scientific order, that is, the metaphysical foundation of democracy. This foundation, which leads philosophy to dissolve into scientific objectivism, has created contemporary framed democracy, where, as Heidegger explained, the "only emergency is the lack of emergency":

> The lack of emergency [*Not*] is the greatest where self-certainty has become unsurpassable, where everything is held to be calculable and, above all, where it is decided, without a preceding question, who we are and what we are to do—where knowing awareness has been lost without its ever actually having been established that the actual self-being happens by way of a grounding-beyond-oneself, which requires the grounding of the grounding-space and its time.[25]

In this condition of lacking of emergency (which we can also call "neutralization"), where Being has been finally replaced by beings, that is, by its technological global organization, philosophy seems forced both to impose its unification and to conserve the established dialogue. This is why Heidegger, in the passage above, finds emergency not only in metaphysics' domination of the world but also in "who we are and what we are to do," that is, in our freedom. *The emergency today is the completion of a condition of neutralization where "freedom" is only possible within the established dialogue.* While the goal of the metaphysical philosophers was to spread Enlightenment scientific objectivism to all the disciplines to assure a more efficient manipulation of external reality, their main task now has become to assure the conservation of established "dialogic realism" against any outsider, parasite, or foreign event. In this condition, only philosophy that can ensure the ontological structure of framed democracy (and all the factors that constitute it: truth, dialogue, institutions) will be rewarded both academically and socially.[26]

Among the many analytic and continental philosophers who directly or indirectly preserve such realism (and therefore also contrast freedom), John Searle has a particular place not only for his original position but also for his debate with Derrida's deconstructive thought.[27] While this debate expressed the fear, insecurity, and danger that realists like Searle see in anyone who questions the scientific dissolution of philosophy, the "social ontology"[28] that the American philosopher outlined exposes (indirectly) the "lack of emergency" emphasized by Heidegger, because it seeks total control through science's objectivistic impositions: Searle, as Barry Smith affirmed, "has defended all along a *basic* realism."[29]

A possible origin of Searle's realism, and therefore of his debate with Derrida, could be found in the dispute between Husserl and Heidegger when they collaborated on the article "Phenomenology" for the fourteenth edition of the *Encyclopaedia Britannica* (1929).[30] Contrary to many politically conditioned interpreters of Heidegger, the only reason why he put an end to his collaboration with Husserl was the metaphysical meaning that phenomenology had acquired for Husserl: the opportunity to dissolve philosophy in a series of regional ontologies. Heidegger could not accept such a dissolution, because it represented the attempt to develop the metaphysical dream that he was trying to overcome and that Husserl also abandoned a few years later.[31] In sum, while Searle radicalized Husserl's early phenomenological project of regional ontologies, Derrida developed Heidegger's fundamental ontology through deconstruction.

Having said this, it should not come as a surprise if in one of his latest books Searle affirms how "several of the standard phenomenological authors seem to me not too phenomenological, but rather not nearly phenomenological enough."[32] Searle is here referring to those philosophers (Heidegger, Hans Blumenberg, and many others) who aborted Husserl's early phenomenological project (to resolve philosophy in a series of regional ontologies) in order to emphasize its fundamental ontology. Among the followers of Husserl's early phenomenological project,[33] Adolf Reinach has a particular place in Searle's realism both because he anticipated John Austin's theory of speech acts and for his regional ontology of "social interactions."[34] Although Husserl and Reinach provided Searle with the appropriate phenomenological approach, the American philosopher managed to submit the realm of human freedom to a scientific political control where, as he says, the "extension of freedom and the extension of rationality are the same."[35] The political project behind Searle's realism is to emphasize, conserve, and control the "Western Rationalistic Tradition" (which is just another name for metaphysics), that is, those standards of objectivity, truth, and rationality that "are essential presuppositions of any sane philosophy."[36] But what is a sane philosophy?

For the American master, in order for a philosophy to be "sane," it must cooperate with empirical science and actually have a general *wissenschaftliche* approach. Such an approach can be achieved by submitting itself to such irrefutable facts as those "stated by the atomic theory of matter and the evolutionary theory of biology."[37] But why must philosophy submit itself exclusively to the latest discoveries of science? The response is simple: because "we live in a world of basic facts, as described by atomic physics, evolutionary biology, and neurobiology."[38] Contrary to what many might expect, Searle openly recognizes that our descriptions of facts change as we learn more through these same sciences; in other words, he recognizes the significance of Thomas Kuhn's theory of scientific-paradigm revolutions.[39] Nevertheless, he does not consider this to be an argument in favor of hermeneutics or relativism: quite the contrary. That our interpretations change is an argument against relativism, because the basic facts' "absolute existence does not by itself guarantee that at any point in our history we have accurately stated them. Facts don't change, but the extent of our knowledge does."[40] This is why Searle gives great significance to our dependence on facts:

> All of our lives, including all of our mental lives, are dependent on the basic facts. Given that, we have an interesting set of questions about how human beings are able to create a meaningful set of semantic, institutional, social, etc., facts out of the basic facts using their consciousness and intentionality. The institutional, social, and other similar facts, etc., have a relative existence. They exist only relative to human beings. But the basic facts do not in that way have a relative existence. They have an absolute existence. They are regardless of what we think.[41]

The most important feature of this passage is not Searle's insistence on the existence of basic facts but rather these other semantic, institutional, and social facts that, just like the basic facts, must be analyzed, systemized, and developed philosophically in order "to get at the basic structure that underlines all institutional reality."[42] But why is it so important to know this basic structure? Searle believes that this basic structure will allow political philosophy in the future to achieve better results because it will finally enable it to "proceed from a prior political ontology,"[43] that is, from science's basic facts. *External realism is the precondition for having theories.* In sum, institutional reality is a matter of collective impositions of what Searle calls "status functions," which are imposed on objects that cannot perform such functions because of their physical nature but demand a collective acknowledgment. But it is not only because of the "collective intentionality" and "assignment of the function" that the object has a certain status (e.g., being a policeman) and, with that, a function (protecting the public). In order for something to have a certain status and, with this status, a certain function, it must also have a "constitutive rule," that is, the possibility "to follow a set of rules, procedures or practices whereby we count certain things as having a certain status."[44]

We believe that the most important feature of Searle's conservative realism rests in his belief that institutional structures, such as government, money, and education, enable us to control our lives within these same structures, when in fact they limit our freedom. This control, according to Searle, should not only increase our power but also provide us with motivations (as "winners," as we will see in the next section) for acting within them. But these motivations are nothing else than Searle's desire to avoid conversions, that is, emergencies within our institutional realities.[45] This must be the reason that he considered it a positive factor that G. W. Bush received the status function of president in the 2000 presidential election regardless of the "fact" (note that this is also an "institutional fact") that many American citizens considered that he had obtained it illegitimately. But the "important thing," explains Searle, "for the structure of deontic power in the US is that with very few exceptions they continued to recognize his deontic powers."[46] As we can see, the priority of Searle's metaphysical realism is to conserve institutional facts in order to submit to power, even though in the end, "perhaps we will have to give up on certain features of our self conception, such as free will."[47]

Contrary to the majority of the interpreters of Searle's debate with Derrida that we mentioned earlier, which arose over Derrida's interpretation of John L. Austin's speech acts[48] (an interpretation that Searle considered not only "lacking in rigor" but also "confusing"),[49] we believe its essence was not linguistic but political. While Derrida's philosophy was primarily focused on overcoming the conservative nature of metaphysics because of the tensions it created against freedom, Searle instead was interested in conserving it against any external events, shocks, or foreign invaders. This is why it was among the French master's philosophical priorities always to pay attention, listen, and recollect such tensions instead of silencing them or, which is the same, submitting them to science, as Searle requested. Searle's inability to follow Derrida's response to his text[50]—where the French master not only ironically renamed Searle as "SARL" (which stands for "*Société à responsabilité limitée*")[51] but also titled his response "Limited Inc abc" (to indicate the "corporation" of the Western rationalistic tradition that the American philosopher defended through Austin)—lies in his vision of "sane" philosophy. As we said above, a "sane" philosophy for Searle must not only have a general *wissenschaftliche* approach but also defend the Western rationalistic tradition, which he circumscribes to followers of "Russell, Wittgenstein and Frege."[52] But by defending such tradition, as Derrida noted, Searle was also abusing the rights of the "other," that is, of other traditions, possibilities, and contexts that belong to our philosophical world. This, after all, is also the meaning of deconstruction: "not yielding to the occupying power, or to any kind of hegemony,"[53] in other words, "a way of reminding the other and reminding me, myself, of the limits of the power, of the mastery."[54]

Instead of summarizing the whole debate, which has already been done a number of times,[55] we are interested in briefly commenting on only one of the many political features that constitute it: Derrida's notion of "iterability." Iterability is the capacity of signs, texts, or words to be repeated in new situations, hence, grafted onto new contexts. A "context is never saturated," because, as Derrida argued, every

> sign, linguistic or nonlinguistic, spoken or written (in the usual sense of this opposition), as a small or large unity, can be *cited*, put between quotation marks; thereby it can break with every given context, and engender infinitely new contexts in an absolutely nonsaturable fashion. This does not suppose that the mark is valid outside its context, but on the contrary that there are only contexts without any center of absolute anchoring.[56]

As we can see, "iterability alters";[57] that is, when texts are inserted into new contexts, they continually produce new meanings that are both different from and similar to previous understandings. But what does this imply? Every sign, text, or word is not possible without what makes its repetitions possible; its constituents are never "really" fully present to themselves. Derrida names this infinite loss of constituents "dissemination," in order to indicate how communication, contrary to Austin, Searle, and most of the Western rationalistic tradition, is never a unified realm because its horizons flee the not wholly present elements of its constituents.

When Searle commented on Derrida's iterability argument, he indicated both what he believed to be its philosophical error (the incomprehension of the type/token distinction) and also the political concession this argument implies, that is, the loss of control. For Searle, the fact that an author loses "control of the meaning of the utterance" implies that "the whole system of distinctions, between sentence meaning and speaker meaning for example, is undermined or overthrown."[58] *Instead of losing control, philosophy should impose further status functions.*

In sum, this debate demonstrated how metaphysical realists are nothing other than servants of the political power, that is, an emergency drill against the "slightest difficulty, the slightest complication, the slightest transformation of the rules." This is why, Derrida continues, their task as "self-declared advocates of communication [is only to] denounce the absence of rules and confusion."[59]

It should not be a surprise that Searle is one of the most distinguished representatives of American analytical philosophy, which in the past decades has managed to take over most of the philosophy departments in the United States, marginalizing other philosophical positions to departments of comparative literature, political sciences, and religion. If prominent philosophers such as Gadamer, Derrida, Rorty, Habermas, Butler, or Žižek have primarily been unwelcome in these departments, it isn't because they are less "professional" than Searle, Strawson, Davidson, Dummett, Bouveresse, or Dennett but rather because they are less inclined to circumscribe philosophy to science. In sum, analytic philosophy, as the completion of scientific realism, legitimizes not only scientific enterprises but also the American government, which in part depends on such enterprises.[60] This is why, according to Derrida, analytic philosophy has an "imperialistic approach" interested in establishing a culture for a descriptive, static, and universal civilization where "no theoretical work, no literary work, no philosophical work, can receive worldwide legitimation without crossing the

[United] States, without being first legitimized in the States."[61] If "linguistic hegemony cannot be dissociated from the hegemony of a type of philosophy,"[62] it shouldn't be a surprise that metaphysical realism has predominantly developed in the United States, where science's latest developments take place and where philosophy has almost disappeared from the public realm.

Derrida might primarily be remembered for having fought against such realism rather than for the enormous effect his deconstructive thought had on literary studies. Together with Rorty, he helped us conceive of both analytical and continental philosophies not as the latest positions, movements, or divisions of contemporary philosophy but rather as the last gasps of the metaphysical dream: a neutralized moral world without freedom. But, as we know, such a dream goes on; that is, in order to conserve this state of neutralization or "lack of emergency," realist philosophers continue to defend truth against other possible philosophies and even against history in general, against any event that could compromise established impositions. Having said this, it should not be a surprise that in 1992 a group (which we could also call "SARL") of metaphysical philosophers led by a known supporter of Searle, Barry Smith,[63] attempted (without success) to convince Cambridge University to avoid honoring Derrida. In their letter, published by the *Times*, Smith and the others declared that the French master's assertions are "either false or trivial" and also that his "originality does not lend credence to the idea that he is a suitable candidate for an honorary degree."[64] By submitting this letter, these professors demonstrated their unfamiliarity with Derrida's writings and provided a clear example of the "winner's history," that is, a desire to avoid different positions or traditions and margins of philosophy, which might threaten the recognition of their own metaphysical brand.

THE WINNER'S HISTORY

Robert Kagan's *The Return of History and the End of Dreams* (2008) is a response to Francis Fukuyama's *The End of History and the Last Man* (1992) and also the latest attempt from the politics of descriptions to situate politics outside history. In order to complete its metaphysical project (after imposing truth and conserving realism), the politics of descriptions also needs to declare victory over those it has defeated, that is, those who do not accept the established framed democracy. The essence of such declarations, like Searle's realism, is conservative, because it intends to conquer any alteration that might question its instituted norms. Although Searle never declared realism's triumph over history, his ontological desire to dissolve philosophy into the sciences inevitably discards everything that does not submit to the Western rationalistic tradition, including different philosophies. But where does this discarding end? And against whom is this victory declared? In order to respond to these questions, it is necessary to individuate these self-declared winners and also the defeated. Our goal in this final section is to suggest how Heidegger's oblivion of Being in favor of beings can be identified with Benjamin's "tradition of the oppressed," that is, the weak. This discarded history reminds us that we are always within history and never above it (as Kagan and Fukuyama suggest), and it also reveals to us where a possible emancipation from framed democracy can take place.

As we mentioned at the beginning of this chapter, the desire for dominion often results in metaphysical thought, not the other way around. Metaphysical democracy is a system sustained by those who find themselves at ease within its order of facts, norms, and institutions. These are the winners, those who believe Being's presence is worthy not only of description but also of contemplation and conservation, since it guarantees their own condition. But such a condition inevitably also includes the defeated history, that is, the oblivion of "Being" and the "weak." While Being refers to Heidegger's oppressed history of metaphysics, the weak, that is, those who are not part of framed democracy's neoliberal capitalism, are a consequence of this same oblivion. In sum, just as Being was discarded in favor of beings, so are the weak oppressed in favor of the winners, that is, in favor of those who dominate within framed democracy's conservative moralized order.[65]

While we will comment on Kagan and Fukuyama's conservative analysis of our current political world in the next chapter, it is important to emphasize now how and why both authors situate politics outside history. The reason is straightforward: they represent the winner's version of history, that is, those who believe that history can be viewed from the standpoint of what Lyotard named "metanarratives."[66] But in order to stand in this view, history must have already become "all it can become," that is, accomplished its continuous rational unification with truth. Framed democracy has now become a metanarrative not only for these two prominent analysts but also for politics of descriptions in general, which must conserve the dominion achieved through science's global control. The desire to declare the end or return of history is bound up with framed democracy, that is, with an order that can legitimize or delegitimize not only history but also other political systems. This is why framed democracy is to Kagan and Fukuyama what basic facts are to Searle: the possibility to "proceed from a prior political ontology."[67] But as we have seen, this "prior political" ontology is just another way to demand that science not only guide philosophy but also dictate all the other domains of culture. While Kagan does not even bother to recognize the subordination of politics, history, or democracy to science, Fukuyama instead openly states how science also dictates history:

> The first way in which modern natural science produces historical change that is both directional and universal is through military competition. The universality of science provides the basis for the global unification of mankind in the first instance because of the prevalence of war and conflict in the international system. Modern natural science confers a decisive military advantage on those societies that can develop, produce, and deploy technology the most effectively, and the relative advantage conferred by technology increases as the rate of technological change accelerates. . . . The possibility of war is a great force for the rationalization of societies, and for the creation of uniform social structures across cultures.[68]

If, as Fukuyama explains, liberal democracy is "the most rational form of government, that is, the state that realizes most fully either rational desire or rational recognition,"[69] and if modern natural science manages to dictate history's directions through military dominion, it should not be a surprise that democracy and science have become indissoluble. And it is this indissolubility that situates framed democracy outside history, where its ideal of objectivity can finally be fulfilled. But now that science has effectively fulfilled in framed democracy its "liberal essence and its ideal of objectivity,"[70] Fukuyama is convinced that "there are no serious ideological competitors left to liberal democracy."[71] In other words, liberal democracy has triumphed over history. As we can see, history has become a synonym for "progress," that is, for improvements not only of different political systems but also of philosophies. *Framed democracy is the completion of history's development, realization, and improvement.* But one might now ask: what is the political goal of declaring the end of return of history?

Although framed democracy is not the first order to declare the return or end of history, as "heirs of prior conquerors"[77] it must continue to impose its victory over the defeated in such a way as to neutralize other possible disruptions of its achieved order. This is why within framed democracy, whatever and whoever refuse to submit to truth, dialogue, or the predictable structure of causes and effects constitute not only an "alteration of history" but also a potential danger, and they must be identified as such. These identifications will become necessary to control the defeated and also to continue to guide the rulers to achieve authority, maintain independence, and most of all, induce indifference toward the defeated. But how is it possible to overcome this winner's history? Is a different history required or just framed democracy's "other history"?

Contrary to many interpreters of Benjamin, we believe it is against this indifference toward the defeated (which has increased tremendously in recent decades) that he emphasized the significance of the "other" oppressed history of framed democracy. The German thinker indicated a substantial difference within Kagan and Fukuyama's commonly accepted historiography: on the one hand, the "history of the winners," which he also called "of the oppressors," and, on the other, that "of the defeated" or "oppressed." According to Benjamin, while the first has always been traditionally considered a "continuous" history, the second has been represented as "discontinuous," that is, entangled in disruptions, emergencies, and alterations. But if the second history is "discontinuous," it is not because it is wrong or irrational but rather because it is defeated and oppressed; in other words, it is a consequence of its oppressors, who are concerned in maintaining intact their rule and oppressive tradition. For this reason, Benjamin believed that whereas "the idea of the continuum levels everything off [*alles dem Erdboden gleichmacht*], the idea of the discontinuum is the basis of a genuine tradition,"[73] that is, of possible emancipations. But as an oppressed history, it encourages the defeated and weak to come forward and also urges framed democracy to suppress its indifference. But where does the defeated history take place, and what possibilities does it include?

As we can see, just as Benjamin's critique of the winner's history was not intended to discover the real continuity of history, neither was Heidegger's destruction of metaphysics concerned with discovering Being's truth. Instead, it sought to discover its political emancipation, that is, the realm within which freedom is effectively possible. This "other" history reveals unnoticed possibilities, projects, and rights that were set aside in favor of Western rationality, but, most of all, it reveals the "emergencies" of framed democracy: "The tradition of the oppressed teaches us that the 'state of emergency' in which we live is not the exception but the rule. We must attain to a conception of history that accords with this insight. Then we will clearly see that it is our task to bring about a real state of emergency, and this will improve our position in the struggle against Fascism."[74]

These emergencies take place outside the metaphysical descriptions of Being, that is, beyond the winner's history (of truth, dialogue, and realism), because they represent dangers that must constantly be suppressed. But, as potential dangers, they are also effective conditions for disruption, that is, of emancipation. As Benjamin argued, the commonly accepted historiography "misses those points at which the transmission breaks down and thus misses those jags and cracks [*Schroffen und Zacken*] which call a halt to those who wish to move beyond it."[75]

Although framed democracy has now achieved a condition of global control where, as we have seen with Heidegger, the "only emergency is the lack of emergency,"[76] it is still possible to disrupt this order through "events of unconcealment" that take place outside the metaphysical descriptions of Being. But what do they look like?

Heidegger, in order to escape the metaphysical violent oppression of truth that silences whatever does not submit to its logical and verbal structure (the defeated oppressed history), individuates in truth's "event of unconcealment" an alternative to its derivative scientific constitution. But contrary to many interpreters, we do not believe that he indicated such disclosedness only to demonstrate the limitations of the correspondence theory of truth. He also revealed the political possibilities of truth when established in this "historical" "event of unconcealment." Heidegger listed some examples where such establishments take place in his famous essay "The Origin of the Work of Art" (1936):

Truth happens only by establishing itself in the strife and space it itself opens up. . . . This happening is, in many different ways, historical. One essential way in which truth establishes itself in the being it has opened up is its setting-itself-into-the-work. Another way in which truth comes to presence is through the act which founds a state. Again, another way in which truth comes to shine is the proximity of that which is not simply a being but rather the being which is most being. Yet another way in which truth grounds itself is the essential sacrifice. A still further way in which truth comes to be is in the thinker questioning, which, as the thinking of being, names being in its question-worthiness [*Frag-würdigkeit*]. Science, by contrast, is not an original happening of truth but always the cultivation of a domain of truth that has already been opened.[77]

As we can see, these events are not different events but only historical events of "unconcealment" that open up a new space. In sum, only what takes place in the discarded metaphysical tradition of philosophy allows a possibility of emancipation from framed democracy—certainly not science, which represents its latest development. The "task of history [is] to take possession of the tradition of the oppressed,"[78] that is, to overcome its oppressions. After all, this is why Derrida exposed the "iterability" argument against Searle: not only to indicate other possibilities at the margins of traditional philosophy of language but also as a way out from the impositions of realism, that is, the winner's history.

2. ARMED CAPITALISM

BUT WHAT I AM SUGGESTING HERE IS THAT MILITARY EXCESSES ARE INSCRIBED
IN THE MISSION OF GLOBAL CAPITAL ITSELF, WITH OR WITHOUT AN EXTREMIST
ADMINISTRATION IN THE UNITED STATES.
—ELLEN MEIKSINS WOOD, *EMPIRE OF CAPITAL* (2005)

ALMOST THREE YEARS AFTER PRESIDENT BARAK OBAMA'S
election, these words by Ellen Meiksins Wood have been confirmed. In
spite of Obama's noble intentions, he not only increased military spending but also intensified the wars in the Middle East.[1] Also, the recent
economic crisis of 2008, like the terrorist attack of 9/11, instead of resulting in an actual change in financial and international relations, produced
an intensification of the existing U.S. dominance; that is, these events
demonstrated how within the system of metaphysically framed democracies, change is almost impossible. Against this interpretation, many
analysts believe that the election of a progressive politician (soon after
also a winner of the Nobel Peace Prize) in the most powerful country of
the world, combined with the 9/11 attacks and the economic crisis, are
actually indications that effective change is possible. Although these

three recent events could be interpreted as effective changes, they are easily explained by the status quo: Obama was always a member of the Washington elite establishment;[2] 9/11 was a response, albeit an unjustifiable response, to decades of Western military constraints in the Middle East;[3] and the economic crisis was created by the same financial speculations that sustain the consumer economy.[4] As we argued in the previous chapter, framed democracy has become the completion of science's liberal ideal of an objectivity able to avoid alterations, shocks, and disruptions; in this condition, Obama's political, economic, and military continuity with his predecessors was inevitable.

If Western capitalist democracies are excessively armed, as we believe, this is the case not only in order to conserve their dominion in the world but also because they no longer have any definite opponent. This is also why the world was a much safer place during the cold war, when there were two superpowers that restricted each other's influence, leaving very little space for unilateral interventions.[5] As Kagan puts it, "American power, unchecked by Soviet power, filled vacuums and attempted to establish, where possible, the kind of democratic free-market capitalist order that Americans preferred."[6] It was this new world order that led Fukuyama to announce the "end of history" in the early 1990s; by this he meant the end of different political, economic, and military systems. As the most successful model for developing societies, Fukuyama stated, "liberal democracies [will] manifest little distrust or interest in mutual domination."[7] Although Fukuyama has now recognized that the "problem, however, is getting economic development started in the first place,"[8] he still believes, together with many other political analysts, that history has ended, at least as far as "liberal democracy" being "the only legitimate form of government broadly accepted."[9]

Against this general optimism, Kagan recently pointed out how commercial ties alone cannot "withstand the forces of national and ideological competition that have now so prominently reemerged. Trade relations don't take place in a vacuum. They both influence and are influenced by geopolitical and ideological conflicts."[10] As we will see, these conflicts will become social conflicts more than geopolitical and ideological conflicts; that is, they will become struggles that take place within rather than between states. Nonetheless, Kagan is convinced that these conflicts demonstrate that we have now entered "an age of divergence,"[11] where "history has returned." This is why he suggests that the goal should be to "establish a global concert or league of democracies [that] could help bestow legitimacy on actions that democratic nations deem necessary."[12] In sum, Kagan does not think that the age of divergence was caused by the reluctance of some states to enter the global neoliberal system (as in South America) but rather that "nationalism" has reemerged, concurrent with the growth of the global economy, with all its dangerous consequences. The possible wars that Kagan foresees will take place between Western democracies and the autocracies of Russia, China, and the Islamist states, regardless of the fact that they are also involved and dependent on the global economy, that is, "responsible shareholders."[13]

Both Fukuyama and Kagan, who are among the establishment's most respected political scientists, have given an account of the current world order where democracy has prevailed over history and must conserve that victory. Against many interpreters of this debate, we do not believe Kagan was contradicting Fukuyama's thesis but confirming it. Kagan's call for a "league of democracies" to "legitimate" their interests against foreign states indicates his fear of change, that is, of the return of history. As we can see, more than in a debate over the end or return of history, Fukuyama and Kagan have engaged in an attempt to present framed democracy as the only legitimate and legitimizing force, regardless of the administration in the White House. What is most interesting about their argument is not the political scenario they present (at the service of framed democracy) but rather what they leave out, that is, what in the previous chapter we called defeated, weak, or other history.

As we mentioned in the previous chapter, the politics of descriptions, in order to impose and justify framed democracy, must eliminate everything that does not submit to its ordering of facts, norms, and institutions. Having said this, it should not be a surprise that Fukuyama and Kagan, together with other establishment intellectuals, forget, neglect, or ignore the oppression caused by neoliberal capitalism. And if they ignore such economic oppression, it is because they themselves sustain it: their condition is also an effect of such oppression. Just as Searle was indifferent to Derrida's arguments, so are Fukuyama and Kagan indifferent to the history of the oppressed, because the priority, in both cases, is always to submit to the scientific or democratic realm of metaphysics. It must be for this reason that when Derrida commented on Fukuyama's thesis in *Specters of Marx* (1993), a great deal of space was given to what he left out of his analysis:

> For it must be cried out, at a time when some have the audacity to neo-evangelize in the name of the ideal of a liberal democracy that has finally realized itself as the ideal of human history: never have violence, inequality, exclusion, famine, and thus economic oppression affected as many human beings in the history of the earth and of humanity. Instead of singing the advent of the ideal of liberal democracy and of the capitalist market in the eupho-

ria of the end of history, instead of celebrating the "end of ideologies" and the end of the great emancipatory discourses, let us
never neglect this obvious macroscopic fact, made up of innu-
merable singular sites of suffering: no degree of progress allows
one to ignore that never before, in absolute figures, have so many
men, women and children been subjugated, starved or extermi-
nated on the earth.[14]

The "inequality, exclusion, famine, and economic oppression" that
Fukuyama and Kagan leave out of their analysis represent framed democracy's effects and also its greatest threat. Although, since the fall of
the Soviet Union, democracies have expanded to the point of achieving
a condition of "lack of emergencies"—that is, of political, financial, and
social emergencies—it does not mean they are not ready for such
events. As we have seen in the past decades, the establishment of democratic free-market capitalist states was not only violent[15] but also ineffec-
tive, considering the dissatisfaction that most Western citizens declare
today.[16] These dissatisfactions have reached such levels that the institutions designed to detect social discontent are no longer limited to the
United Nations (International Labour Organization, World Trade Organization, or the Food and Agriculture Organization) but have expanded to states' ministries of defense. These ministries have been producing reports that not only confirm this situation but also prepare to
confront it. As Mike Davis explained in *Planet of Slums*, the Pentagon
war-fighting doctrine "is being reshaped accordingly to support a low-
intensity world war of unlimited duration against criminalized segments of the urban poor."[17] And Rear Admiral C. J. Parry (the director
general of a recent UK Ministry of Defense report) has indirectly explained why:

Differentials in material well-being will be more explicit through globalization and increased access to more readily and cheaply available telecommunications. Disparities in wealth and advantage will therefore become more obvious, with their associated grievances and resentments, even among the growing numbers of people who are likely to be materially more prosperous than their parents and grandparents. Absolute poverty and comparative disadvantage will fuel perceptions of injustice among those whose expectations are not met, increasing tension and instability, both within and between societies and resulting in expressions of violence such as disorder, criminality, terrorism and insurgency. They may also lead to the resurgence of not only anti-capitalist ideologies, possibly linked to religious, anarchist or nihilist movements, but also to populism and the revival of Marxism.[18]

Although reports from many other states also warn of a future rife with wars (over water, immigration, and infectious diseases),[19] the fact that "absolute poverty" and "comparative disadvantage" are now also considered threats for the security of framed democracies inevitably poses "other" alarms than the ones indicated by Fukuyama and Kagan. As we can see, the coming threats are not limited to Russia, China, and India, which, as Kagan explains, have become "responsible shareholders," but rather come from everyone who is not part of framed democracy's neoliberal capitalism. This is why we do not believe the next wars will primarily be against other states[20] but rather against those "useless shareholders," who, for the most part, are the weak, poor, and oppressed citizens, as highlighted in the defense reports. As we argue, the weak do not possess a different history but rather exist at history's margins; that is, they represent the discharge of capitalism and are present not only in the Third World but also in the slums of Western metropolises. These slums are not only becoming larger as we write but also are where the majority of the population is forced to live because of the concentration of capital. While in the West the slums are becoming battlegrounds, in some South American states, as we will see in chapter 4, they have become territories for social improvement through communist initiatives. In sum, the conflicts of the twenty-first century will not be caused by the return of history, as Fukuyama and Kagan predict, but rather by its own ends: liberal states.

The fact that framed democracy is already preparing to fight and win such urban wars indicates how within our democratic system change is almost impossible and also how the oppressive effects of capitalism are predicted to increase. As Meiksins Wood explained, whether "national or global, [capitalism] is driven by a certain systemic imperatives, the imperatives of competition, profit-maximization and accumulation, which inevitably require putting 'exchange-value' before 'use-value' and profit before people."[21] These are systemic imperatives of dominion, supremacy, and control over others, and they result in such metaphysical systems as liberalism, where the power of the individual becomes the only substance. Our goal in this chapter is to demonstrate how framed democracy's liberal, financial, and security measures regulate one another in order both to conserve our current "lack of emergencies" and to impose necessary emergencies.

THE IMPOSITIONS OF THE LIBERAL STATE

If the democracies' chief priority is to conserve what Heidegger called the "lack of emergencies," that is, the neutrality achieved through science's liberal essence, modern states still have an essential function, contrary to the opinion of many contemporary thinkers.[22] This function is not limited to the historical, racial, or linguistic identification of a state's citizens but extends to other states: "liberal states" are also "liberating states"; that is, they liberate other states from undemocratic regimes. The recent imposed liberalization of Iraq and Afghanistan (also called "state building") occurred under the orders of other liberal states and as a consequence of the essence of liberalism. It is also in the name of this essence that democracy is imposed today as the best system of government even when it becomes corrupt. As we mentioned in the previous chapter, the "liberal essence" of science consists in its ideal of objectivity, that is, establishing "truth" or "freedom" as only what legally enters within the established, recognized, and framed democratic order.

It must be for these reasons that Carl Schmitt viewed "liberalism as a coherent, all-embracing, metaphysical system"[23] and that Heidegger viewed it as another product, with fascism, capitalism, and communism, of subjectivist metaphysics.[24] This is why within metaphysically framed democracies liberalism avoids change: while democratic elections are procedures for possible change, liberalism is the realm within which such change presents itself through elections, finance, and institutions. Liberal electoral results represent humanity's unconditional self-legislation, in other words, the focus on "the I"[25] from which stems liberalism. But this vision from a pure "I," according to Heidegger, is impossible to achieve, because

there are no experiences that ever set man beyond himself into an unentered domain from within which man as he is up to now could become questionable. That is—namely, that self-security—

that innermost essence of "liberalism," which precisely for this reason has the appearance of being able to freely unfold and to subscribe to progress for all eternity. . . . Thus, it now took only a few years for "science" to realize that its "liberal" essence and its "ideal of objectivity" are not only compatible with the political-national "orientation" but also indispensable to it. And hence "science" as well as "worldview" must now unanimously agree that the talk of a "crisis" of science was actually only a prattle.[26]

As we saw in the previous chapter, such self-security is a consequence of the "unconditional relationship" of metaphysics, where "the *present that is present to itself* becomes the measure for all beingness."[27] This is why, as Richard Polt pointed out, "liberalism [for Heidegger] can go on 'progressing' forever precisely because its basis is static."[28] Having said this, if the liberal worldview, capitalism's systemic imperatives, and states' identification measures are unified by static desires of progress, control, and domination, they must also be unified in the fear of possible foreign shocks, disruptions, or emergencies, which Searle, Smith, Fukuyama, and Kagan express in their politics of descriptions.

If, in addition to Schmitt and Heidegger, contemporary thinkers such as Edgar Morin, Enrique Dussel, and Richard Sennett have also criticized liberalism, it is not because it defends individual liberties but, on the contrary, for its particular view of freedom, which has already decided who we are. It is on this basis that radical defenders of liberalism such as Robert Nozick promote the "minimal state," that is, a realm within which only "individuals have rights."[29] Such a minimal state is not very different from our framed democracies, as both are constituted in such a way as to avoid individual alterations and conserve their stability. A state "limited to the functions of protection against force, theft, fraud, enforcement of contracts, and so on," explains Nozick, "is justified; any more extensive state will violate person's rights."[30] It is also within this liberal realm that the political changes that occur in framed democracies such as Italy or the United States are relevant as a measure of liberty only against rubrics established by institutions in the same state that are charged with verifying such measures.[31] In Italy, parties lose their political identity as soon as they join coalitions (which have the only chance to govern); in the United States, the coalitions are the parties. Here "lack of emergency" is translated into a lack of alternatives before elections and a lack of opposition after them. This is not a consequence of the parties' radical positions but rather of the lack of positions created by liberalism's all-embracing system. If Nozick, together with most liberal individualists, endorses wide political coalitions or capitalism, it is not only because of their stability and ability to accumulate wealth but because the "logic of liberal individualism," as Eric Hobsbawm emphasizes, "is perfectly compatible with the free market."[32] But how does such compatibility arise in our globalized world?

A recent example can be found in the invasions of Iraq and Afghanistan in 2001 and 2003, where liberal states imposed their own "compatible" systems of market and government: neoliberal capitalism and democracy.[33] Even though there has been a significant change in the administration of the White House since the wars began, both countries are still occupied militarily, economically, and culturally by a number of liberal states under the guidance of NATO.

While the economic and strategic intentions behind the invasion of Iraq have been scrupulously investigated,[34] little consideration has been given to the "liberal" scientific and political justifications of the invasion. If, as we have analyzed above, science manages to realize its liberal essence of objectivity within a political state, then liberal states were indispensable to the objective presence of weapons of mass destruction upon which the war was launched. This is also why it never really mattered whether these weapons existed objectively; much more significant were the liberal states' self-righteous justifications to invade. As Chomsky reminds us:

> The United States and United Kingdom proclaimed the right to invade Iraq because it was developing weapons of mass destruction. That was the "single question" that justified invading Iraq, the president declared in a March 2003 press conference, a position stressed repeatedly by Blair, Bush, and their associates. Eliminating the threat of Iraq's WMD was also the sole basis on which Bush received congressional authorization to resort to force. The answer to the "single question" was given shortly after the invasion, as Washington reluctantly conceded. Scarcely missing a beat, the doctrinal system concocted new pretexts and justifications, which quickly became virtual dogma: the war was inspired by President Bush's noble visions of democracy, shared by his British colleague.[35]

This event demonstrated how the objective existence of WMD and the vision of democracy can be indistinguishably used to invade a country and also the interest they share in creating another liberal state where the liberal essence of science will also progress.[36] But as we have seen above, such progress is static; that is, it will transform Iraq into another liberal state capable in the future of imposing the same sort of invasions.[37] In sum, if we look into the changes that are planned for Iraq by the former head of the Coalition Provisional Authority, Paul Bremer, we will see that they all focus on "the I" from which stems liberalism.

His orders were all centered on the cardinal neoliberal "assumption that individual freedoms are guaranteed by freedom of the market and of trade,"[38] that is, a complete privatization of the state. Following these assumptions, one could easily envisage a full privatization of "public enterprises, full ownership rights by foreign firms of Iraq businesses, full repatriation of foreign profits . . . the opening of Iraq's banks to foreign control, national treatment for foreign companies, and the elimination of nearly all trade barriers."[39] As J. E. Stiglitz and L. J. Bilmes point out in their account of the cost of the war, this "privatization plan was part of the mantra of the Bush administration from the beginning."[40]

After hundreds of thousands of civilian causalities in Iraq alone,[41] Afghanistan[42] is also being forced to follow the same liberal imposition through President Obama's recent intensification of the 2001 invasion.[43] This intensification has been justified through the same logic of liberalism that supported Bush's original invasion of Iraq and Afghanistan: "a cause that could not be more just."[44] The president specified the reasons and goals of this "just cause" on March 27, 2009:

> Al Qaeda and its allies—the terrorists who planned and supported the 9/11 attacks—are in Pakistan and Afghanistan. . . . We are not in Afghanistan to control that country or to dictate its future. We are in Afghanistan to confront a common enemy that threatens the United States, our friends and our allies, and the people of Afghanistan and Pakistan who have suffered the most at the hands of violent extremists. So I want the American people to understand that we have a clear and focused goal: to disrupt, dismantle and defeat al Qaeda in Pakistan and Afghanistan, and to prevent their return to either country in the future. That's the goal that must be achieved. That is a cause that could not be more just.[45]

This justification inevitably implies liberalism's "self-security," that is, that "who" we are has already been decided. As we mention above, together with this decision comes the certainty of "what" there is, of the necessary measures that must be taken for the Afghan people. Having said this, liberal states will impose themselves wherever their own democratic frame is not present. But the presence of this democratic frame means not only the imposition of our systems but also the exclusion of the invaded state's cultural and political systems. *Instead of systems rising through democratic elections, democracy is framed within our own liberal system, which imposes elections.* These elections, both in Iraq and Afghanistan, have failed and have increased the population's suspicions of our frame. As Robert Fisk reminds us, although both the Iraqis and Afghanis wanted to vote for freedom, voting for freedom "is not necessarily the same as democracy," since "ethnically divided societies vote on ethnic lines."[46] This has been evident in both Iraq and Afghanistan, where the support of ethnic tribes is essential for electoral success, indicating, perhaps, that the country should be allowed to exercise "internal generated reforms," as Jamie Metzl and Christine Fair suggested, after serving as observers during the 2009 Afghan elections, instead of submitting to "the international community," which finances the government's "official corruption."[47]

As we can see, regardless of the fact that al Qaeda is still dangerous, the self-security of Obama's declarations is not very different from Bush's convictions regarding the existence of WMD in Iraq. Both follow the logic of liberal individualism, where self-certainty becomes the measure for action. Perhaps the most interesting feature of the presence of WMD in Iraq and of al Qaeda in Afghanistan and Pakistan is not their effective danger but rather the emergency they create for framed democracies by refusing to comply with these frames.[48] This alteration provided both presidents with alarming justifications to invade and intensify their presence in these states, obtaining not only popular support at home but also further economic and imperial control.[49]

Liberalism's self-security, that is, the decision of who we are, becomes the measure of liberal states. But these measures are violent for other states, as with Iraq and Afghanistan, and also for the liberal states themselves, which conserve at any cost the condition of lack of emergency. The 2008 world financial crisis indicated at what cost such a lack would be maintained.

CONSERVING FINANCIAL RECESSIONS

As Joseph Stiglitz explains, financial markets are supposed to assure "a more prosperous and stable economy as a result of good allocation of resources and better management of risk." In the financial crisis of 2008, however, "financial markets didn't manage risk, they created it."[50] The 2008 economic crisis demonstrated not only the extent to which states depend on financial markets but also their interest in the conservation of such a system, that is, their interest in a systemic lack of emergencies. Although the 2008 crisis seemed to be an emergency within framed democracies, it was actually used as an opportunity to preserve the financial system, at the cost of taxpayers. Given that distinguished economists such as Nouriel Roubini, Bradley R. Schiller, and Dean Baker predicted the crisis—while others sounded the alarm over the structural vulnerability of the financial system—this crisis most likely could have been avoided. But it was not, and neither were the violent policies of the International Monetary Fund prevented, which created much greater damage even than the 2008 crisis did. The continuity between the economic policies, strategies, and appointments of Bush and Obama also indicate that the priority is not to reform but rather to conserve the financial system.[51] Perhaps this is why, during the first G20 meeting in Pittsburgh, Obama dismissed the protesters as "generic opponents of capitalism" because they believe that the "free market is the source of all ills."[52] While the financial free markets might not be the "source of *all* ills," they are certainly responsible for the 2008 financial crisis and for the economic ills of the other 170 states not invited to the G20 summit.[53] The financial measures taken at this summit further enforced the policies of the IMF, already the cause of worsened economic conditions in many states, which have been forced to live under a condition of permanent recession.

In order to understand why the current financial economic system has been preserved, regardless of its responsibility for the 2008 crisis, it is first necessary to stress how capitalist imperatives (of competition, profit maximization, and accumulation) are bound together with the metaphysical nature of economics. It is in this context that Paul Krugman recently criticized those economists who "mistook beauty, clad in impressive-looking mathematics, for truth." By this Krugman means that most economists are

> seduced by the vision of a perfect, frictionless market system. If the profession is to redeem itself, it will have to reconcile itself with a less alluring vision—that of a market economy that has many virtues but that is also shot through with flaws and frictions. . . . When it comes to the all-too-human problem of recessions and depressions, economists need to abandon the neat but wrong solution of assuming that everyone is rational and markets work perfectly.[54]

This "seduction" is the result of the need for domination, and this often results in metaphysical thought, which, as we mentioned in chapter 1, worships truth, science, and the global organization of all beings within the predictable structure of causes and effects. Krugman believes that the greatest problem of the professional economists is not that most of them did not predict the 2008 crisis but rather the "profession's blindness to the very possibility of catastrophic failures in a market economy."[55] This blindness comes not only from the selfish interest of each economist in obtaining a powerful job within framed democracies but also from the submission of their discipline to the "secure path of science,"[56] where alternatives, changes, or shocks are impossible, given that "modern financial economics [has] everything under control."[57]

As we can see, this insistence on control or self-security is also a characteristic of John Searle's metaphysical realism, which is inclined not only to circumscribe philosophy to science but also to legitimize scientific political enterprises. It should not come as a surprise that among the followers of Searle is the economist Hernando De Soto, who sees in the rationality of free markets the capacity of self-regulation and also the potential to lift developing countries from poverty, by bringing them into this same free market.[58] But what is missing from this rational economy, in which capitalism becomes the motor that allows "sane" individuals to interact in "perfect" markets and where everyone who does not enter this scheme is destined to remain in poverty? First, what is missing is the recognition of limitations of human rationality, which may, among other consequences, lead to economic bubbles; second, the acknowledgment of the "imperfections of all financial markets"; and third, an understanding of the "dangers created when regulators don't believe in regulation."[59]

According to Krugman, it is just this belief in the power and rationality of free financial markets that "blinded many if not most economists to the emergence of the biggest financial bubble in history."[60] But the most disturbing factor is not that this crisis was not predicted—it was—but rather how the measures taken in its wake are actually worsening and prolonging the recession.

The current recession was created by the 2001 Internet bubble, the cost of the U.S.-led coalition invasion of Iraq, the 2008 housing bubble, and, most of all, by capitalist imperatives of competition, profit maximization, and accumulation, which inevitably guide the logic of liberal individualism that we mentioned earlier.[61] If banks, which grew to be "too big to fail," began to adopt incentive structures that were designed to induce excessively risky behavior, it is because they believed in the rational self-regulation of the market and also because the "regulatory authorities [mostly the Fed] allowed the financial markets (including the banks) to use the abundance of funds in ways that were not socially productive."[62] This is why Stiglitz believes the recession is not a crisis of the housing bubble but rather of our whole "economic and political system":

Each of the players was, to a large extent, doing what they thought they should do. The bankers were maximizing their incomes, given the rules of the game. The rules of the game said that they should use their political influence to get regulations and regulators that allowed them, and the corporations they headed, to walk away with as much money as they could. The politicians responded to the rules of the game: They had to raise money to get elected, and to do that, they had to please powerful and wealthy constituents.

There were economists who provided the politicians, the bankers, and the regulators with a convenient ideology: According to this ideology, the policies and practices that they were pursuing would supposedly benefit all.[63]

This ideology is nothing other than the conservative measures that all of these players (seduced by the financial-market ideology of perfection, rationality, and self-regulation) were already forced to adopt in order to succeed in the capitalist system. According to this system, government ought to be blamed not for doing too much but rather "for doing too little,"[64] that is, for limiting its encouragement of a deregulatory process that is supposed to "benefit all." But this deregulatory process contrasts sharply with framed democracies' effort to sustain an absence of emergencies, disruptions, and shocks.

If we look into the measures taken by both Bush and Obama, we see that the crisis was used as an opportunity to conserve the current financial system;[65] their response "has led to a consolidation of the big banks increasing the risk of surviving banks becoming 'too big to fail.' "[66] This is counterproductive, both because a bank that becomes "too big to fail" will inevitably affect other institutions (intensifying the interdependency of the global system) and because its survival will have to be guaranteed for the well-being of the whole system, regardless, as we have seen in this crisis, of its inevitable losses. This is why with the "bailout of AIG," as Stiglitz explains, "we have officially announced that any institution which is systematically significant will be bailed out."[67] The fact that the U.S. Treasury Department together with both Bush and Obama decided to spend billions to preserve the financial system indicates that we have become even more dependent on banks than we were before the crisis. Having said this, it should not come as a surprise if the IMF was reinforced by the G20, that is, by these same framed democracies interested in preserving the financial system.

Together with the World Bank and the U.S. Treasury, the IMF (all located in Washington, D.C.) both represents the so-called Washington Consensus and imposes its economic policies.[68] In exchange for economic assistance during the past decades, the IMF has forced developing countries to raise interest rates and to "reduce deficits by cutting expenditures and/or raising taxes. . . . This led to a weakening of national economies, when the point of IMF assistance was to strengthen them."[69] As Stiglitz points out, these policies significantly increased the recessions in which these countries already found themselves, forcing many to decline any assistance from the IMF. But why has the IMF, which was created to promote global economic stability, failed to perform the task for which it was designed? The reason lies in the IMF's

> focus on saving the Western creditors rather than on helping the countries in crisis and their people. There was money to bail out Western banks but not for minimal food subsidies for those on the brink of starvation. Countries that had turned to the IMF for guidance failed in sustained growth, while countries like China, which followed its own counsel, had enormous success. Deeper analysis exposed the role that particular IMF policies such as capital market liberalization had played in the failures.[70]

Although the IMF, especially after the G20 summits in 2009, now allows new economic powers such as China and India to determine its policies,[71] it still functions for the well-being of the conservative ideology Stiglitz mentions: the financial market ideology of perfection, rationality, and self-regulation.

If the G20's response to the 2008 crisis in developing countries relied principally on the IMF (tripling the resources available to it, to $750 billion), it was not only to maintain recessions in those countries but also to oppose the rising prominence of multinational funding in the developing world, which was becoming an effective alternative to the dominance of the G20 nations. As Baker indicates, the most "explicit alternative to the IMF is the Bank of the South that has been established with the support of most of the countries in Latin America. However there is also an East Asian bailout fund . . . and also China's own efforts to act as an IMF-like source of funds."[72] Although these new funds must also operate within the neoliberal global markets, that they have been established at all indicates the need for alternatives, that is, economic representations other than the IMF. While the economic policy of both the framed democracies and the IMF cannot be exclusively responsible for the current crisis and the level of poverty throughout the world, that the framed democracies and the IMF confirmed their neoliberal policies during the crisis indicates their interest in preserving this condition. But in order to maintain the neoliberal global economy, which inevitably increases the numbers of the discharge of capitalism (the population of the poor, weak, and oppressed), the framed democracies must reshape and expand their security measures.

FIGHTING THE WEAK

Framed democracies are interested in the conservation of their liberal impositions and financial system and in protecting this global condition against any change. While an "emergency" for framed democracies represents the possibility of change, "emergency" for the weak is precisely a "lack of emergency," that is, a lack of change, alteration, or modification of the current state of affairs. As we argued in the first chapter, the weak are the losers of history. They are those who instead of being framed within the scientific political organization of all beings (realism or, which is the same, the neoliberal system) are left at its margins. In this way, they represent Kagan's fear of the "return of history," Heidegger's unpredicted "event of unconcealment," and Benjamin's discontinuous "tradition of the oppressed." These marginal peoples occupy both those states (such as Iraq, Afghanistan, or Iran) that do not comply with liberal measures and the slums of the cities of the framed democracies; that is, they occupy those places where history continues, where events are unpredicted, and where the population is discontinuous. Framed democracies have begun to reshape their security measures not because the weak have started attacking them but, on the contrary, because they have not yet begun to attack. In order to understand why and how the Pentagon war-fighting doctrine is preparing for "low-intensity world wars of unlimited duration against criminalized segments of the urban poor,"[73] it is first necessary to indicate why, together with states, the urban poor may also be considered "weak."

As we argued earlier, Iraq was invaded because it became a threat to framed democracies; that is, it was outside the control of the neoliberal system. But among the many reasons it was "out of control" was its forced isolation from the liberal, cultural, and financial measures of framed democracies.[74] This precarious condition forced it to remain both economically inferior and incapable of becoming the real technological threat that Saddam Hussein's government wanted the West to believe it already was. But Iraq is not the only state to have been discarded; many other states in other regions of the world also faced similar impositions, becoming not only financially oppressed through the

IMF but also useless for the development of liberal science.[75] Although the chances that these states could become effective threats to neoliberal states are minimal, because of their precarious condition and the unequal balance of power, they still constitute emergencies for framed democracies, because they include elements that are not fully recognizable or controllable by those states. These useless, insignificant, weak elements represent both the discharge of framed democracies and the possibility of emancipation from its control. But more importantly, this weak condition does exist in both foreign states and also at the margins of framed democracies, in all those slums that have also become useless and insignificant. The weak populations in these slums have also become an emergency and a threat: they are closer than the disenfranchised populations of foreign states and, most of all, because their numbers have drastically increased in the last fifty years because of the social ineffectiveness of capitalism.

Just as Fukuyama and Kagan left the weak out of their debate because they were not "responsible shareholders" in the international political landscape, so do the GDP measurements exclude them because they do not reflect the capital growth of the state. If growth is to be sustainable, then inequality in the distribution of wealth should be an integral factor of GDP as an effective measure of economic growth.[76] But, as Stiglitz explained, market change in most states represents an increase in inequality; that is, as "bankers get much richer, average income can go up, even as most individuals' incomes are declining. So GDP per capita statistics may not reflect what is happening to most citizens."[77] Rising GDP figures ignore wealth inequalities, both creating the illusion of constant economic growth and, most of all, ejecting the weak from economic standards.[78] If the precarious condition of three-quarters of the world's population is related to the huge differences in income and wealth, which can be seen at international, national, and regional levels, then the GDP measures only the winners living in the framed democracies, that is, those who will always increase the GDP because of their established level of income and wealth.[79] The inequality between the "useful" contributors to the GDP and the weak has increased because of capitalism's systemic imperative of accumulation, and the gap now seems to deny any possibility of bringing the two groups together. The Italian sociologist Luciano Gallino recently estimated that the

inequality of income between the most well-off quintiles and the poorest quintile in the world's population is 90 to 1. If instead of the strata of the population we consider the 20 richest nations and the 20 poorest, the inequality rises to 120 to 1. The 20 richest men of the world possess wealth equal to that of the 1,000,000,000 poorest. In those countries where the per capita GPD appears uniformly well off, as in the United States and Italy, the inequalities of income and wealth, both real and financial, between the richest 10 percent of the population and the poorest 10 percent are evident and increasing. To achieve the same income as the top managers of the big industrial and financial enterprises in twelve months (considering incomes, bonuses, stock options), an Italian, French, British, or American worker with a gross income of 25,000 euros (equivalent to 23,000 pounds or 32,000 dollars in the 2008 exchange) would have to work between 400 and 1,000 years. In 1960 they would only have needed, more or less, 40 years.[80]

These inequalities demonstrate both the condition in which the majority of the population finds itself and the essential condition of the weak. The extreme low end of wealth distribution is not restricted to the informal-employment sector or citizens living in extreme poverty but includes "vulnerable employees." Although the ILO's *Global Employment Trends* report distinguished between the "working poor" and "vulnerable employees," both groups not only exist at the margins of framed democracies but also are at its "service," considering that the service sector has surpassed the agriculture sector as the world's most prevalent source of jobs.[81] This report also specifies that while the "working poor" numbered up to 1.4 billion in 2009, that is, 45 percent of the world's employees, when "vulnerable employees" are included, the level of endangered workers rises to 53 percent of the employed population.[82] What effect does this increasing poverty have on the security measures of framed democracies?

Among the many consequences of international, national, and regional economic impoverishment are overurbanization and the relocation of populations to the margins of framed democracies, that is, into urban slums. If these slums have mushroomed, it is not because the weak have overbred but, on the contrary, because of their "inclusion into the global economy."[83] Overurbanization, as Josef Gugler and Mike Davis explain, is not driven by the concentration of jobs, as neoliberals would have us believe (for example, in the service sector), but rather by the reproduction of poverty.[84] Considering that "half of humanity now lives in cities, and within two decades, nearly 60 per cent of the world's people will be urban dwellers,"[85] it should not come as a surprise if slum populations are growing by an overwhelming 25 million per year.[86] In this new "planet of slums," vulnerable employees are becoming an integral and essential component, along side of the urban poor.[87] Although these slums differ significantly across the world's cities, one common element is that their residents, the weak, are the necessary workforce (civil servants, laborers, and former peasants) for the neoliberal global economy both because of their low-cost services and because resources are not expended on their social security or health coverage. *Slums have become containers of indispensable specters for framed democracies.* Contrary to the traditional definitions, a slum is not only a run-down area of a city characterized by substandard housing, filth, and insecurity. It is also a population; it is a functioning social community beyond the controls of framed democracies. As Davis explains in *Planet of Slums*:

> Even within a single city, slum populations can support a bewildering variety of responses to structural neglect and deprivation, ranging from charismatic churches and prophetic cults to ethnic militias, street gangs, neoliberal NGOs, and revolutionary social movements. But if there is no monolithic subject or unilateral trend in the global slum, there are nonetheless myriad acts of resistance. Indeed, the future of human solidarity depends upon the militant refusal of the new urban poor to accept their terminal marginality within global capitalism. . . . The demonizing rhetorics of the various international "wars" on terrorism, drugs, and crime are so much semantic apartheid: they construct epistemological walls around *gecekondus*, *favelas*, and *chawls* that disable any honest debate about the daily violence of economic exclusion.[88]

These "epistemological walls" have been constructed not only to discourage debate and therefore increase indifference toward the weak but also out of fear of "myriad acts of resistance."[89] Just as Searle's fear of Derrida's philosophy grew out of the lack of control and information it implied, so do framed democracies fear the weak because they imply elements that are not fully present, recognizable, and, most of all, controllable. This is also why the wars in Iraq and other recent international conflicts have been preemptive, that is, launched in anticipation of possible alterations caused by this lack of control. Among the many consequences of these invasions, the "urban battles" of Sadr City (which is now one of the world's largest slums) and before that of Mogadishu have forced the Pentagon to venture "where most UN, WB, or departments of States types fear to go: down the road that logically follows from the abdication of urban reform."[90] While this was a real concern forty years ago during the cold war,[91] the only interest today is in developing adequate weapons[92] with which to fight the slum and its weak.

If military powers are now venturing into the urban discharge of capitalism, it is because the future of warfare lies in these city slums. "Our recent military history," declares Major Ralph Peters, "is punctuated with city names—Tuzla, Mogadishu, Los Angeles, Beirut, Panama City, Húe, Saigon, Santo Domingo—but these encounters have been but a prologue, with the real drama still to come."[93] After all, it should not come as a surprise if the various sophisticated systems of control now used as part of the militarization of many Western cities correspond to the ones used in occupied nations such as Iraq and Afghanistan.[94] *Fighting the weak is nothing else than confronting and containing any change, emergency, and emancipation from the impositions of the framed democracies.*

In sum, framed democracies are not afraid of these "myriad acts of resistance" as much as what they might lead to: "The resurgence of not only anti-capitalist ideologies, possibly linked to religious, anarchist or nihilist movements, but also to populism and the revival of Marxism."[95] This, as we will see in chapter 4, is what is happening in South America, where an alternative to neoliberal global control has began to take shape through democratic communist procedures. Having said this, it should not come as a surprise if the bulk of the discharge of capitalism, that is, slums and the weak, are in the southern hemisphere. But, as we mention above, if the weak, as in Derrida's philosophy, do not want to conserve this condition of "lack of emergencies," it isn't because it is untrue but rather because the absolute poverty, comparative disadvantage, and social constrictions it imposes over the majority of the population renders it *unfair*.

PART II

HERMENEUTIC COMMUNISM

3. INTERPRETATION AS ANARCHY

YES, I THINK THE HERMENEUTICAL OR GADAMERIAN ATTITUDE IS IN THE
INTELLECTUAL WORLD WHAT DEMOCRACY IS IN THE POLITICAL WORLD. THE TWO
CAN BE VIEWED AS ALTERNATIVE APPROPRIATIONS OF THE CHRISTIAN MESSAGE
THAT LOVE IS THE ONLY LAW.

—RICHARD RORTY, *THE FUTURE OF RELIGION* (2005)

THROUGHOUT THE HISTORY OF POLITICAL PHILOSOPHY,
interpretation and politics have been considered two separate domains.
Kant regarded interpretation as the social function that mediates between people and the sovereign, Hobbes conceived it as a subordination to the demands of the state, and Weber saw in politics and interpretation two exclusively different domains of culture.[1] While interpretation
became a central problem of philosophy, psychology, and science by
the beginning of the twentieth century, only recently have the political
consequences of hermeneutics begun to emerge. For example, in 1982
the interdisciplinary journal *Critical Inquiry* ran an issue entitled "Politics of Interpretation," inviting several distinguished scholars to discuss
the relation between politics and interpretation; a few years later, Stanley Rosen published *Hermeneutics as Politics*, Patrick Colm Hogan *The*

Politics of Interpretation, and Georgia Warnke *Justice and Interpretation.* Although these, together with other publications,[2] have further developed the relation between the interpreter and politics while producing insightful analyses of the political meaning of a reader's interpretation of a text, none has investigated the revolutionary political project that hermeneutics embodies. Our goal in this chapter is to outline not only the essence of this political project but also, and most of all, the emancipation it entails from the bearers of power.[3]

But why has such a politics of interpretation, that is, the political project of hermeneutics, not been explored systematically until now? The first explanation is social-historical: the modern masters of hermeneutics, Nietzsche, Heidegger, and Gadamer, were traditionally, culturally, and politically conservative. And the fact that the ontological dimension of hermeneutics was systematically investigated for the first time by Heidegger, who had been a member of the Nazi regime, must have induced many authors, such as Popper, Habermas, and others, to distance themselves from all the intuitions of the German thinker. Gadamer's hermeneutics met a similar fate: it was accused in 1971 by Habermas and his followers from the 1968 German student revolt of being too conservative. This accusation was rooted in the idea that hermeneutics relied too much on an uncritical acceptance of tradition. But this dependence cannot be employed without also criticizing existing practices; in other words, hermeneutics is more a "critical theory" than the work of the Frankfurt School, since it does not need to ground its critical function on metaphysical ideals, such as Habermas's communicative or Apel's transcendental conditions of rationality. Hermeneutics, as we will see in Luther and Freud, for example, is committed to overcoming institutionalized conventions, norms, and beliefs and certainly not to accepting existing practices. But for the generations of philosophers that had to come to terms with Germany's responsibilities after the end of the war, any allusion to figures such as Heidegger or Gadamer also implied an evaluation of their activities during the Nazi regime. Although we are not interested in justifying the political choices of Nietzsche, Heidegger, or Gadamer (because this would require other studies justifying David Hume's consideration of negroes being naturally inferior to whites, Gottlob Frege's declared anti-Semitism, or André Glucksmann's support of the 2003 invasion of Iraq), we would like to point out that while hermeneutics as a philosophical discipline would not have been possible without them, none of them developed its political dimensions, what we prefer to call its "political project."

By "political project" we do not mean that hermeneutics actually represents a political position that no one has yet explicated systematically, but rather that it is political in itself. If politics, as Hannah Arendt explained, is not exclusively conflicting assertions of truth, claims to recognition, and power relations but rather the action necessary to create a public realm in which individuals coexist freely while protecting the private space required for their personal development, then hermeneutics is also political. It relies on a plurality of individual developments, that is, active interpretations. A philosophy that relies on a plurality of interpretations must avoid not only any metaphysical claims to universal values, which would restrict personal developments, but also that passive, conservative nature that characterizes descriptive philosophies in favor of action. While these descriptive philosophies have always been concerned with regulating objectifying processes in order to impose them, hermeneutics instead is motivated by an active *techne*, that is, the opposite of *theoria* as conservation, neutralization, and violence. More than descriptive philosophies, interpretation often implies a call for emancipation, which is politically revolutionary; in other words, it is opposed to the objective state of affairs. This is why hermeneutics has always been the latent backbone of cultural revolutions against bearers of power, that is, the most productive movements against imposed truth. Although these movements are also always accused of being oppressive in that they try to impose their own agendas, it should be noted that there is an anarchic vein in hermeneutics that, as Reiner Schürmann explained, does not involve the absence of rules but of the unique universal rule. As the resistance to principles, conventions, and categories, anarchy is not the end of the political project of hermeneutics but its beginning.

Perhaps one of the main reasons that the political project of hermeneutics has at last become central is that politics is finally becoming aware of the end of metaphysics, that is, of the impracticality of adhering to, aspiring to, and promoting "objective truth," "universal values," and "ideological revolts." The end of metaphysics means the end of object-originated knowledge as the unique measure for truth. This understanding of truth is common not only to science, where the subject is valid only to the extent that it mirrors whatever is objective, but also for those politics of descriptions that violently impose certain systems. The 2003 invasion of Iraq in order to impose democracy and the 2008 bank bailout are the most recent paradigmatic examples of this politics of truth and also examples of its failure, that is, the failure of metaphysical politics. The dissolution of the politics of descriptions can also be found in the end of colonialism and in the rise of cultural anthropology: when cultural anthropology took shape as a discipline, it dissolved the myths of humanity's linear progress guided by the "more civilized" Western countries and allowed other interpretations to come forward. The end of metaphysics goes hand in hand with the end of modernity and the recognition of the interpretative nature of descriptions. In this postmodern condition, politics, instead of relating to truth, must be guided by the interplay of minority and majority, that is, by democratic consensus. This procedural democratic consensus is not very different from the essence of hermeneutics, that is, the contingent, free, and perilous nature of interpretation, which excludes any imposition of truth. This truth knowledge upon which a politics of descriptions stands is transformed in a politics of interpretation by the right of the weak to interpret. In sum, hermeneutics is the only philosophy that reflects the pluralism of postmodern societies, which, on the political level, is expressed in progressive communist democracies (as we will see in the next chapter), where achievements are not measured in relation to truth but rather in relation to others. But in order to systematically delineate its political project, we need to explore the work of the masters of hermeneutics (Dilthey, Nietzsche, Heidegger, and Gadamer), the origins of hermeneutics (Luther, Freud, and Kuhn), and its radical political developments (Schürmann, Lyotard, and Rorty), which together will lead to an understanding of the political emancipation for the "weak" that interpretation embodies.

THE ANARCHIC VEIN OF HERMENEUTICS

Some histories situate the creation of philosophical hermeneutics in the seventeenth century, when Johann Dannhauer introduced for the first time the Latin word "*hermeneutica*" as a necessary requirement for those sciences that relied on the interpretation of texts. Others proclaim that it was formed two centuries earlier by Flacius, in *Clavis scripturae sacrae*, or even centuries earlier by Aristotle, in his treatise *Peri hermeneias* (*De interpretatione*). While this might raise doubts that there is such a thing as an origin, history, or any unified development of hermeneutics, it also indicates the system's anarchic vein, that is, its opposition to established historical canons. But one of the few agreements that can be found among the historical accounts of hermeneutics is its practical action, in contrast to the conservative impositions that constitute the descriptive philosophies we explored in the first chapter.

This practical action directly refers to the discipline's origin in Hermes (whose name points back to his winged feet), the messenger of the gods renowned for his speed, athleticism, and swiftness and who exercised the practical activity of delivering the announcements, warnings, and prophecies of the gods of Olympus. This is why in Plato's *Ion* (534e) and *Symposium* (202e) hermeneutics is presented both as a theory of reception and "as a practice for transmission and mediation":[4] Hermes must transmit what is beyond human understanding in a form that human intelligence can grasp. But in this transmission, Hermes was often accused of thievery, treachery, and even anarchy, because the messages were never accurate; in other words, his interpretations always altered the original meanings. More than an error, this alteration is the real contribution of interpretation; unlike descriptions (which pursue the ideal of total explanation), interpretation adds new vitality to the meaning. For this reason, Dilthey (who was the first to trace systematically the history of hermeneutics) saw in the vitalist essence of hermeneutics the priority of interpretation over scientific inquiry, theoretical criticism, and literary construction.

While examples of hermeneutic alterations can be found throughout the historical record of hermeneutics (in Origen, Augustine, and Schleiermacher), there are three thinkers from different centuries whom we want to emphasize because in them the anarchic vein of the political project of interpretation is particularly evident: Martin Luther for fifteenth-century religion, Sigmund Freud for nineteenth-century psychology, and Thomas Kuhn for twentieth-century science.

Luther's hermeneutic operation was directed against the hegemony of the Catholic Church's magisterial establishment, which pretended to be the only valid interpreter of the biblical text. His *Ninety-Five Theses* (1517) and translation of the Bible into German (1534) provoked a general revolt against the papacy, because until then the ecclesiastical hierarchy had forced every believer to turn to its officials for readings, interpretations, and elucidations of the text. Against such spiritual, cultural, and political dominion Luther instead believed that the literal meaning of the Bible contained its own proper spiritual significance, which should be interpreted by each believer: the Bible is *per se certissima, apertissima, sui ipsius interpres, omnium omnia probans, indicans et illuminans*; that is, "it interprets itself."[5] In asserting this, Luther was valorizing both the linguistic text and one's own linguistic act, the interpreter's capacity to judge for himself. If, as Luther said, "Scripture is not understood, unless it is brought home, that is, experienced,"[6] then interpretation cannot be dictated from above and must be experienced from within. Interpretation, as we will see especially in Heidegger, is part of existence, because by bringing new vitality to the text (as with Hermes' alteration of original meaning), it also reinforces the interpreter's own faith.

For these reasons, Luther decided to translate the Bible, a translation that brought about a revolutionary political operation through hermeneutics, that is, from the vital nature of interpretation. He transformed it from a foreign book in a foreign tongue accessible only through an establishment imposed from above into a document open for all literate people's interpretation from within. After his translation (followed by other Protestant versions in French, Dutch, and English), the Bible could be read without the permission or intervention of the Catholic Church. With Luther's impact in Germany comparable to if not greater than that of Dante in Italy or Rousseau in France, Hegel could affirm that if Luther had done nothing besides this translation, he would still be one of the greatest benefactors of the German-speaking race. Although the traditions of the Church should not be put aside, since they are also an effect of the Bible's history, Luther should be recognized for his political action, that is, for depriving for the first time the Roman pontifex of his absolute authority over the Bible. By recognizing everyone's right and contribution to interpret for himself, Luther not only defended the weak but also exercised the latent anarchic nature of interpretation.

Just as Luther's hermeneutic operation began as a rejection of ecclesiastical imposition, so Freud's psychological revolution was set in motion in order to overcome the imposed facts of the positivist scientific culture of the early twentieth century. One of his chief targets was the empiricist theory of modern science, which conceived the human mind as a tabula rasa, a blank surface upon which impressions could be inscribed and from which descriptions could be made. This scientific understanding of the mind, common also to Descartes, presupposed certain moral values that were supposed to find a correlative in the social world the mind inhabited; in other words, objectivity prevailed over the subject, which was considered merely a mirror of nature. Against these common beliefs of modern science, Freud suggested that our actions are motivated not by pure, rational, and logical mechanisms but rather by many different unknown forces, motives, and impulses constantly clashing within and between our conscious and unconscious minds. For these reasons, familiar forms of irrationality such as self-deception, depression, ambivalence, or even weakness of the will, all of which were problematic in the Cartesian model of invisible unitary consciousness, became in Freud part of the normal manner of human beings. Freud anarchically transgressed the accepted line of demarcation between the "rational/normal" and the "irrational/abnormal" human being.

But Freud did not limit his discoveries to explaining the normality of the "abnormal," which by itself produced great progress for civilization. He also emphasized how the dynamically interchangeable relation between the two is the same as that of the human being and his society. In this structure, problems might emerge from oppressed instincts (imposed from above by society), from unconscious determinations (death or sexual drives upwelling from within), or from their objective interpretations, in other words, from the positivist psychologies of the time. These psychologies believed that a patient's sufferings came only from objective ignorance, in other words, from a lack of information about his or her own life. If this were actually true, then a better description of the patient's dreams would be enough to cure him. But the mind implies unconscious factors that not only determine the conscious ones but also reject the expression of certain ones. In this condition, interpretation is required to inform the patient of those memories he has repressed. Therefore, interpretation is the only available approach to the human mind and to those nonobjective, unconscious factors that demonstrate that the mind cannot be considered a tabula rasa. Against the traditional "dream book" mode of interpretation in terms of fixed symbols, Freud applied "free association," which obliged the patient (not the interpreter) to report hidden or forgotten thoughts. The emancipation that Freud brought about by stressing unconscious mental processes and the analysis of the human psyche through the vital exercise of interpretation spread irreversible doubts upon the objective formation of human rationality.

Against the rationalist psychologies of the time, in 1900 Freud published *The Interpretation of Dreams*, which recognized, among other things, how conscious, reflective meditation cannot be imposed on dreams because they are "the royal road to a knowledge of the unconscious."[7] This is a road that descriptive psychologies are incapable of traveling, because they limit themselves to present, consciously recalled expressions of the dream. Although Freud has not received enough recognition in the histories of hermeneutics, his project was really a development and radicalization of the previous psychological hermeneutics of Schleiermacher and Dilthey, who doubted that the author of a work would be able to reconstruct its meaning if informed of all the techniques used to produce it.[8] Just as a complete reconstruction of a patient's life would not necessarily solve his problems, nor would the history of the production of a work of art explain the meaning of the work to the author. As Habermas rightly noted, Freud goes beyond the art of interpretation insofar as his system of analysis must grasp "not only the meaning of a possible distorted text, but the *meaning of the text-distortion itself.*"[9]

Another author who used the anarchic vein of interpretation to free his field of research from objectivism is Thomas Kuhn. But unlike Luther and Freud, neither of whom defined their own work as "hermeneutical," Kuhn explicitly recognized in various autobiographical passages the fundamental effects that the philosophy of interpretation exercised over his innovative view of scientific revolutions. For this reason, Richard J. Bernstein saw in Kuhn one of the first examples of "the recovery of the hermeneutical dimension of science,"[10] that is, its interpretative nature.

When the American scientist published *The Structure of Scientific Revolutions* in 1962, logical empiricism's dominion over the philosophy of science was unquestionable. Scientific innovation could come only from an accumulation of knowledge, that is, as a closer approximation to the truth than any earlier theory achieved. But this normative orientation, by presupposing truth as the only common measure of scientific development, not only discredited the history of science but also considered it useless, because it just indicated past errors. For logical empiricism, these historical changes were nothing more than the account of uniform progress toward better science, but for Kuhn they were a confirmation that science is not uniform but shifts through different phases. But in these shifts, the sciences are not so much making "progress toward truth" as "changing paradigms"; in other words, older theories become different rather than incorrect. Kuhn explained this relation to previous scientific theories with his idea of "incommensurability," which he shared with Feyerabend: sciences driven by different paradigms do not share any common measures, because the standards of evaluation are themselves subjected to change. Incommensurability, then, is interpretation. If this were not the case, then ancient, medieval, and contemporary scientists would all have deduced the same results when looking at the moon. Instead, every epoch has brought about its own scientific progress through different, incommensurable paradigms.

Scientific progress for Kuhn is really an alternation between what he called "normal," "revolutionary," and "extraordinary" phases of science. While "normal science" is very much like puzzle solving, where success depends on whether the rules are strictly followed, "revolutionary science" instead involves the revision of these beliefs and methods, and this inevitably detaches it from normal science and shifts science into its "extraordinary" phase. This detachment (or revolution) takes place when a dominant paradigm is left behind and when universally recognized scientific achievements that for a long period of time provided the model of problems, methods, and solutions for a community of scientists reach a crisis. Such crises become evident when anomalies and discrepancies resist the expected solutions of normal scientific experiments, making progress impossible. In this condition, the very paradigm that has guided normal science until then is questioned, and when a rival paradigm emerges, "extraordinary science" is the result. But Kuhn does not consider this rival paradigm a mere substitution for the previous one, because at first it will only allow a certain amount of progress, which must still be accepted by the community of scientists. Kuhn calls this phase a "pre-paradigm," that is, a paradigm lacking the consensus the previously normal science could depend upon. But once a larger number of scientific communities begins to accept the new paradigm, collective progress will again be possible, making science ready for new puzzle solutions.

The conclusion that derives from Kuhn's hermeneutic intuitions is twofold: truth is not the main concern that drives scientific progress, and scientific knowledge does not change through confrontation with hard facts but through a social struggle between contending interpretations of scientific communities. Luther's revolt against the Roman pontifical authority and Freud's dismantling of traditional psychology's rational constitution of the mind are not very different from Kuhn's transgression against the dominion of logical empiricism over science's unilinear development. All are not only anarchic for resisting conventions, structures, and principles but also hermeneutic, because they presuppose the possibility of, project of, and right to interpret differently. It is just in this right to interpret differently that the weak emerge politically as bearers of new vitality. While this new vitality challenges the conservative norms of descriptive philosophies, it also becomes the project upon which Heidegger and Nietzsche define the human being's essence.

EXISTENCE IS INTERPRETATION

It is not a surprise that the standard bearers of hermeneutics we evoked in the previous section are also revolutionary figures. Each presented a new vision of the world and, most importantly, asserted that there could no longer be a single "vision of the world." This thesis was explicitly developed in Heidegger's essay "The Age of the World Picture" (1938), which concludes that today it is impossible to obtain a unitary, organized, and systematic image of the world because of the multiplication of special sciences, which does not allow any sort of unified vision.[11] The world of hermeneutics is not an "object" that can be observed from different points of view and that offers various interpretations; it is a world in continuous revolution. This is also why hermeneutics is an ontology, a theory of Being that thinks of the world only in terms of event, an event that does not reveal itself to the eyes of the human beings as a show because they are engaged as performers.

The first thinker to emphasize radically this condition was Nietzsche, in his famous thesis from his notebooks of 1883–1888:

Against positivism, which halts at phenomena—"There are only facts"—I would say: No, facts is precisely what there is not, only interpretations. We cannot establish any fact "in itself": perhaps it is folly to want to do such a thing. "Everything is subjective," you say; but even this is interpretation. The "subject" is not something given, it is something added and invented and projected behind what there is.—Finally, is it necessary to posit an interpreter behind the interpretation? Even this is invention, hypothesis.[12]

This passage and its distillation ("there are no facts, only interpretations, and this is also an interpretation") not only refer to a general problem of knowledge wherein nothing could be considered an objective fact, because even when we talk about facts we actually express interpretations, but they also assert that "facts" "do not exist," at least as external independent objects as an objectivist, scientific, or positivist mentality would imagine them. Or better, there are facts only if we comprehend them as events or happenings in the constitution of which we, as interpreters, contribute in a determined way. As we know, Nietzsche, far from organizing his philosophy into a clear and performable theoretical system, developed his hermeneutics essentially as a vitalistic thought. This choice was probably determined by his proximity to positivism and the inheritance of the Enlightenment, which induced him to see the world and man in terms of expression and the increase of vital forces. These vital forces conserve life by continuously overcoming the degrees it has achieved. In this world where there are no facts but only interpretations, life conserves itself not only by developing but also by destroying (or putting aside) what it has little by little produced, in order to construct new things. In this way, it also overcomes what came before. Nietzsche, who was also a historian of literature and culture, began to elaborate in his first major philosophical work, *The Birth of Tragedy* (1872),[13] the thesis according to which in order to create, one must also destroy.[14] Although this model of ontology remains constant throughout almost all of Nietzsche's work, he did move away from its providentialistic historicism, which considered the will to power as will to "progress" toward a state of perfection (which for him would be equivalent to death), and also from a biological conception of the will to power as a demand to empower man (*"der bisherige Mensch,"* "the man so far") in his "constitutive" capacities and faculties.[15]

But the most important feature of Nietzsche's intuitions is what we wish to call his "ontology of event," which not only anticipates but also clarifies *ante litteram* Heidegger's analysis of Being. In order for interpretation to make sense as the constitutive dimension of Being, it is necessary to understand Being as an event and not an object. This nihilistic meaning that Nietzsche grants to hermeneutics makes him a sort of *avant la lettre* interpreter of Heidegger's thought. Although many would object that this is a paradoxical thesis, it indicates the complex relation that Heidegger always had with Nietzsche's philosophy. Heidegger, overturning a consolidated tradition that regarded Nietzsche mainly as a political critic (Alfred Bäumler) and a biological thinker (Ludwig Klages), was the first to suggest considering him a metaphysical philosopher of the same dignity of Plato, Aristotle, or Hegel, with the difference being that he was writing as a metaphysical philosopher at the end of metaphysics. It is in just this way that Dilthey presented Nietzsche as a *"Lebens philosoph,"* a "philosopher of life," who practiced philosophy only as existential wisdom, because the great philosophical systems had declined.[16] Although Heidegger—who was always very close to Dilthey, from whom he inherited the comprehensive vision of the history of Western philosophy as the triumph and dissolution of metaphysics—considered Nietzsche from this perspective, he never explicitly accepted that the end of metaphysics could be Nietzschean nihilism, which he believed he had overcome. This is why we believe that the relation between Heidegger and Nietzsche is both complex and ambiguous: there is in Heidegger no real overcoming of Nietzsche's positions but rather a reading that twists and frees him from those positivistic and vitalistic remains so visible in the notion of will to power. In very synthetic terms: Heidegger and his theory of interpretation allow us to understand Nietzsche's hermeneutics; Nietzsche and his nihilism and ontology of event allow us to read Heidegger in a manner faithful to his theory of the ontological difference.[17] In sum, Nietzsche closes all the remaining metaphysical temptations that consider Being as something that is "out there."

Heidegger and Nietzsche, regardless of Heidegger's explicit attitude toward Nietzsche, are the guides we choose to outline the meaning of hermeneutics and its political implications. Hermeneutics, in the configuration it obtains through Nietzsche and Heidegger, becomes modernity's proper philosophy. It would not have been possible for Nietzsche to formulate such a statement as "there are no facts, only interpretations, and this is also an interpretation" without the expansion of the world horizon that had taken place as a consequence of geographic discoveries, intensified relations with other cultures through the imperialistic ventures of the West, and the historical-anthropological awareness that prevailed over most of the culture of the late 1800s. All this is expressed in Dilthey who, insisting on knowledge of the human sciences (particularly historiography), also constructed the basis of contemporary hermeneutics.

Historiographies have always tried to explore historical epochs with certain rigorous and objective pretensions to the reality of those in the world before us. But historiography became challenging precisely at the end of the 1800s mainly because of the expansion and multiplication of modernity's horizons, to which Dilthey and many other authors of the end of the century dedicated so much attention. It is also true that debates in the late 1800s over the human sciences (history and humanistic disciplines) in contrast to the natural sciences were inspired mainly by the need of historians and humanists to obtain a specific position in the academic world, which was becoming increasingly dominated by techno-scientific disciplines.[18] But the emphasis on the notion of "understanding" or "comprehension" as characteristic of the human sciences makes also more urgent the problem of the extraneity of objects, which belongs to so many products that these sciences study. It is just in this atmosphere that the centrality of interpretation matures as a philosophical problem. Even though human sciences must "understand," which implies a certain form of involvement, how can such involvement take place in "objects" as distant as those that ethnology and anthropology venture into?

The realm of human sciences—which also bear a strong "political" component because of the academic corporations they face (that is, the financial power of scientists, obtained through universities and private enterprises)[19]—becomes an essential aspect of the objectivity crisis. However one explains and characterizes hermeneutics (its historic and cultural components are various: from the dispute over readings of sacred texts with Luther to the Marxist notion of ideology), it is at the end of modernity that the crisis of (the notion of) objectivity is fully engaged. This crisis should not only be understood as the essential feature of the modern discourse but must also be considered the triumph of historicism: the real is not the object but rather history. But if the real is history, which cannot be thought as a determined external object, instead of responding to an act of knowledge it will only offer itself to interpretation. Luigi Pareyson—who, from an aesthetic thought, developed a general theory of interpretation—defined interpretation as the "form of knowing in which receptivity and activity are inseparable, and where the known is a form and the knower a person."[20] We should read this definition while thinking of Nietzsche's idea of the will to power (only if the subject does not pretend to disappear, the "object," the thing, reveals itself) and also of Heidegger's notion of interpretation as existence.

Although in *Being and Time* (1927) Heidegger defined human existence as a "thrown project," already in Kant the human subject was not considered a tabula rasa but rather said to encounter the world perceiving things within a priori frames: categories of space, time, and the intellect. According to Kant, man only knows phenomena, that is, what appears within those a priori schemes that constitute his own reason. In knowledge there is not only the object but also, and most of all, the subject. But Kant never called knowledge "interpretation," because he still thought that those a priori schemes with which the human being is equipped are fixed and identical at all times and for all men. Against Kant, we must observe that this character of stability belongs to phenomenal objects but cannot be attributed to the structure of the human subject. Between Kant and Heidegger there is also Kierkegaard and cultural anthropology, that is, the awareness of the inevitable finitude of human existence (which is not pure reason but involved interest, passion, and history) and the knowledge of different cultures. In sum, "thrown project" means for Heidegger that human existence is in the world not as pure reason but as an individual with interests, expectations, and cognitive instruments that he inherits from a world, culture, and language. He is an interpreter: someone who looks at things with interest. Only in this way will he avoid the appearance of things as an indistinct stack and instead frame them in a comprehensible order, that is, in a world and without falling into subjectivism. But just as his world is not distinct from the subject, neither is he, as a subject, distinct from the world that would be his "object." This transobjective dimension, which can still seem imperfect and dubious in *Being and Time*, is developed further in Heidegger's later writings, starting from his *Letter on Humanism, Contributions to Philosophy,* and other texts.

This brief venture into Nietzsche's and Heidegger's hermeneutics allows us to confirm the political significance of hermeneutics as a conception of Being that does not offer itself to descriptions but that rather involves us from the beginning as interpreters. Outside the prejudice of knowledge as the mirror of nature, one can no longer imagine a world given objectively but only one always given through someone's involvement. There are no facts; there is never anything that presents (by itself) as obvious or evidently in the phenomenological sense. The thrown project looks into the world through a number of instruments that serve or hinder its existential interest. But what is called "world" is an outcome not only of interpretation but also of history: it is the result of the interpretative processes of others. Just like the subject is not something primordial or original, neither is the world that is always given as the outcome of other interpretations.

Hermeneutics is a way of looking at Being as an inheritance that is never considered as ultimate data. Capitalism has always grown by considering, or forcing another to consider, as a "natural" possession what is inherited. The great dominating families are really the inheritors of the strongest pirates, thieves, and bandits, and they consider themselves entitled to command through a divine or natural law, when they really are only the result of a forgotten "violence."

The divine rights of kings, applicable in many ways also to the logic of class societies and capitalistic growth—although only one example among many others—demonstrates eloquently how and why hermeneutic ontology alone opens the horizon of emancipation, an emancipation from the demand for more original rights for priests, monarchs, and owners. But if the logic of dominion cannot simply be overcome in this way, how is it possible to bring forward such emancipation? Expressed in metaphysical "terms," if Being is only history, then the recip rocal is also valid: all history is Being. But then wouldn't any hegemony that had successfully imposed itself also be legitimate? We are here venturing into all the problems that belong to Nietzsche's and Heidegger's nihilism: those unsolvable issues for which metaphysics—the idea that an objective order exists independently from us and to which we ought to conform to know (mirroring) and act (rights and "natural" ethics)— still pretends to value as inevitable. We do not consider it a coincidence that the radical problem of the opposition between metaphysics and hermeneutics presents itself just where we pose the ethical-political problem of emancipation. It is mostly in the ethical and political spheres that the unsustainability of metaphysics becomes evident. Those that preach that there "is" an order of the world to which we must all conform are really its consumers, that is, its satisfied and therefore most rabid defenders.

If Being is history and nothing else—not an eternal objective structure—we would say that only what is history is Being. This would leave out everything that pretends to avoid history. This is not very different from saying that emancipation means openness, transformation, and projected interpretation instead of what already is; this, after all, is probably why Rorty used to say, "If you take care of freedom, truth will take care of itself."[21]

In sum, we prefer the idea of Being as "event," since without it we could not "exist" (as projects) for the simple purpose of living. Shouldn't such a principle also function for the holders of power, the defenders of the world as a stable structure that ought to be respected? We may at least recommend such an idea to them with the hope they will endorse it; nevertheless, we must remain ready to fight also in concrete ways in order to prevent the obstruction of such practice.

HERMENEUTICS AS WEAK THOUGHT

Hermeneutics, particularly in the radical version we present here, because it is not a metaphysical theory—with pretensions to describe the stable structures of Being that thought could capture with a sort of Platonic rise—only has contingent historical motivations at its disposal to claim any reasonable validity.

The nihilism that Nietzsche discusses is the result of history, the same history of Western metaphysics that he resumes in a well-known chapter of *Twilight of the Idols*, "How the 'Real World' at Last Became a Myth."[22] It is not necessary to remind everyone that the end of metaphysics that takes place in this history is not a "fact" but is instead always an interpreter's narration that not only is within this history but also does not presume to discuss it objectively. As this passage suggests, the various stages through which the world became a myth move from Platonism (which thinks the things of the world as ideas provided with a sort of Cartesian certainty) through Kant's a priori and positivism, which identifies objectivity with the result of the experiment. The real world, which was supposed to be a world of pure forms and ideas, has actually been reduced to the production of a subject. The scheme outlined in this brief chapter of *Twilight of the Idols*, in different terms, holds all of Heidegger's analyses in one of his courses on Nietzsche regarding the transformation of the idea of truth. Nevertheless, in both Nietzsche and Heidegger, the end of metaphysics is not a theoretical discovery but the interpretation of a history that belongs to and is part of each philosopher. In many ways, the end of metaphysics is the death of God, which Nietzsche discusses in *The Gay Science*; believers have killed God by following his command not to lie. Faith in God allowed the construction of a more secure, organized, and peaceful world, in which faith becomes an unnecessary lie.

Hermeneutics did not begin because of a theoretical discovery; it is an interpretative response to the end of metaphysics. Interpretation, following Nietzsche and Heidegger, means an interested involvement. But the end of metaphysics is not something we must inevitably accept as a fact; it is the meaning we attribute, for our interest, to the vicissitudes that Nietzsche and Heidegger narrate. We read such vicissitudes as the dissolution of objective metaphysics because we are against objectivity, which makes impossible the history and freedom of existence.

Recent Italian philosophy calls this way of tying hermeneutics to nihilism and to the end of metaphysics "weak thought."[23] Initially, "weak" primarily denoted the abandonment of pretensions to absolutes that had characterized the metaphysical traditions. But the weakness of thought could not halt this critical-negative characteristic, just as Nietzsche's nihilism could not be only negative and reactive. Together with Heidegger we consider the vicissitudes of metaphysics as the history of Being, which has to be interpreted as a process of weakening absolutes, truths, and foundations. In sum, weak thought becomes a (strong) theory of weakening as an interpretive sense of history, a sense that reveals itself as emancipative because of the enemies it has attracted. Weak thought can only be the thought of the weak, certainly not of the dominating classes, who have always worked to conserve and leave unquestioned the established order of the world.

Contrary to weak thinkers, when defenders of metaphysical realism face the postmodern condition (where principles, absolutes, and dogmas are critically questioned),[24] they tend to dismiss the political difference this condition implies in favor of a second-rate cultural difference. But for weak thinkers, philosophical debate can here become political struggle. Instead of yet another system of thought, such a struggle must rely on "weak thought," that is, the idea of the impossibility of overcoming[25] metaphysics while at the same time establishing the capacity to live without legitimizations or grounding values. This is why Charles Taylor recently affirmed that "once we see this, we can break the spell of the narrow moral rationalism whose supposed strength and rigour merely hides a fundamental weakness. Thinking straight requires that we admit the full '*debolezza*,' weakness, of our thought."[26]

Weak thought allows philosophy to correspond to the dissolution of metaphysics (through hermeneutics) and to search for new goals and ambitions within the possibilities of the "thrown" condition of the human being: instead of an understanding of the eternal, philosophy redirects humanity toward an interpretation of its own history. It is important to emphasize that the negative connotation of the term "weak" does not allude to a failure of thinking as such but rather to the consequences of the transformation of thought brought about by the end of metaphysics, hence, as a possibility of emancipation. Weak thought is a very strong theory of weakness, where the philosopher's achievements do not derive from enforcing the objective world but rather from weakening its structures. Weak thought does not become strong once it weakens the structures of metaphysics, since there will always be more structures to weaken, just as there will always be subjects to psychoanalyze, beliefs to secularize, or governments to democratize. In sum, the weakness of "weak thought" should not be interpreted in contrast to "strong thought" or as the result of a discovery (that there is no objective description of truth) but rather as an awareness of our postmodern condition.

Although Schürmann, Lyotard, and Rorty exposed postmodern antifoundationalism in very different ways, they all belong to the hermeneutic *koiné*, where the legitimization of foundations is substituted by an antifoundational hermeneutics. Therefore, it should not come as a surprise that they all can be considered as inspirers of weak thought in the late 1980s, because their intuitions also helped create this postmetaphysical attitude of thought. Schürmann individuated the "absence of foundations" for practical action after metaphysics, Lyotard defined the "postmodern" condition, and Rorty exposed "conversation" as its ethical guiding thread instead of truth. These three philosophical intuitions have become essential points of reference not only for hermeneutic weak thought but also for the weak in general, to whom this thought belongs. If existence is interpretation, human beings must learn to live without legitimizations and grounding values, that is, within antifoundationalism. But how is it possible to think, that is, proceed philosophically, without facts, objects, and truth? Is politics without truth possible?

Among the first to try to answer this question was Schürmann, who in the 1980s published *Heidegger on Being and Acting: From Principles to Anarchy* and *Broken Hegemonies*. According to Schürmann, until now we have lived by following foundations and paradigms, because each epoch was guided by legitimate (and legitimating) principles that would never change. But as he analyzed in these studies, epochs ("Greece," "Latinity," "Modernity") did create different principles ("one," "nature," "conscience") that at the same time legitimated new practices ("religions," "science," "psychology") that would have been inappropriate in the past. For Schürmann, Western metaphysics becomes a succession of epochal principles that determined hegemonically the different periods of the history of thought. When an epoch changes, a new principle installs itself hegemonically in order to legitimate new practices. Here is a clear example of different epochs dominating through their principles and practices the same sacred space:

> The Parthenon: within the network of actions, things, and words, the way an entity like the Acropolis is present epochally assumed a well-defined, although complex character—when rhapsodes prepared for the Panathenean festival, when the Parthenon served as a Byzantine church, when the Turks used it as a powder magazine. Today, when it has become a commodity for tourist consumption and when UNESCO plans to protect it from pollution with a plastic dome, it is present in an epochal economy in yet another fashion—a mode of presence certainly inconceivable for its architect, Ichtynos. At each moment of this history, the edifice was present according to finite, unforeseeable, uncontrollable traits. And each entailed the irremediable disappearance of such an epochal physiognomy.[27]

Why are we now aware of this alternation of epochs? Schürmann does not consider the end of metaphysics outlined by Nietzsche and Heidegger as the theoretical awareness of another, previously unknown structure of Being (which would just legitimate another principle) but rather as the existential assumption of the absence of foundations. This is the meaning of "anarchy" referred to in his book's title:[28] the "economies of Being" (the substitution of old principles in favor of new ones) do not follow a rational course in history but rather, on their turn, an "anarchic" one.

The problem that emerges from this analysis of the end of metaphysics is what to do once we have individuated not only the mechanism of grounding principles but also its absence. But, as we argued at the beginning of this chapter, for Schürmann the anarchic vein of hermeneutics does not involve the absence of all rules but of a unique rule that could guide all practices. This is why, in the absence of ultimate metaphysical principles, we can only live through the acquisition of a particular anarchic existential disposition: only by becoming "unaccustomed" to living according to legitimizations and grounding values can thought be practiced in a postmetaphysical or, as Lyotard calls it, a "postmodern" world. This is why for Schürmann to ask today, "What ought I to do? is to speak in the vacuum of the space deserted by the successive representations of an unshakable ground."[29] As we will see, both Lyotard and Rorty indicate how it is possible to live without legitimizations and grounding values and point out the opportunities that come from it.

In the 1970s, the government of Quebec commissioned Lyotard to write a report on knowledge, but instead of a simple report, the French master came up with one of the most discussed philosophical texts of the past half century: *The Postmodern Condition*. While this condition was outlined for the first time by Ihab Hassan in 1976 to refer to the social condition of Western civilization, it is Lyotard who a few years later managed to expose the philosophical innovations that this terminology implied. In this text, Lyotard indirectly outlines the condition of weak thought, that is, how its epoch differs from that of modernism (metaphysics), but, contrary to Schürmann, who limited himself to delineating why we entered this "shakable ground," Lyotard went further, describing the condition for thought that this new ground implies for us.

Although Lyotard agreed with Schürmann that modernity was characterized by "legitimating" norms, he saw this process take place not through principles but rather "metanarratives," that is, as founding myths that present themselves as global narratives such as positivism, Marxism, and Hegelianism. In sum, while modernity was the age where norms were legitimized through metanarratives, in postmodernity these same metanarratives have been bankrupted. Communication technology in our societies—both as the exchange of news and the possibility for entire masses of people to transfer—has vertiginous, multiplicated perspectives. But such bankruptcy does not mean that these metanarratives do not exist anymore but rather that we began to lose interest in them after the technological advances since World War II. Among the various effects produced by these technological transformations, the most important concern the end of the ideas of history as a development toward social emancipation and of knowledge as a progression toward accomplishment and truth. Instead of legitimating history and knowledge through metanarratives, we tend today to follow a plurality of interpretations, a practice that has reached its peak through the Internet. But what happens once we can no longer legitimate our thoughts in terms of progress toward truth? The same concept of truth is weakened into its various interpretations, making it impossible to regard human events as proceeding toward an end, hence, making it impossible to realize a rational program of improvement.

In order to explain this new postmodern condition of truth, Lyotard used Wittgensteinian language games, where the antifoundational nature of hermeneutics becomes evident. In the second period of his thought, Wittgenstein developed his notion that reality is not described by an overarching theory but rather by a number of language games. Lyotard comments on the implications of these games:

> The first is that their rules do not carry within themselves their own legitimation, but are subject to a contract, explicit or not, between players (which is not to say that the players invent the rules). The second is that if there are no rules, there is no game, that even an infinitesimal modification of the one rule alters the nature of the game, that a "move" or utterance that does not satisfy the rules does not belong to the game they define. The third remark is suggested by what has just been said: every utterance should be thought of as a "move" in a game.[30]

Unlike some interpreters, we believe there is a political motivation behind Lyotard's use of these language games, because they are used to represent the status of knowledge in postmodernity and also the plurality of truth this society presupposes. If we substitute the word "rule" in the passage above with "truth," then truth must respect the contingency within the processes with which it deals; in other words, each game implies a different truth that cannot delegitimize other games. This has a deep political import, for now politics cannot be based on accurate representations of reality but rather on singular different events that cannot be represented by rational theory. The revolutionary political project of hermeneutics here becomes evident, making Lyotard one of the pioneers of interpretation's call for emancipation.

Lyotard's deprecation of grand narratives has been welcomed by political, cultural, and intellectual minorities because it demands that difference is a principle to follow rather than to reject and also is an indication of civilization. These minorities have always been marginalized by rational politics on the basis of their difference; that is, their difference has been used as a factor of discrimination. Lyotard believes that the difference of each linguistic game (truth) should not only be incorporated into but also become a goal of social organization. But once we recognize how difference becomes a condition we must pursue instead of reject, conversation substitutes for truth in order to cope with the plurality of linguistic games that surround us. The concept of conversation allows us to dismiss the modern grand narratives that tried to explain the totality of social practices in terms of their conformity to a universal pattern even when they encountered cultures different from their own. While many believed that the concept of conversation undermined our intellectual and moral hierarchies in favor of relativism, Rorty saw it as enforcing the possibilities of freedom from such hierarchies, because there is no position outside our historically situated language games from which to distinguish mind from world.

Before indicating some possibilities that will come from conversation as the guiding ethical thread, it is important to remember that Rorty is the philosopher who demonstrated how Anglo-Saxon analytic philosophy is really one of the last gasps of descriptive philosophies. Analytic and continental realist philosophies are theoretically responsible for limiting the democratic ambitions of freedom, through their epistemological imposition of truth and state liberalism. This is probably why Rorty, in *Philosophy and the Mirror of Nature* (1979), after indicating how analytic philosophy was conditioned by a desire to imitate not only the natural sciences but also their technical agenda, saw in hermeneutic philosophy "an expression of hope that the cultural space left by the demise of epistemology will not be filled."[31] For this reason,

Rorty is among the first supporters of hermeneutic weak thought, because it does not pretend to fill any cultural space but rather advocates the discovery of different interpretations, descriptions, and understandings of the world. Rorty specified this, alluding to Nietzsche:

> What Nietzsche—and, more generally, "hermeneutics"—has to tell us is not that we need a new method, but rather that we should look askance at the idea of method. He and his followers should not be viewed as offering us a new set of concepts, but rather as offering a certain skepticism about all possible concepts, including the ones they themselves use . . . they should be seen as urging us to think of concepts as tools rather than pictures—problem-solving instruments rather than firm foundations from which to criticize those who use different concepts.[32]

Knowledge, explains Rorty, after Nietzsche, Heidegger, and Derrida's deconstruction of metaphysics, cannot be acquired by deciding which propositions are true and which are false but only through "conversation," which has become the "ultimate context within which knowledge is to be understood."[33] The American philosopher demands that the paradigm change from truth to conversation for the same ethical reasons that Nietzsche and Heidegger had to overcome metaphysics: because to "see the aim of philosophy as truth—namely, the truth about the terms which provide ultimate commensuration for all human inquiries and activities—is to see human beings as objects rather than subjects."[34] Rorty's main philosophical operation has been to develop all the consequences of leaving the idea of truth as a matter of mental or linguistic representation of reality. He invites all philosophers to substitute for "philosophy as the mirror of nature" an "edifying hermeneutic philosophy" that guides, projects, and maintains the conversation of mankind.

Like Schürmann and Lyotard, Rorty also believes that nothing legitimizes or grounds our practices, since there is nothing that shows how they are in touch with the way things are. He believes it is much more productive to accept as justified practices those agreed upon by our epistemic community; in other words, it's better to make practical decisions on the basis of our history, education, and experiences instead of on the basis of truth or principles. Traditional principles have always been beyond the realm of human justification; they are metaphysical matrixes that presuppose that at a certain point in the process we will reach a goal (which could take various forms, such as eternal life, justice, or wealth). But Rorty, following Nietzsche's intuitions, reminds us that these goals do not exist; they are only projections of an insecure humanity in search of extreme reassurances. While these principles are not relative to anything we can experience, human finite justifications are always relative to a "language game community." It is in these individual and free communities that Rorty sees the potentiality for us to become historical contingencies, that is, determined for the cause of freedom instead of the significance of truth. As we can see, the guiding ethical thread behind Rorty's philosophy does not depend on a strong conception of morality but rather on a weak one:

> In a "weak" conception, morality is not a matter of unconditional obligations imposed by a divine or quasi divine authority but rather is something cobbled together by a group of people trying to adjust to their circumstances and achieve their goals by

cooperative efforts. . . . This humility will encourage tolerance for other intuitions and a willingness to experiment with ways of re-fashioning or replacing intuitions.[35]

Rorty, together with Schürmann and Lyotard, has found in herme-neutic weak thought an ethics without principles and a politics without truth. For all three, genuine liberalism is only possible if human beings are given infinite freedom for their own re-creation. This is the reason that a tolerant society is one in which achievements will be determined by the plurality of conversations with different linguistic communities instead of the imposition of a liberal state, as with the invasion of Iraq. But this is only possible once we leave aside those legitimatizing norms, foundational beliefs, and traditional principles that assured the links be-tween our rational certainty and Truth, Nature, or God.

The main accusation leveled against hermeneutic weak thought is that it supports a politics without truth, that is, relativism. But contrary to what many think, the relativism of interpretation favored by postmo-dernity does not imply a progressive accumulation of points of views but rather the impossibility of declaring once and for all the primacy of one interpretation over others. Although a given interpretation could be preferable to others, this preference will not depend on anything ex-ternal and capable of guaranteeing its objectivity but only on a positive recollection of its premises, that is, the history that produced it. The relativism of hermeneutic weak thought cannot be absolute, since in its essence this is a thought against every claim to absoluteness, including "absolute relativism," which would inevitably translate into political op-pression. This is also why the "real" still exists for hermeneutics, but only within certain paradigms, as Kuhn explained: it is always possible to establish whether an interpretation or a proposition is true or false, but only within a historical condition, a certain scientific discipline, or a political epoch.

For all these reasons, hermeneutic weak thought is the thought of the weak, of those who are not satisfied with the established principles imposed on them and who demand different rights, that is, other interpretations. In this politics of interpretation, conversation becomes the realm where the powerful describers of the world can listen to the requests of the weak and perhaps change their selfish priorities. But if they do not listen, today the weak can finally come together. Perhaps Rorty foresaw this when he stated that what is "important about representative democratic government is that it gives the poor and weak a tool they can use against the rich and powerful, especially against the unconscious cruelty of the institutions the powerful have imposed upon the weak."[36]

4. HERMENEUTIC COMMUNISM

IN THIS REGARD, COMMUNISM HAS ALWAYS BEEN AND WILL REMAIN SPECTRAL: IT
IS ALWAYS STILL TO COME AND IS DISTINGUISHED, LIKE DEMOCRACY ITSELF, FROM
EVERY LIVING PRESENT UNDERSTOOD AS PLENITUDE OF A PRESENCE-TO-ITSELF,
AS TOTALITY OF A PRESENCE EFFECTIVELY IDENTICAL TO ITSELF. CAPITALIST
SOCIETIES CAN ALWAYS HEAVE A SIGH OF RELIEF AND SAY TO THEMSELVES:
COMMUNISM IS FINISHED SINCE THE COLLAPSE OF THE TOTALITARIANISM OF
THE TWENTIETH CENTURY AND NOT ONLY IS IT FINISHED, BUT IT DID NOT TAKE
PLACE, IT WAS ONLY A GHOST. THEY DO NO MORE THAN DISAVOW THE UNDENIABLE
ITSELF: A GHOST NEVER DIES, IT REMAINS ALWAYS TO COME AND TO COME-BACK.
—JACQUES DERRIDA, *SPECTERS OF MARX* (1993)

COMMUNISM WAS A SPECTER AT THE TIME OF *THE
Communist Manifesto*—a ghost that frightened the upper middle class
and the governors of the epoch. And it is still spectral today, because it
has lost the ability to frighten the status quo after the complete domination of capitalistic framed democracies. These democracies managed to
reduce communism to a residue of the past, a trace of a conquered fear,
demonstrated by its complete absence in recent Western electoral politics (especially in the United States). Communism has become a ghostlike presence, and when it is noted at all, it is simply as a remote, rigid
system of thought and history. Why has this happened, and why does
hermeneutics carry the possibility of renovating the potential of communism in our world? It is in answering these questions that our work
must conclude.

Hermeneutics should not be considered a miraculous philosophical discovery in a long history of breakthroughs in human thought. It lacks such an excessive ambition, and it cannot be reduced to such a simple level. It does not aim to be a more "real" or objective representation of the world than other philosophies; neither does it pretend to be an interpretation of the world among others. We are not talking about hermeneutic communism because we are pretending to add to communism the energy of a philosophy (as with Lenin's definition: "Communism is Soviet power plus electrification")[1] that would enforce its status as truer than other systems. Instead, we see in communism and in hermeneutics the destiny of an event, a sort of appeal of Being (excluding mysterious and transcendent factors) that hermeneutics does not invent or discover but rather receives and struggles to respond to. In this way, hermeneutics is like the communism that the *Manifesto* talked about: a specter that haunts us, a voice that calls from the events that we live in. In this way, it does not require a philosophical investigation to be acknowledged but only to be an unforeseen appeal that is not submitted to the metaphysics that has dominated the past as the theory of the ruling classes. Hermeneutics is similar to communism because its truth, Being, and necessity are entirely historical, that is, not the outcome of a theoretical discovery or a logical correction of previous errors but rather the result of the end of metaphysics. Although this end implies certain conceptual disarrays (produced by such thinkers as Marx, Nietzsche, Heidegger, Derrida, and Kuhn), it could not have happened without the series of social transformations that accompanied, directed, and determined this same disarray. In sum, hermeneutics would not have been possible without the end of Eurocentrism, which has also always been the sociopolitical correlative of Western metaphysics. No one could have come up with affirmations such as Nietzsche's "there are no facts, only interpretations" in a social, cultural, and anthropological milieu other than the colonial epoch of the late 1800s, which was also becoming more uncertain regarding its own supremacy. Just as the bloodbath of World War I decisively confirmed the disarray of the Eurocentric convictions, so were the various crises of the dissolution of metaphysics in the twentieth century accompanied not only by wars but also by technological revolutions unimaginable in the past.

If we hold the end of metaphysics accountable for the wars and violence of the twentieth century, we should also recognize that the experiences of Soviet communism were an aspect of this epochal phenomenon. Although the two aspects of the response that we are trying to define are strictly interconnected, if not identical, to achieve a better comprehension it is best to discuss them separately. First of all: why does the end of metaphysics, that is, the end of Eurocentrism and its pretense to universal "Western" rationality, which Searle defends in his debate with Derrida, provide a chance for the return of communism? We could summarize the answer by paraphrasing one of Heidegger's responses in his interview with *Der Spiegel*: "Only communism can save us."[2] We do not believe this is a ludicrous paraphrase, since it could even be justified by quoting the Gospel: "For where two or three are gathered together in my name, there am I in the midst of them" (Matthew 18:20). After all, "in my name" means in the name of justice, fraternity, and the solidarity of the weak. But without moving toward a "theological communism"—which would be completely legitimate—it seems evident that the postmodern condition that the dissolution of absolutes imposes for the survival[3] of the human species demands that we assume communism as the horizon of any possible liberation for the human being. In a Nietzschean-Christian style, one could say: *Now that God is dead and the absolute truth is not credible anymore, love for the other is possible and necessary.* Can anyone continue to doubt that love for the other can coincide with a communist politics? Although the arguments that sustain this doubt are numerous, they are either founded on the idea that there is an absolute truth with which communism contrasts, such as the "natural" rights of private property,[4] or on the tragic experience of Soviet communism. But while the actions of the Soviet state cannot be justified, it should be kept in mind that they were also a development of the October revolution, born of the resistance to the attack of the entire capitalist world, that is, the so-called industrial democracies together with fascism and Nazism.

Paradoxically, though only to a certain extent, we affirm the historical (not theoretical) necessity to recapture communism in the moment in which its "spectrality" seems to have reached its peak. World public opinion believes communism's corpse definitively buried, to the point of not noticing its presence in the form of a specter. Derrida dedicated one of his last books to just this theme,[5] from which we wish to recover at least the justification of the necessity of the return to communism in a world dominated by framed democracies, that is, communism as the highest "weakness." This is our *Abendland*, "land of the sunset," which, while it is setting, ought to do so consciously and openly toward the future, without being dragged away by our contemporary logics of war, that is, armed capitalism. It is in these wars (which, as we saw in the previous chapter are not only limited to fights of nation against nation but also are fought in our slums) that the oppressed, the weak, the losers of history are discharged, ignored, and left to perish[6] by the cruelty of the winners.[7]

Our argument is not only similar to Derrida's but actually hopes to recapture his in order to show how and why communism, which is excluded from the horizon of our culture and so-called public opinion, should be rehabilitated and listened to. As we can see, recourse to spectral communism becomes an objective necessity today both because of the discharge of capitalism and because capitalism continues to impose itself with the absolute certainty of having "realized itself as the ideal of human history."[8] In order to justify why communism can become an alternative and model for the twenty-first century, when the "ideals of human history" are losing their credibility, we must first expose its weakened essence, then its alternative manifestation in some of the democratically elected governments of South America, and finally how these same Latin American politics (so effective for the weak) can also become a possible model for the West to pursue.

WEAKENED COMMUNISM

Our suggestion of a hermeneutic communism is aware of but also takes into account the weakness of communism in our world. Such weakness is probably attributable to the violent connotations of historical communism (as its Russian-Soviet realization demonstrated). Although we believe that these connotations were justified, considering the conditions in which Lenin and Stalin had to govern, especially the latter, with Hitler at his doorstep,[9] they were admittedly in stark contrast to communism's promises of emancipation. Here lies the meaning of the youth and proletarian "revolution" of 1968: a revolt against those oppressions that communism demanded against the desires of happiness and friendship. The events of historical communism, which culminated with the fall of the Berlin Wall in 1989, are developments of this revolt, which can also be seen as having spread the economic crisis that today, twenty years later, has also ruined the capitalism that triumphed over historical communism. We believe that both the fall of the Berlin Wall and the current crisis of capitalism are aspects of the general dissolution of metaphysics, in other words, of those socioeconomic policies that were founded on the objective truth of history. *To Soviet communism's absolute scientific claims, capitalism opposed the truth of market laws.* Both of these ideological positions, with all their concrete political implications, were outcomes of absolute philosophies of history dominated by the idea of development.

While communism tried to understand better the laws of economics, liberal capitalism opposed such knowledge through its functionality. Although Marx never stated explicitly that political economics is not a natural science, he did point out how the structures and laws of economics are always historical products put to work by some class, dominating group, or institutionalized establishment. This is why these structures and laws must always be challenged and changed when the collective sensibility or technological innovations render obsolete existent forms of social relations. Marx, in his *Theories of Surplus Value* (volume 4 of *Capital*) criticized the Physiocrats for their inability to historicize materialism:

> The analysis of *capital*, within the bourgeois horizon, is essentially the work of the Physiocrats. It is this service that makes them the true fathers of modern political economy. In the first place, the analysis of the various *material components* in which capital exists and into which it resolves itself in the course of the labour-process. It is not a reproach to the Physiocrats that, like all their successors, they thought of these material forms of existence—such as tools, raw materials, etc.—as capital, in isolation from the social conditions in which they appear in capitalist production; in a word,

in the form in which they are elements of the labour-process in general, independently of its social form—and thereby made of the capitalist form of production an eternal, natural form of production. For them the bourgeois forms of production necessarily appeared as natural forms. It was their great merit that they conceived these forms as physiological forms of society: as forms arising from the natural necessity of production itself, forms that are independent of anyone's will or of politics, etc. They are material laws, the error is only that the material law of a definite historical social stage is conceived as an abstract law governing equally all forms of society.[10]

Questioning the social relations of production does not occur automatically. The errors and violence of many communist regimes were caused precisely by their failure to consider these aspects of collective subjectivity, which have to be interpreted in order to innovate those mutations of the productive forces. The scientific pretext of socialism was predestined to miss this interpretative stage; class consciousness, too, which certainly had a determined weight in theories of revolution, was imagined as a mechanical and necessary outcome of the proletariat's condition of exploitation when, in fact, it wasn't.

As we can see, introducing the "interpretative" element into Marxism and communism is not a theoretical game; the crisis of Soviet communism (parallel to the crisis of neoliberal capitalism today) requires from Marxism a hermeneutic turn.[11] Such a turn is necessary both in order to recuperate those elements of subjectivity that "vulgar" materialism (where only economic structures count) has always left aside and because it brings about all the antimetaphysical vigor of hermeneutics, that is, its rejection of any political plan wherein objective truth ought to guarantee results. As we saw in chapter 2, Krugman held economists' belief in an absolute truth responsible for capitalism's current crisis, that is, their belief in a realm where "everyone is rational and markets work perfectly."[12] In sum, if there is no "objective" truth behind society's structures, then the communist goal of a society without classes, differences, and conflicts can never come about, because such a society would be the equivalent of Fukuyama's fantasy (the "end of history as triumph of democratic capitalism"), which we analyzed at the beginning of chapter 2. Communism's promise of a society "without classes" must be interpreted as "without dominion," that is, once again, without an imposed unique truth and compulsory orthodoxy. This could also be called a society of "dialogue," had this term not been abused so much by the dominating classes to justify the conservation of the status quo. The "Soviet power plus electrification" that Lenin proposes does not imply that the Soviet, workers, and peasant councils are gathered together only to acknowledge a unique truth. These are realms of discussions and regulated conflict between positions and different interests that also move within a frame that lacks a unique dominating power. This is probably why Nietzsche considered "nihilism" (the positive nihilism in which conversations develop instead of dialogues)[13] as "the devaluation of 'supreme values' "[14]—not every value, decision, or preference but rather those constricting ones such as truth, nature, and ethical principles.

We are well aware that Marx, Lenin, or any of their theoretical or practical successors never solved the problem of the complete "realization" of a communist society.[15] The problem is that the so-called cultural battles (conflicts between different ideologies, religions, ethnicities, and political systems) that we see in our daily experience become "polluted" when ownership takes place. Is it possible to imagine a society where this polluting factor is eliminated or at least reduced to a minimum? What we do know from our experience is that the battle to eliminate or reduce the polluting weight of ownership is still taking place; perhaps this is why the phase of communism that calls for the dictatorship of the proletariat was never overcome within Soviet communism. While we cannot imagine a world where communism is completed, neither can we renounce this ideal as a regulative and inspiring principle for our concrete decisions. But wouldn't we lose in this way the meaning of the regulative ideal? Kant's lesson of practical reason also has this meaning: the union between virtue and happiness is not only the end that gives meaning to moral actions but also something impossible to carry out in the world. Nevertheless, this impossibility does not remove the obligation toward the categorical imperative. In sum, communism is utopia or, as Benjamin would say, a project of the "*weak* messianic power, a power on which the past has a claim."[16] After all, the messiah, as Jesus teaches in the Gospels, never allows himself to be indicated positively. The messianic power of the utopia is also a critical and indispensable limit; it is only when the revolution is considered completed (or, which is the same, when Being is identified with being as a present fact) that it becomes despotic power, hegemony, and violence against any disclosure toward a different future.

A society without classes and therefore capable of living in peace is the regulative ideal of any communist battle in the world. The fact that its complete realization is not imaginable is in part a function of the indissoluble link between theory and praxis: only by approaching the realization of the ideal will its traits appear more clearly.

The point is that all these features constitute the weakness and spectrality that are the indispensable characteristic for communism's rebirth. We must recall that communism was a powerful dominion not only in the historical event of the Soviet state but also, though in much more domestic terms, when it believed it could become a "force of government" in the advanced industrial democracies, such as the center-left Italian governments (and many European social democratic regimes) of the last decades of the twentieth century. But the left that referred to communism underwent a process of corruption, leaving the left unrecognizable to its own followers, as recent electoral results in various states in Europe have demonstrated, by bringing to power right-wing governments in Germany, France, and England.[17] It could be objected that a weak and spectral communism of the leftist parties accepts "compromises" with moderate or bourgeois political parties in order to obtain at least some improvement of the proletarian condition. This objection is especially valuable if one thinks about the positive meaning it takes in the role of the unions, which must always, as is commonly said, "bring home the contracts." Thus communism can never present itself as a revolutionary radical force.

The same could be said about the leftist reformist governments that have certainly obtained important partial transformations of the social order by aligning themselves with bourgeois, moderate, and conservative parties. Ignoring these relative successes would mean neglecting the improvements in the lives of so many of the "weak." But there are now many signs that reformism has come to an end and is no longer capable of winning ground. Reformism today will not gain those partial transformations that have marked its history without the sturdy support of a movement that radically questions the existent capitalist armed order. As we have seen, framed democracies, which include these reformist parties, have complied with the establishment's demands to conserve the banking and financial systems, at the cost of the tax contributions of the weak. These contributors were told that this was the only way to avoid the total collapse of the economy, which jives with the reformist fixation on "relative successes." In addition to defrauding the taxpayers with these bailouts, the reformists have supported or joined the military interventions that have served since the fall of the Berlin Wall to conserve not only capitalism but, most of all, the global corporations.[18] These compromises have destroyed the possibility of meaningful reform.

Although reformism in Italy and other European "democracies" has been discarded by the ruling right-wing governments, this does not mean that it is no longer practicable. In order for reformists to hope for productive results within nation-states, they must find the support of strong social-dissent movements on an international level instead: for example, in the popular democratic experiences recently realized in South America. Although it is obvious that these new socialist governments, starting with the Bolivarian regimes of Hugo Chávez and Evo Morales, do not have any direct effects on Europe's framed democracies, their simple presence on the international scene is an important element for a diverse and more open international climate. After all, these alternative governments' efforts to increase their economic, social, and political power (especially Brazil and Venezuela) are direct efforts to limit the excessive multinational capitalist power centered in the United States. While Obama has certainly not been "objectively" helped in his campaign for president by Castro's resistance, Chávez's initiatives, and the other Latin American communist achievements, haven't they provided a real example of change? It is just in these examples that we can talk about a "spectral" presence of communism, a promise that, as Derrida indicated, circulates in the air, does not identify itself with any concrete element, but can be sensed through public opinion and in the spreading suspicions over the capitalism of the framed democracies. In Derrida's words:

> It is a link of affinity, suffering, and hope, a still discreet, almost secret link, as it was around 1848, but more and more visible, we have more than one sign of it. It is an untimely link, without status, without title, and without name, barely public even if it is not clandestine, without contract, "out of joint," without coordination, without party, without country, without national community (International before, across, and beyond any national determination), without co-citizenship, without common belonging to a class.[19]

What these considerations imply for the return of communism in its spectral or hermeneutic form is still to be discovered, especially in the union of theory and praxis, without which no real social transformation can take place. Framed industrial democracies express two very different features: while the parliamentary majorities are following a right-wing conservative course throughout the Western world, European social movements (concerned with the most elementary needs, such as civil, health, and ecological rights)[20] instead follow with hope the socialist renovation of South America. In sum, the South American experience is providing the weak not only in Europe but also in the United States with a productive alternative to the condition of lack of emergency created by capitalism (Obama's popular health-care reform battle is another indication). As we have seen, this lack of emergency implies that states submit to a development in favor of the GDP, discharging the majority of the population and creating the enormous differences of income that Gallino discusses. In a condition where the weak are increasing, the neoliberal road of a capitalist economy, with its focus on intensified development, is confirmed as not only socially unproductive but also destructive for humanity in general.

If we take these factors into account, we can see why communism must function as a "specter," that is, not as a political program that proposes more "rational" ways for unfettered development (which were part of the agenda of scientific socialism) but rather as a movement that embraces the programmatic cause of "degrowth"[21] as the only way to save the human species. In this way, the function of the specter—which disturbs and shocks the serene routine of those who, as in the case of Hamlet, must reap the fruit of violence—is useful for shocking into awareness those who prefer not to recognize capitalism's consequences. Leaving aside any metaphors, we believe that hermeneutic communism today, that is, a programmatically "weak" communism, can hope for a different future only if it has the courage to act as a specter by refusing to follow capitalism's emphasis on rational development. And if hermeneutic communism does not imply immediate violent revolutions, this is both because armed capitalism is impossible to defeat and because a violent acquisition of power would be socially counterproductive. After all, as the new South American governments have demonstrated, communist access to power may still take place within the framework of the formal rules of democracy.

THE SOUTH AMERICAN ALTERNATIVE

Weak communism is not dead. It has begun to rise in South America through Chávez, Morales, and other democratically elected politicians who are creating an international emergency for framed democracies. This is why renowned intellectuals, writers, and journalists, such as Moisés Naím, Mario Vargas Llosa, and Thomas L. Friedman, and the mainstream world media are bound together by an obsession to portray these democratically elected South American politicians as evil, violent, and undemocratic.[22] If these intellectuals and media figures are obsessed with this region, it is because its governments represent a political alternative to the global capitalism of framed democracies and, most of all, because they govern through communist programs in an age where capitalism has apparently triumphed.[23] These programs not only benefit the weak (which is the most prevalent population sector in the region) but also draw the attention of the European social movements mentioned above. But contrary to the reports of our Western media, this new weak communism differs substantially from its previous Soviet (and current Chinese) realization, because the South American countries follow democratic electoral procedures and also manage to decentralize the state bureaucratic system through the *misiónes* (social missions for community projects). In sum, if weakened communism is felt as a specter in the West, it is not only because of media distortions but also for the alternative it represents through the same democratic procedures that the West constantly professes to cherish but is hesitant to apply;[24] this must be why Chomsky recently declared that in "Latin America, people just take democracy more seriously than in the West, certainly the United States."[25]

Although there are several states in South America that have elected socialist or communist governments, the world media seems to focus most of their attacks on the president of Venezuela. This is probably because Chávez, just like the United States does,[26] influences elections in other countries of the region. While Chávez, for example, supports the indigenous people of Bolivia in electing someone of their own ethnic majority (and someone who intends to nationalize their resources against foreign corporations),[27] the United States imposes a neoliberal government in Iraq. But in order to explore Chávez's South American alternative, or what he calls the "Bolivarian Revolution," it's first necessary to briefly recall how Chávez managed to become president,[28] since too often his (failed) coup d'état in 1992 is confused with his democratic victories (in elections and referendums) of 1998, 2000, 2004, 2006, and 2009.[29] For example, the referendum of 2009, which ended presidential term limits, is often described as a way that Chávez found to remain in power, even though elections still have to be won democratically (the prime minister of England can also be reelected indefinitely).[30] Another oft-repeated accusation is the revocation of the broadcasting license to RCTV (Venezuela's second largest TV channel) after it was demonstrated that it supported the coup against him in 2002.[31] Regardless of this revocation, today the majority of the media in Venezuela is still in the hands of the opposition,[32] and RCTV is allowed to broadcast via cable and satellite.[33]

The world media continue to portray Chávez as a dictator because of the political emergency he represents: the alternative to U.S. neoliberal impositions. But where did Chávez obtain this political consciousness? As Nikolas Kozloff explains in his up-to-date study on Latin America, when Chávez (who joined the military to get out of poverty) toured Venezuela as a "young soldier, he was moved by the plight of Venezuela's dirt-poor Indians and the rampant social injustice he saw."[34] This is why in 1992 he

organized a coup d'état against C. A. Pérez, in an effort to overturn rampant corruption and the "dictatorship of the Monetary Fund."

Though the coup was a failure, it established Chávez as a prominent figure and underscored growing political tension within the
ranks. Cruising to victory in 1998, this time as a civilian, Chávez
broke military ties with the US. . . . The Venezuelan opposition,
led by wealthy globalizing magnates, conservative army officers,
and oil industries executives opposed to Chávez's nationalistic petroleum policy, rebelled. In April 2002 the opposition, which had
been receiving money from the US through the taxpayer-funded
National Endowment for Democracy, took the streets of Caracas to demand Chávez's resignation. Taking advantage of street
violence and political confusion, dissident officers kidnapped
Chávez. P. Carmona, a former petrochemical executive, took
power, dissolving the Supreme Court and eliminating the country's constitution. However, officers loyal to Chávez, aided by massive street protests by pro-Chávez demonstrators, soon returned
the president to power. Chávez's return came as a stinging rebuff
to Washington and allowed the Venezuelan president to consoli-
date his position over the state oil company. With the money from
the petroleum industry, Chávez has been able to deepen the Bolivarian Revolution by undertaking ambitious programs in such
areas as health and education.[35]

The "Bolivarian Revolution" is Chávez's commitment to twenty-
first-century socialism.[36] Named after Simón Bolívar, the early-
eighteenth-century Latin American revolutionary leader in the South
American wars of independence, the "Bolivarian Revolution" names
the desire to bring about Bolivar's dream of a united Latin America.
While for Bolivar the union of Latin America was against the Spanish
oppressors, for Chávez the unification is against the U.S. neoliberal and

military impositions that, together with the "dictatorship of the Monetary Fund," have reduced the region to a great slum, that is, the discharge of capitalism. As we can predict, it is just from these slums that Chávez receives most of his electoral support, as his political initiatives are all directed toward the weakest population.

When Chávez finally managed to secure control over the oil resources after the coup against him in 2002, he obliged Venezuela's largest oil company, PdVSA, to distribute oil wealth throughout the country.[37] This weak communist plan is called the "Oil Sowing Plan,"[38] and it invites communities to design their own development projects, for which PdVSA provides the funding. In 2005, social programs such as Barrio Adentro (for community health), Sucre (for university scholarships), and others received more than 6.9 billion dollars from PdVSA. Perhaps the most famous social program is Misión Milagro, which performed free eye surgery on thousands of Venezuelans. This program is part of the greater Cuban-Venezuelan agreement where, in exchange for subsidized petroleum, 14,000 Cuban doctors were sent to help the country transform "the situation of the poor districts, where 11,000 neighborhood clinics have been established and the health budget has tripled."[39] As a consequence of this weak communist political program, extreme poverty has been reduced by 72 percent since 2003, infant mortality has dropped by more than one-third, and Venezuela has now become a territory free of illiteracy.[40] This cooperation with Cuba is also a defense against common enemies: the United States and the IMF.

As we have said, Chávez's Bolivarian Revolution is not limited to his country[41] but takes interest in the whole region. Together with Castro (who quickly also became his "mentor"),[42] Chávez began to support other politicians who shared these common enemies and were also interested in favoring the weakest citizens of their countries. Inspired by

Chávez's democratic election and social revolt against neoliberalism in 2002, Lula was (democratically) elected president of Brazil, Kirchner in Argentina in 2003, Bachelet in Chile in 2005, Morales in Bolivia in 2005, Correa in Ecuador in 2006, Ortega in Nicaragua in 2006, Lugo in Paraguay in 2008, Funes in El Salvador in 2009, and Mujica in Uruguay in 2009.[43] While most of these politicians enacted, in different ways, weak communist programs, the most representative politician and closest ally of Chávez is Evo Morales,[44] who only three months after taking office withdrew from the IMF and World Bank because of their tendencies "to settle disputes in favor of international corporations and against governments."[45]

As Forest Hylton and Sinclair Thomson point out, although "Latin America has been the site of the most radical opposition to neoliberal restructuring over the past five years, Bolivia has been its insurrectionary frontline."[46] Morales not only has become the first president of Bolivia from the country's ethnic majority (Aymaras) but also is among the first in the region to undertake a radical nationalization of his country's resources (oil, natural gas, and almost half of the world's reserves of lithium), against exploitation by foreign corporations (BP, General Motors, Bechtel) and in favor of control by native Indians.[47] But in order to recover control over Bolivia's natural resources, Morales was obliged (through a referendum held on January 25, 2009) to change the constitution, which had been written by the descendants of the Spanish colonizers. These colonizers, who today, as then, represent the ethnic minority, live in the eastern provinces of Bolivia, which contain most of the country's resources. As we can predict, Morales's greatest obstacle came from these white minorities, who, as Richard Gott of the *Guardian* explains, still "have a racist and fascist mentality and, after centuries in control, dislike the prospect of their future being dominated by the formerly suppressed indigenous majority."[48] Nevertheless, the referendum passed with 61.43 percent of the vote, enabling a reform of the land and judiciary systems "for the benefit of the people. Yet more important—and at the heart of the new constitutional charter—are the clauses that strengthen the rights of the country's indigenous peoples."[49] Unfortunately, to win approval, the new constitution needed more than popular democratic support, because the eastern provinces of Santa Cruz, Tarija, Beni, and Pando not only tried to boycott it but also violently threatened to declare their independence from Bolivia. Although the European Union deployed a group of observers during the election,[50] it was UNASUR (Union of South American Nations) that managed, after an emergency summit held in the Chilean capital, to obtain respect from the eastern provinces for their democratically elected president and receive assurances of their peaceful participation in the referendum. After the summit, which allowed the referendum to take place, Morales declared that this was the first time in the history of the region "that the countries have decided to resolve the problems of South America themselves. In the past, even to deal with some internal or bilateral . . . Latin American issues, they were discussed in the United States."[51]

In sum, both Chávez's initiatives and Morales's nationalizations are paradigmatic examples of weak communism. They decentralize the state bureaucratic system, which was so counterproductive in the Soviet Union: while the independent counsels increase community involvement, nationalization returned land, dignity, and rights to the weakest segments of the population.[52] But if Chávez and Morales managed to enact these progressive policies in their own countries, it is also because the whole region has been able to resist some of capitalism's most "extreme characteristics and even set up innovative arrangements outside of formal market structures."[53] Most of these arrangements are monitored by organizations such as ALBA (Bolivarian Alliance for the Americas), Mercosur (Southern Common Market), Banco del Sur (Bank of the South), and UNASUR, among others.[54] With these organizations, South America is providing an alternative not only for the weak among its population but also for other continents searching for a different political, economical, and ecological system.[55] This is why Banco del Sur was recently endorsed by Stiglitz against the IMF impositions and why UNASUR was praised by Chomsky as an "alternative" to U.S. dominance in the region.[56] *Weak communism is the political alternative to the neoliberal impositions of framed democracies.*

After years of submission to capitalist market policies that obliged South American countries, among other entities, to remove obstacles to foreign investments, weak communism has began to take control. This is why in 2009 Lula preferred to skip the Davos meeting in order to participate again, together with Chávez, Morales, and other South American leaders, in the World Social Forum in Belem. Over the past ten years, this forum has become both an effective alternative to the Swiss meeting and the driving engine of those social movements without which Lula, Chávez, and other politicians would not have been elected. Although these social movements "differ in many respects from country to country, they all share antipathy towards US political, economic, and military control,"[57] an opposition that is at the essence of weak communism's economic programs. This is why Lula, discussing the recent economic 2008 crisis at the social forum, felt compelled to emphasize how it was "not caused by 'the socialism of Chávez' or by 'the struggles of Morales' but by the bankrupt policies and lack of financial control of wealthy states outside the continent."[58] Given that "neoliberal methods . . . created the third world,"[59] South American citizens will probably continue to vote for these communist leaders. As Mark Weis-brot has pointed out, they have "succeeded where their neoliberal pre-decessors failed" and

> changed their economic policies in ways that increased economic growth. Argentina's economy grew more than 60% in six years and Venezuela's by 95%. These are enormous growth rates even taking into account these countries' prior recessions, and allowed for large reductions in poverty. Left governments have also taken greater control over their natural resources (Ecuador, Bolivia, Venezuela) and delivered on their promises to share the income from these resources with the poor. This is the way democracy is supposed to work: people voted for change and got quite a bit of what they voted for, with reasonable expectations of more to come. We should not be surprised if most Latin American voters stick with the left through hard times. Who else is going to defend their interests?[60]

South American governments manage to defend their citizens' eco-nomic interests because they have been detaching themselves not only from neoliberal impositions but also from the attendant military pres-ence, that is, armed capitalism.

UNASUR, which was modeled after the European Union (prior to the creation of a common parliament, currency, and passport for all of its member states), has tried, through its member states, to evict the remaining U.S. military bases present in the region. While there are U.S. military bases throughout Europe, in South America only Peru, Para-guay, Honduras, and Colombia,[61] which has the sole remaining conser-vative government in the region, recently agreed to an increase in U.S.

military presence, in exchange for billions of dollars and privileged access to military supplies. Regardless of Colombia's poor human-rights record, the United States continues to sponsor President Uribe not only in exchange for these bases (which also house nuclear weapons) but also for general political support, given the prevailing antipathy toward the United States in the region.[62] But this is not the only indication that the United States is trying to regain control over South America. In 2008, the Fourth Fleet was reestablished in the region's waters, and in 2009 a military coup against the democratically elected president of Honduras was allowed.[63] While this coup could have been easily avoided, considering that the United States still has a base in the country, the United States instead supported the newly imposed president, because the "constitutional reform process that Zelaya hoped to set in motion could easily lead to voters' rejection of foreign troops on their soil."[64] All these are examples of U.S. interest in the region, an interest that goes far beyond its natural resources, even considering that the "US gets half its oil from Latin America."[65]

Nevertheless, instead of a military response to these provocations, UNASUR instructed its Defense Council to investigate the danger that these bases in Colombia pose for the region and declared (after the summit held in Bariloche, Argentina, on August 29, 2009) that "South America must be kept as 'a land of peace,' and that foreign military forces must not threaten the sovereignty or integrity of any nation of the region."[66] If the region's prevailing communist governments lose electoral support one day, it will not be because of the impositions of armed capitalism but rather because its own social movements have ceased to support them. After all, weak communism was chosen because of the overwhelming poverty that dominates the region after decades of neoliberal impositions—the same poverty that now is also starting to appear in Western states. In sum, the United States feels the need to regain control over South America not only because of its vital natural resources but also, and most of all, because its social, economic, and democratic model is again summoning the specter of communism throughout the world.[67]

CHÁVEZ: A MODEL FOR OBAMA?

As we have seen, the problem for U.S. neoliberalism is that South America's weak communism, guided by Chávez, has become an "emergency," that is, an effective economic and political alternative to framed democracies. The Venezuelan president has managed to help the region elect other politicians who enacted communist models in favor of the weak, and he has also attracted Western social movements unsatisfied with their left-wing reformist politicians. Fukuyama must have noticed all of this, because he recently felt compelled to express that the "idea that contemporary Venezuela represents a social model superior to liberal democracy is absurd."[68] Contrary to Fukuyama, Greg Grandin, in a recent article for *The Nation* (which covered the increasing U.S. militarization of South America under Obama's administration), instead emphasizes how throughout Latin America

a new generation of community activists continues to advance the global democracy movement that was largely derailed in the United States by 9/11. They provide important leadership to US environmental, indigenous, religious and human rights organizations, working to develop a comprehensive and sustainable social-justice agenda. Latin America does not present a serious military danger. No country is trying to acquire a nuclear weapon or cut off access to vital resources. . . . Obama is popular in Latin America, and most governments, including those on the left, would have welcomed a demilitarized diplomacy that downplays terrorism and prioritizes reducing poverty and inequality—exactly the kind of "new multilateralism" Obama called for in his presidential campaign. . . . Unable or unwilling to make concessions on these and other issues important to Latin America—normalizing relations with Cuba, for instance, or advancing immigration reform—the White House is adopting an increasingly antagonistic posture.[69]

The reasons for concluding this book by directing our attention to the recent South American revolutionary examples, in particular that of Chávez, should be quite evident to anyone who is unsatisfied with framed democracies. Chávez, together with his allies, provides an alternative and a model we could follow. However, our attention has been drawn not only by South American social politics but also by the excessive interest that the Obama administration (from which we are all still waiting for innovative changes)[70] is putting into improving, consolidating, and establishing the U.S. military presence in South America. The recent U.S.-supported coup in Honduras, together with the new and powerful bases being opened in Colombia, are alarming, considering that none of these states, as Grandin explains, represents any military danger to the United States. This brings to mind "Operation Condor," that is, of those politics that in the 1970s sustained the worst South American military dictatorships.[71] It is clear that the U.S. obsession with this region is motivated not only by strategic interest, that is, fear of extracapitalist political and economic formations, but also by a fear of the democratic example that these communist states provide. If "hermeneutic communism" must be proven practically, we are convinced that it can be found in these Latin American democracies that have constructed themselves along the lines of the Cuban resistance. This explains the particular tenacity that characterizes U.S. foreign policy toward Venezuela, which has become the guiding force in Latin America. Although Venezuela's exemplary social and democratic model is presented only here, at the end of our book, it constitutes the key of our thesis.

Hermeneutic communism is not a theoretical discourse aiming merely to offer philosophical perspectives on those ideas of revolution or radical transformation of society that still manage to survive in our imaginary and imaginations. Rather, it is a theory capable of both updating classical Marxism and again rendering believable the effective possibility of communism. While at a theoretical level we have argued that a revolution may be correctly thought about only outside the scientific and metaphysical horizons that still dominate classical Marxism, at the practical level such a theoretical possibility can be linked to the effective examples of "new" communism in Latin America. In sum, this theory is nothing other than a reevaluation of our Marxist inheritance, stimulated and inspired by those realities that have been outlined in the "real America" of Chávez, Morales, and Lula; it must be pointed out that although Lula had to deal with Brazil's vast and complex history, which forced him to apply the same communist ideals in a much more circumscribed way, he still became an alternative voice in international affairs.[72]

Although we are not certain, it is quite possible that Cuban resistance, after fifty years of U.S. terrorist attacks and embargos,[73] made possible the birth of Chávez's Bolivarian socialism and the other political transformations in Latin America. As Noam Chomsky explained:

> Cuba has become a symbol of courageous resistance to attack. Since 1959 Cuba has been under attack from the hemispheric superpower. It has been invaded, subjected to more terror than maybe the rest of the world combined—certainly any other country that I can think of—and it's under an economic stranglehold that has been ruled completely illegal by every relevant international body. It has been at the receiving end of terrorism, repression and denunciation, but it survives.[74]

The Cuban revolution represents a small country's triumphant resistance to moral exploitation, through which U.S. imperialism and the Batista regime forced it to become the "brothel for American businessmen."[75] Just like Cuba, our weak or ghostlike communism is capable of resisting the dominant capitalist world. Belief in these effective alternative Latin American politics renders hermeneutic communism a seed of philosophical resistance to the impositions of conservative realist philosophies (and not the other way around); philosophical positions still convinced that the only possible order of the world is the capitalistic one are always prepared to exploit and dominate with a "human face," as Žižek often emphasizes. And it is just through this human face that the excessive manipulation of the media (dependent and compromised by European pseudoleftist parties) has rendered unthinkable the idea of political transformations through communism. Such a possibility can only be thought about in those regions where European colonial dominance is resisted by original communities, in other words, where it is possible to construct true alternatives upon the ruins of Western industrial capitalism.

Many might object that indicating this communicative spirit, which is still alive in so many regions of South America, is simply "mythologizing" the third world. But such a claim forgets that the origins of our financial crisis are also rooted in Western modernity, that is, in the spirit that dominated European colonialism. This spirit involves the exploitative capitalist relation with natural resources and also a wider issue that concerns general culture and the way we relate to others. Although Chinese or Indian societies could also function as a model for the West, what we see in them now are not new forms of capitalism, socialism, or communism but rather the incarnation of Max Weber's "iron cage of capitalism." If these societies have assimilated and rendered neoliberal practices more effectively than the West, it is not because they have applied a better method but because they function within much more rigid frames. Without venturing into a comparative anthropological analysis of different cultural models, South American socialism appears to be the realm in which a possible alternative to the dominant capitalist vision of the world can take place, because it is not framed within a disciplinary or, as we have called it throughout this book, metaphysical vision of the world.

The idea that has guided us throughout this text is rigorously materialistic: the structural changes we ascertain in South American societies are inseparable from a collective culture and structure that are very different from the one that characterizes the West. But thinking that this difference is only an expression of underdevelopment or the incomplete assimilation of modernity would be a prejudiced result of colonial beliefs. Regardless of its actuality today, it is the postmodern thinking of

Lyotard, Derrida, and others that liberated us from those modern dogmas that imposed the Western form of development on "underdeveloped" populations. If international institutions such as the IMF continue to conceive of their aid to the third world as following just this idea of development, the South American alternative shakes up this modern, Eurocentric frame.

The democratically elected governments of South America are also an indication of how Western democracies have submitted to those private interests without which politicians could not finance their political campaigns. The intention of our book, though it explores the status of communism, is also to provoke a reflection on the value of democracy as it is practiced in the West. We should stop considering as scandalous the idea that a revolution can occur without a previous authorization by the citizens as expressed in a referendum; after all, no modern constitution was ever born "democratically," starting with that of the United States, whose constitution was drafted by a group of progressive intellectuals. Although it is a tricky argument, one should ask oneself whether, today, U.S. citizens are actually freer than Cubans. After all, the freedoms that Cubans have missed in these recent years are not constitutional but rather depend on the limitations imposed on their economy by years of U.S. embargo. This is why progressive American public figures such as Michael Moore, Oliver Stone, and Noam Chomsky have repeatedly emphasized how the effective possibilities of a fair life are all in favor of Cubans today. Although these South American governments have not yet betrayed parliamentary democracy, we are convinced that they ought to be defended even if eventually they do have to violate these rules. As Mao said: "A revolution is not a dinner party, or writing an essay, or painting a picture, or doing embroidery; it cannot be so refined, so leisurely and gentle, so temperate, kind, courteous, restrained and magnanimous. A revolution is an insurrection, an act of violence by which one class overthrows another."[76]

We do not know how the relationship between the armed capitalism of framed democracies and Latin American governments will develop, but we must all hope it will not become a violent conflict, even though the United States seems to countenance this option. The problem we must ask ourselves at the end of this book, which tries to regain faith in a radical transformation of our current order, is well summarized in Mao's affirmation: "a revolution is not a dinner party." Regardless of our admiration for a vision of history that progressively excludes violence, we are not very hopeful, as the recent social, economic, and military levels of inequality caused by capitalism continue to increase, threatening any project of social transformation.

History, as the dialectical conflict of authorities, classes, or entire populations, has not ended. Neither has the universal proletarianization (upon which Marx made the communist revolution depend) been exorcised by the well-being spread by globalization, because globalization has not spread wealth. With the pretext of possible terrorist attacks, the intensification of control will end by forcing us to live in the "imprisoned" world that Nietzsche called "accomplished nihilism": a world where in order to survive as human beings we must become *Übermensch*, that is, individuals capable of constructing our own alternative interpretation of the world instead of submitting to the official truths. This is also why the *bisheriger Mensch*, "the man so far," is the man of modernity, who needs to emerge from his enslavement to metaphysics in order to encounter other cultures of the world and propose alternative ways of life.

Contrary to metaphysical conservative realism, hermeneutic communism allows other cultures to suggest different visions of the world, visions not yet framed within the logic of production, profit, and dominion. Although the revolt of colonial populations is still largely dominated by Western capitalism, these revolts are increasingly aware of the possibility of becoming a cultural revolt rather than a method for an equal redistribution of wealth. While European modernity claimed to be the bearer of universal values and therefore viewed with suspicion any demand from individual communities or identity populations, today we cannot believe anymore in the necessity of, say, international proletarianism, that is, of a universal value. The world will not cease to be alienated by finding its identity but rather by being open to the multiplicity of identities. Nevertheless, if in order to construct such a world we must "unite all the proletarians of all the world," then it will eventually become necessary to plan the foundation of a Fifth International, as Chávez has recently suggested.[77] While we also endorse Chavez's suggestion, the communist project must always bear in mind its hermeneutic inspiration against all those metaphysical temptations and the horrors of those universalisms that have shed blood throughout the world.

Unfortunately, hermeneutic communism cannot assure peaceful existence, dialogue, or a tranquil life, because this "normal" realm already belongs to the winners within framed democracies. In these democracies, the weak have been discharged so that the winners may preserve a life without alterations; this, after all, must be why the word "stability" or "bipartisanship" is so often used by Obama and other presidents in international and domestic summits. But, as the recent economic crisis has demonstrated, the so-called stable world is not stable at all. As this instability increases, so do the possibilities of world revolution, a revolution that hermeneutic communism is not waiting for at the border of history but rather is trying (paradoxically) to avoid. If we prefer to circumvent such revolution, it is not because we do not believe in the necessity of an alternative but rather because the powers of armed capitalism are too powerful both within framed democracies and in its discharge. As we have seen above, these same territories at the margins of framed democracies are also part of the mechanism of armed capitalism and are therefore subjected to what Danilo Zolo calls "humanitarian wars" in order to guarantee stability.

As we indicated in chapter 3, hermeneutics is not an assessment of tradition but most of all an ontology of the event, a philosophy of instability. In this context, communism's dialectical conception of history is not dominated, as in the metaphysical systems, by the moment of conciliation but rather by the awareness that Being as event continuously questions again the provisional conciliations already achieved. As a dialectic theory, hermeneutic communism does not consider itself the bearer of metaphysical truths or a metaphysics of history as conflicts and clashes. Instead, it is convinced that in the current situation of increasing universalization, lack of emergency, and the impossibility of revolution, philosophy has the task of intensifying the consciousness of conflict, even though everything ("stability," cultural "values," and analytic philosophy's "realism") seems to prove it wrong.

In sum, hermeneutic communism proposes an effective conception of existence for those who do not wish to be enslaved in and by a world of total organization. Although we are not thinking about the professional revolutionary figure as the only possibility for authentic existence, we are not going to exclude that such an idea is interesting. Heidegger's thesis, according to which existence is a thrown project, is the only one we manage to suggest as an alternative to the pure static discipline of the politics of descriptions, founded on dominion in all its forms. That the transformation of the world cannot be projected in the form of a violent engagement, which would only provoke increased repression, makes much more difficult the goal of resistance and opposition and therefore communism. After all, great revolutions of the past, such as the Russian and Chinese revolutions, seem today like events that had to adopt the arms of their enemies, leading to regimes as violent and repressive as the ones that they had set out to destroy. But we do not accept the desperate vision of Sartre in his *Critique of Dialectical Reason*, according to whom any form of renovation, after the great experience of "groups in fusion," must fall again into the routine of dominion, in a triumph that he regarded as "practico-inert." Today, the global integration of the world offers different forms of resistance than the armed revolts of the past. Examples of nonviolent methods, from Gandhi to the "pressure" exerted by the simple existence of the communist democracies of Chávez and Lula, may operate to limit the current dominion of the great empire of capitalism. These are the most productive alternatives at our disposal today. Other forms of passive resistance, such as boycotts, strikes, and other manifestations against oppressive institutions, may be effective, but only if actual masses of citizens take part, as in Latin America.[78] These mass movements might avoid falling back again into the practico-inert, which is the natural consequence of those revolutions entrusted to small and inevitably violent avant-garde intellectuals, that is, those who have only *described* the world in various ways. The moment now has arrived to *interpret* the world.

NOTES

INTRODUCTION

1. M. Heidegger, "Overcoming Metaphysics," in *The End of Philosophy*, trans. J. Stambaugh (New York: Harper and Row, 1973), 91.

2. R. Rorty, *Achieving Our Country: Leftist Thought in Twentieth-Century America* (Cambridge, Mass.: Harvard University Press, 1998), 139. Göran Therborn, in his account of contemporary Marxism, points out that although "Marx and Engels saw no tension between science and critique, the Western, mainly Anglophone, post-1968 academic reception of Marx drew a distinction between 'critical' and 'scientific' Marxism" (*From Marxism to Post-Marxism* [London: Verso, 2008], 71). This distinction is also captured in the essays written on Derrida's *Specters of Marx* by Antonio Negri, Fredric Jameson, Terry Eagleton, and others in *Ghostly Demarcations: A Symposium*

on *Jacques Derrida's* Specters of Marx, ed. Michael Sprinker (London: Verso, 1999), and also in some of the contributions to *The Idea of Communism*, ed. S. Žižek and C. Douzinas (London: Verso, 2010).

3. A guide to the contemporary Marxist philosophers is available in chapters 2 and 3 of Therborn, *From Marxism to Post-Marxism.*

4. Slavoj Žižek, *In Defense of Lost Causes* (London: Verso, 2008), 1.

5. Yu Wujin, "Marx's Philosophy as Practical Hermeneutics," *Fudan Journal* (June 2009).

6. Although most Latin American governments define themselves "socialist" rather than "communist," the fact that President Hugo Chávez of Venezuela recently called for the Fifth International indicates how this region also represents the twenty-first-century communism.

7. E. Hobsbawm, "El comunismo continúa vigente como motivación y como utopía," interview by Aurora Intxausti, *El País* (April 12, 2003). It should be pointed out that Hobsbawm, together with Naomi Klein, Eduardo Galeano, John Pilger, Alexander Cockburn, José Bové, and many others, signed a manifesto in support of Chavez in 2004 that stated: "We wish to denounce the disinformation campaign that is being orchestrated by the major media and that attempts to characterize Chavez as a tyrant, a President who has consistently respected the rule of law and the country's Constitution" (Sharmini Peries, "Venezuela's Chavez Triumphant: History Making Democracy in Latin America," Venezuelanalysis.com [August 16, 2004]). See also Peter Beaumont, "History's Man," *Guardian* (August 15, 2004).

8. There "are very few things held in common in the fragmented field of contemporary philosophy," explains Jean Grondin, "except perhaps for this very fact that we do live in a 'fragmented field' of philosophical discourse, that is, one that is inescapably characterized by interpretation" (J. Grondin, *Sources of Hermeneutics* [Albany, N.Y.: SUNY Press, 1995], 1). Accounts of the fragmentation that characterizes contemporary philosophy are avail-

able in Franca D'Agostini, *Analitici e continentali* (Milan: Cortina, 1997); C. Prado, ed., *A House Divided: Comparing Analytic and Continental Philosophy* (Amherst, N.Y.: Humanity Books, 2003); and also in the last chapter of Michael Dummett's recent book *The Nature and Future of Philosophy* (New York: Columbia University Press, 2010).

9. R. Rorty, "What Is Religion's Future After Metaphysics?" in R. Rorty and G. Vattimo, *The Future of Religion*, ed. S. Zabala (New York: Columbia University Press, 2005), 74.

10. "Humanitarian wars" is a term coined by Danilo Zolo to indicate the violent nature the so-called democratic wars that we have grown accustomed to in the West. According to the Italian philosopher, the great powers have managed to "neutralize" the notion of "aggression" by alternating the notion of "self-defense" expressed in article 51 of the Charter of the United Nations. "In the majority of the cases the concept of 'aggression' has been distorted and converted in the opposite idea of a war conducted to defend humanity against the menace of 'global terrorism.'" Zolo specifies that the 1991 Gulf war and interventions in the Federal Republic of Yugoslavia, Afghanistan, Iraq, Lebanon, and Palestine have all managed to simulate the triumph of the humanitarian war through a terrorist use of military power. In particular, the 1999 war against the Federal Republic of Yugoslavia and the 2003 U.S. invasion of Iraq are archetypes of a war of aggression skillfully covered under the cloak of humanitarian war. These wars were actually aimed at realizing an imperialistic project of global hegemonic dimension on political, military, and economic grounds. See D. Zolo, *Terrorismo umanitario: Dalla guerra del Golfo alla strage di Gaza* (Reggio Emilia: Diabasis, 2009), 13–14. Unfortunately, a similar process took place after the earthquake in Haiti in 2010, as the U.S. government has given priority to the accumulation of foreign soldiers over the distribution of emergency supplies. As Ashley Smith reported, a month "into the disaster, the US and UN were managing to feed

only 1 million people, leaving more than a million people without relief aid. Instead of mobilizing to provide water, food, and housing for the victims, the US focused on occupying the country with 20,000 US troops and surrounding it with a flotilla of US Navy and Coast Guard ships" (A. Smith, "Imperialism with a Human Face: Haiti After the Quake," in *International Socialist Review* 70 [March–April 2010]: 9–20).

11. See G. Vattimo, *Ecce Comu. Come si ri-diventa ciò che si era* (Milan: Fazi, 2008) and G. Vattimo, "Communisme faible?" in *L'idée du communisme*, 287–289.

1. IMPOSING DESCRIPTIONS

1. http://www.neh.gov/news/archive/20041117.html.

2. R. Rorty, *Objectivity, Relativism, and Truth* (Cambridge: Cambridge University Press, 1991), 22.

3. M. Heidegger, *Contributions to Philosophy (From Enowning)* (1989), trans. P. Emad and K. Maly (Bloomington: University of Indiana Press, 1999), 140.

4. W. V. O. Quine, "Mr. Strawson on Logical Theory" (1953), in *The Ways of Paradox and Other Essays* (Cambridge, Mass.; Harvard University Press, 1976), 151.

5. R. Rorty, *Philosophy and the Mirror of Nature* (1979; Princeton, N.J.: Princeton University Press, 2008), 384.

6. Heidegger, *Contributions to Philosophy*, 103.

7. I. Berlin first coined the term "Counter-Enlightenment" in his essay of 1973. See I. Berlin, *The Proper Study of Mankind*, ed. H. Hardy and R. Hausheer (New York: Farrar, Strauss and Giroux, 2000), 243–268.

8. H. Marcuse, *Heideggerian Marxism*, ed. R. Wolin and J. Abromeit (Lincoln: University of Nebraska Press, 2005), 158. On the relation or possible dialogue between Marx and Heidegger, see chapter 5, "Heidegger and Marx-

ism: 'A Productive Dialogue,'" in M. Lewis, *Heidegger Beyond Deconstruction: On Nature* (London: Continuum, 2007), 128–151.

9. "Framed" (*Ge-Stell*) is Heidegger's term to indicate science and technology's objectivist nature, that is, how "man's essence is framed, claimed, and challenged by a power which man himself cannot control" (Heidegger, "Only a God Can Save Us: *Der Spiegel's* Interview" (1976), in *Philosophical and Political Writings*, ed. Manfred Stassen, trans. M. P. Alter and J. D. Caputo [New York: Continuum, 2003], 38). We will apply Heidegger's use of this term to democracy to show how the democratic procedures have also become "framed" within the rational organization of technology.

10. R. Rorty and P. Engel, *What's the Use of Truth?* ed. P. Savidan, trans. W. McCuaig (New York: Columbia University Press, 2007), 47–59.

11. Rorty, *Objectivity, Relativism, and Truth*, 21.

12. A. Tarski, "The Semantic Conception of Truth and the Foundations of Semantics," in *Philosophy and Phenomenological Research* 4 (1944), 341–75. See also Tarski, *Introduction to Logic and to the Methodology of the Deductive Sciences*, ed. Jan Tarski (New York: Oxford University Press, 1994), 33.

13. M. Heidegger, *Being and Time* (1927), trans. Joan Stambaugh (Albany, N.Y.: SUNY Press, 1996), 207–208.

14. Specifically in the section "Existence Is Interpretation" in chapter 3.

15. M. Heidegger, *Logic: The Question of Truth* (1925–1926), trans. T. Sheehan (Bloomington: University of Indiana Press, 2010), 113.

16. Heidegger, *Being and Time*, 211.

17. M. Heidegger, *On Time and Being*, trans. J. Stambaugh (Chicago: University of Chicago Press, 2002), 70.

18. E. Tugendhat, *Self-Consciousness and Self-Determination*, trans. P. Stern (Cambridge, Mass.: The MIT Press, 1986), 214. A historical account of these affirmations on *Time and Being* by Tugendhat, Habermas, and Apel are available in the second chapter of S. Zabala, *The Hermeneutic Nature*

of Analytic Philosophy: A Study of Ernst Tugendhat, trans. S. Zabala and M. Haskell (New York: Columbia University Press, 2008).

19. Heidegger specified this nontheoretical essence of hermeneutics: "What hermeneutics is really meant to achieve Is not merely taking cognizance of something and having knowledge about it, but rather an existential knowing, i.e., a Being [*ein Sein*]. It speaks from out of interpretation and for the sake of it. . . . As far as I am concerned, if this personal comment is permitted, I think that hermeneutics is not philosophy at all, but in fact something preliminary which runs in advance of it and has its own reasons for being: what is at issue in it, what it all comes to, is not to become finished with it as quickly as possible, but rather to hold out in it as long as possible. . . . It wishes only to place an object which has fallen into forgetfulness before today's philosophers for their 'well-disposed consideration'" (M. Heidegger, *Ontology—the Hermeneutics of Facticity* [1923], trans. J. van Buren [Bloomington: University of Indiana Press, 1999], 14).

20. The first formulation of this thesis is expressed in G. Vattimo, *Farewell to Truth,* trans. William McCuaig (New York: Columbia University Press, 2011).

21. J. Searle, *Freedom and Neurobiology* (New York: Columbia University Press, 2007), 32.

22. M. Heidegger, *Introduction to Metaphysics,* trans. G. Fried and R. Polt (New Haven, Conn.: Yale University Press, 2000), 97.

23. This difference is analyzed in chapter 2 of S. Zabala, *The Remains of Being* (New York: Columbia University Press), 78–86; and S. Zabala, "Being Is Conversation," in *Consequences of Hermeneutics,* ed. J. Malpas and S. Zabala (Evanston, Ill.: Northwestern University Press, 2010), 161–176.

24. A recent confirmation of this accomplishment of metaphysics in individual sciences can be found in S. Psillos and M. Curd, eds., *The Routledge Companion to Philosophy of Science* (London: Routledge, 2008), where the edi-

tors state in the introduction how the "philosophies of the individual sciences have acquired an unprecedented maturity and independence over the past few decades" (ix).

25. M. Heidegger, *Contributions to Philosophy*, 140. While P. Emad and K. Maly translated "*Not*" as "distress," we prefer R. Polt's suggestion of "emergency" (R. Polt, *The Emergency of Being* [Ithaca, N.Y.: Cornell University Press, 2006]).

26. This prize that Searle was awarded by President Bush is just one of the many institutional recognitions of objectivist philosophers at the service of science in recent years. Similar recognitions are listed in note 63.

27. Among the continental philosophers who defend such realism through phenomenology and also engaged in a debate with Derrida we should point out J.-L. Marion. This debate is now available in *God, the Gift, and Postmodernism*, ed. J. D. Caputo and M. J. Scanlon (Bloomington: University of Indiana Press, 1999).

28. Searle outlined this ontology for the first time in *The Construction of Social Reality* (New York: The Free Press, 1995).

29. B. Smith, "John Searle: From Speech Acts to Social Reality," in *John Searle*, ed. B. Smith (Cambridge: Cambridge University Press, 2003), 2.

30. A complete account of the collaboration between Husserl and Heidegger and of all the drafts of the *Encyclopaedia Britannica* article can be found in E. Husserl, *Psychological and Transcendental Phenomenology and the Confrontation with Heidegger (1927–1931)*, ed. and trans. T. Sheehan and R. Palmer (Dordrecht: Kluwer Academic Publishers, 1997).

31. This occurred with the publication of *The Crisis of European Sciences and Transcendental Phenomenology* in 1934, where Husserl emphasized the historical nature of the European sciences and philosophy itself.

32. J. Searle, *Philosophy in a New Century* (Oxford: Oxford University Press, 2008), 2.

33. We are here referring to the "Munich phenomenology" group, that is, A. Reinach, J. Daubert, A. Pfänder, and M. Geiger. For a complete account of all the phenomenological movements, see E. Spiegelberg, *The Phenomenological Movement: A Historical Introduction* (Berlin: Springer, 2007).

34. A. Reinach, *A Priori Foundations of the Civil Law* (1913), trans. J. Crosby, *Aletheia* 3 (1983): 1–142.

35. J. Searle, in *Conversations with John Searle*, ed. G. Faigenbaum (Montevideo: Libros En Red, 2001), 146.

36. Searle, *The Construction of Social Reality*, iii.

37. Searle, *Philosophy in a New Century*, 25.

38. Ibid., 131.

39. Kuhn's theory will be analyzed in the first section of chapter 3.

40. Searle, *Philosophy in a New Century*, 132.

41. Ibid., 131.

42. Searle, in *Conversations with John Searle*, 151.

43. Ibid., 150.

44. Searle, *Freedom and Neurobiology*, 89.

45. "The form of motivation that goes with a system of accepted status functions is essential to our concept of the political" (Ibid., 99).

46. Ibid., 103. Searle has also recently made this point in an interview with *La Stampa*: "La libertà è figlia del linguaggio," interview by Alberto Papuzzi, *La Stampa*, 19 May 2008.

47. Searle, *Freedom and Neurobiology*, 5. In the next chapter we will see how the liberal economist H. De Soto developed Searle's institutional-fact realism to continue the imposition of capitalism.

48. J. Austin, *How to Do Things with Words*, ed. J. O. Urmson (Oxford: Clarendon, 1962).

49. Searle, *Conversations with John Searle*, 166.

50. J. Derrida, "Limited Inc," supplement to *Glyph* 2 (1977): 162–254; reprinted

in J. Derrida, *Limited Inc.*, ed. G. Graff (Evanston, Ill.: Northwestern University Press, 1988), 29–110; J. Searle, "Reiterating the Differences: A Reply to Derrida" *Glyph* 1 (1977): 198–208.

51. "SARL" is equivalent to a private company limited by shares ("Ltd.") in the United Kingdom or a "corporation" in the United States.

52. Searle, *Conversations with John Searle*, 169.

53. Derrida, *Paper Machine*, 115.

54. J. Derrida, "A Discussion with Jacques Derrida," *Writing Instructor* 9, nos. 1–2 (Fall 1989–Winter 1990): 18.

55. For a complete history of the development and essence of the debate, see Raoul Moati, *Derrida/Searle: Déconstruction et langage ordinaire* (Paris: PUF, 2009); J. Culler, *On Deconstruction: Theory and Criticism After Structuralism* (1982; Abingdon: Routledge, 2008), 110–134; and Ian Maclean, "Un dialogue de sourds? Some Implications of the Austin-Searle-Derrida Debate" (1985), in *Jacques Derrida: Critical Thought*, ed. I. Maclachlan (London: Ashgate, 2004), 49–66.

56. J. Derrida, "Signature, Event, Context" (1971), in *Margins of Philosophy*, trans. A. Bass (Chicago: University of Chicago Press: 1982), 320.

57. Derrida, *Limited Inc.*, 62.

58. Searle, *Conversations with John Searle*, 166.

59. Derrida, *Limited Inc.*, 158.

60. J. Derrida, *Ethics, Institutions, and the Right to Philosophy*, ed. P. Pericles Trifonas (Lanham, Md.: Rowman & Littlefield, 2002), 29.

61. Derrida, *Ethics, Institutions, and the Right to Philosophy*, 29. This imperialistic nature of analytic philosophy was also stated by Searle in an interview with the *Harvard Journal of Philosophy*, where he expressed his desire to write a book on the "ontology of civilization" (Z. Sachs-Arellano, "Interview with Searle," *Harvard Review of Philosophy* 12 [2004]: 132–133).

62. Derrida, *Ethics, Institutions, and the Right to Philosophy*, 29.

63. Barry Smith is probably the best representative of the dissolution of philosophy into science; that is, he is a defender of realism through phenomenology and analytic philosophy. In his applications of ontology in relation to biomedical terminologies, electronic health records, property rights, and social development, ontology is reduced to a theory of objects. Through these investigations he managed to receive funding from many national and private science foundations (such as the Volkswagen Foundation, the European Union, and the U.S., Swiss, and Austrian National Science Foundations), confirming the political alliance between the scientific ideal of objectivity and the owners of societies.

64. B. Smith et al., "Derrida Degree: A Question of Honour," *Times* (London) (May 9, 1992).

65. Recently, the Italian philosopher Danilo Zolo has emphasized the how such order is also an international juridical order imposed on other by the winners. See D. Zolo, *Victors' Justice: From Nuremberg to Baghdad*, trans. M. W. Weir (London: Verso, 2009).

66. Lyotard's "metanarratives" will be analyzed in the section "Hermeneutics as Weak Thought," in chapter 3.

67. Searle, in *Conversations with John Searle*, 150.

68. F. Fukuyama, *The End of History and the Last Man* (New York: Free Press, 1992, 2006), 73. Fukuyama goes on to specify how "scientific development makes possible the enormous increase in productivity that has driven modern capitalism and the liberation of technology and ideas in modern markets economies" (Fukuyama, "Afterword," in *The End of History and the Last Man*, 343).

69. Ibid., 211–212.

70. Heidegger, *Contributions to Philosophy*, 103.

71. Fukuyama, *The End of History and the Last Man*, 211.

72. W. Benjamin, "On the Concept of History" (1939), in *Selected Writings: 1938–1940*, ed. H. Eiland and M. W. Jennings (Cambridge Mass.: Belknap Press of Harvard University Press, 2003), 4:391.

73. W. Benjamin, *Gesammelte Schriften*, ed. R. Tiedemann and H. Schweppenhäser (Frankfurt: Surhkamp, 1972), 1:1236.

74. Benjamin, "On the Concept of History," 392.

75. Benjamin, *Gesammelte Schriften*, 1:658.

76. Heidegger, *Contributions to Philosophy*, 140.

77. M. Heidegger, "The Origin of the Work of Art" (1936), in *Off the Beaten Track*, ed. and trans. J. Young and K. Haynes (Cambridge: Cambridge University Press 2002), 37.

78. Benjamin, *Gesammelte Schriften*, 1:1236.

2. ARMED CAPITALISM

1. "Barack Obama, winner of the Nobel Peace Prize," explains David Whitehouse, "has taken ownership of the war he always said the US should fight. In his first eleven months in office, he ordered troop escalations in Afghanistan of 21,000 and 30,000, to effectively double the US fighting force— while military contractors will continue to outnumber those in uniform. The annual cost for the war is also set to double, from $50 billion in 2005 to some $100 billion in 2010" (D. Whitehouse, "Afghanistan Sinking Deeper," *International Socialist Review* 69 [January–February 2010]: 23–29). Travis Sharp, who is a military-policy analyst at the Center for Arms Control and Non-Proliferation in Washington, D.C., reported that the Obama administration's 2009 budget "included $534 billion for the Department of Defense, as well as $130 billion for the wars in Iraq and Afghanistan. At $534 billion, President Barack Obama's Pentagon budget is $9 billion, or 1.7 percent, greater than the previous year's budget after adjusting for inflation" (Travis

Sharp, "The Worst Kind of Stimulus," *Foreign Policy* [March 2009], available at http://www.iiss.org/whats-new/iiss-in-the-press/march-2009/the-worst-kind-of-stimulus/). This was confirmed by C. Drew and E. Bumiller of the *New York Times* on April 6, 2009, when, during a press briefing at the Pentagon, Defense Secretary Robert M. Gates and the vice chairman of the Joint Chiefs of Staff, Gen. James E. Cartwright, announced the "first broad rethinking of American military strategy under the Obama administration, which plans to shift more money to counterterrorism in Iraq and Afghanistan while spending less on preparations for conventional warfare against large nations like China and Russia." This is probably why Jeffrey D. Sachs was keen to point out how Obama's budget in military spending is "an amount that exceeds US budget spending in all other areas except so-called 'mandatory' spending on social security, healthcare, interest payments on the national debt and a few other items. Indeed, US military spending exceeds the sum of federal budgetary outlays for education, agriculture, climate change, environmental protection, ocean protection, energy systems, homeland security, low-income housing, national parks and national land management, the judicial system, international development, diplomatic operations, highways, public transport, veterans' affairs, space exploration and science, civilian research and development, civil engineering for waterways, dams, bridges, sewerage and waste treatment, community development and many other areas. This preponderance of military spending applies to all 10 years of Obama's medium-term scenario. By 2019, total military spending is projected to be $8.2tn, exceeding by $2tn the budgeted outlays for all non-mandatory budget spending" (Jeffrey D. Sachs, "Obama's Military Conundrum," *Guardian* [May 22, 2009]).

2. Since the available bibliography on Obama is not only excessive but also unreliable, we prefer to rely on different commentaries that indicate not only how he was always a member of the establishment but also how he

continues its politics: D. Moisi, "Barack Obama's American Revolution," *Japan Times Online* (December 29, 2007); N. Chomsky, "Elections 2008 and Obama's Vision," *Z Magazine* 22, no. 2 (February 2009); N. Wolf, "The Bush in Obama," *Sunday Times* (August 2, 2009).

3. For a history of the roots of 9/11, see P. Bennis, *Before and After: U.S. Foreign Policy and the War on Terrorism* (New York: Olive Branch Press, 2003). Commenting on the *9/11 Commission Report*, Howard Zinn indicated how it ignored the fundamental question: what were the causes of 9/11? "The 9/11 Commission dodges the issue of relationships between American foreign policy and the creation of enormous anger in the Middle East—an anger which is felt by millions of people in the Middle East, which then leads to a small number of fanatics engaging in terrorist attacks. To point to the way in which American foreign policy has inflamed people against us and therefore led to terrorist attacks is not therefore to justify, of course, the terrorist attack; it's simply to say we need to look for more profound causes of 9/11 than intelligence failure" (H. Zinn, "About the Book," in *A People's History of the United States: 1492–Present* [New York: HarperCollins, 2005], 8).

4. The financial market system will be analyzed in the second paragraph of this chapter. A clear explanation of this recent crisis can be found in D. Baker, *Plunder and Blunder: The Rise and Fall of the Bubble Economy* (Sausalito, Calif.: PoliPointPress, 2009), and in J. Stiglitz, *Freefall: America, Free Markets, and the Sinking of the World Economy* (New York: Norton, 2010).

5. Justifications of this thesis can be found in W. Blum, *Killing Hope: U.S. Military and CIA Interventions Since World War II* (Monroe, Maine: Common Courage Press, 2008).

6. R. Kagan, *The Return of History and the End of Dreams* (New York: Random House, 2008), 49. Kagan goes on to specify how "since September 11, 2001, the United States has built or expanded bases in Afghanistan, Kyrgyzstan, Pakistan, Tajikistan, and Uzbekistan in Central Asia; in Bulgaria, Georgia,

Hungary, Poland, and Romania in Europe; as well as in the Philippines, Djibouti, Oman, Qatar, and of course, Iraq" (91). E. Meiksins Wood points out how the disappearance of the Soviet Union "removed the last remaining reality-check on US global ambitions" (*Empire of Capital* [London: Verso, 2003], 163). As Chomsky emphasizes, although the "United States spends almost as much as the rest of the world combined on its military and . . . is far more advanced in the technology of destruction . . . [and] the world is unipolar militarily, since the 1970s it has become economically 'tripolar,'" with comparable centers in North America, Europe and northeast Asia. The global economy is becoming more diverse, particularly with the growth of Asian economies. A world becoming truly multipolar, politically as well as economically, despite the resistance of the sole superpower, marks a progressive change in history" (N. Chomsky, "Barak Obama and the 'Unipolar Moment,'" *In These Times* [October 6, 2009]).

7. F. Fukuyama, *The End of History and the Last Man* (New York: Free Press, 1992, 2006), 263.

8. Afterword to ibid., 350–351 (included in the second paperback edition in 2006).

9. F. Fukuyama, "Back to the End of History," interview with M. Phillips, *Newsweek* (September 29, 2008).

10. Kagan, *The Return of History and the End of Dreams*, 80.

11. Ibid., 4.

12. Ibid., 98–99.

13. Ibid., 26.

14. J. Derrida, *Specters of Marx*, trans. P. Kamuf (New York: Routledge, 1994), 85.

15. "Between 1989 and 2001, the United States intervened with force in foreign lands more frequently than at any other time in its history" (Kagan, *The Return of History and the End of Dreams*, 50).

16. According to a poll by the *Financial Times* and the Harris Institute, large majorities of people in the United States and across Europe believe that "economic globalization, that is, neo-liberalism, is not only an overwhelmingly negative force, but also is having a negative rather than a positive effect on their own countries. The public surveyed in all six rich countries (US, UK, France, Spain, Italy, and Germany) apart from recognizing how neoliberalism is not beneficial to them as it isn't to poor countries, also expressed the wish that their own governments increase taxation on those with the highest incomes" (C. Gilles, "Poll Reveals Backlash in Wealthy Countries Against Globalization," *Financial Times* [July 23, 2007]).

17. M. Davis, *Planet of Slums* (London: Verso: 2006), 205.

18. Rear Admiral C. J. Parry, *The DCDC Global Strategic Trends Programme: 2007–2036*, 3.

19. Peter Schwartz and Doug Randall, *An Abrupt Climate Change Scenario and Its Implications for United States National Security*, www.environmental defense.org/documents/3566_AbruptClimateChange.pdf.

20. As we mentioned in note 1, the Pentagon is planning "to shift more money to counterterrorism in Iraq and Afghanistan while spending less on preparations for conventional warfare against large nations like China and Russia" (*New York Times* [April 6, 2009]).

21. Wood, *Empire of Capital*, 14.

22. Among the various defenders of the end of the nation-state we recall J-M. Guéhenno, *The End of the Nation-State* (1993), trans. V. Elliott (Minneapolis: University of Minnesota Press, 1995); K. Ohmae, *The End of the Nation State* (New York: The Free Press, 1995); P. Bobbitt, *The Shield of Achilles* (London: Allen Lane Penguin, 2002); and M. Hardt and A. Negri, *Empire* (Cambridge, Mass.: Harvard University Press, 2000).

23. C. Schmitt, *Die Geistesgeschichtliche Lage des Heutigen Parlamentarismus* (Berlin: Dunker and Humblot, 1926), 5. For a complete exposition of

Schmitt's political thesis, see M. Marder, *Groundless Existence: The Political Ontology of Carl Schmitt* (New York: Continuum, 2010).

24. R. Polt has exposed a very clear description of Heidegger's liberalism in *The Emergency of Being* (Ithaca, N.Y.: Cornell University Press, 2006), 227–236.

25. M. Heidegger, *Contributions to Philosophy (From Enowning)* (1909), trans. P. Emad and K. Maly (Bloomington: University of Indiana Press, 1999), 36. Heidegger also specified how " 'Spirit' is thereby always taken to be 'reason,' as the faculty of being able to say 'I.' In this regards even Kant was further along than this biological liberalism. Kant saw that person is more than the 'I'; it is grounded in self-legislation. Of course, this too remained Platonism" (37).

26. Ibid., 38, 103. A historical reconstruction of the various meanings of liberalism can be found in D. Losurdo, *Controstoria del liberalismo* (Roma-Bari: Laterza: 2006); and A. Wolf, *The Future of Liberalism* (New York: Knopf: 2009).

27. Heidegger, *Contributions to Philosophy*, 140.

28. R. Polt, "Metaphysical Liberalism in Heidegger's Beiträge Zur Philosophie," *Political Theory* 25, no. 5 (October 1997): 663.

29. R. Nozick, *Anarchy, State, and Utopia* (Malden: Blackwell, 1974), ix.

30. Ibid.

31. A recent critique of Italian political ineffectiveness can be found in G. Vattimo, *Ecce Comu* (Rome: Fazi, 2008). On the U.S. electoral system, see chapter 6 of N. Chomsky, *Failed States* (London: Penguin, 2006).

32. E. Hobsbawm, *The New Century: In Conversation with A. Polito*, trans. A. Cameron (London: Abacus, 2000), 50.

33. Numerous other examples can be found in J. Stiglitz, *Globalization and Its Discontents* (New York: Norton, 2002); and N. Klein, *The Shock Doctrine* (London: Penguin, 2007), not only for other nations (e.g., Chile) but also for entire regions, such as the former Soviet Union states.

34. While the most plausible economic and strategic justifications for invading Iraq, as N. Klein, explained, still rest in its "vast oil reserves [and] a good central location for military bases now that Saudi Arabia looked less dependable" (*The Shock Doctrine*, 329), the "attack on Afghanistan," according to E. Meiksins Wood, "was undertaken with an eye to the huge oil and gas reserves of Central Asia" (*Empire of Capital*, 165). See also P. Cockburn, *The Occupation: War and Resistance in Iraq* (London: Verso, 2007); and G. Achcar and N. Chomsky, *Perilous Power: The Middle East and U.S. Foreign Policy Dialogues on Terror, Democracy, War, and Justice*, ed. S. R. Shalom (Boulder, Colo.: Paradigm, 2007).

35. Chomsky, *Failed States*, 24.

36. The same goes for the invasion of Afghanistan, considering that the allegations that the Taliban were implicated in the 9/11 attack are still fragile, in that most of the attackers were from other nations. On the plotting of 9/11, see J. Burke, *Al-Qaeda: The True Story of Radical Islam* (London: Penguin, 2007), 236–238, 244–248; and P. Bennis, *Before and After: U.S. Foreign Policy and the War on Terrorism* (New York: Olive Branch Press, 2003); and N. Chomsky, *9/11* (New York: Seven Stories Press, 2011).

37. According to E. Margolis, "In the U.S., Pentagon hardliners are drawing up plans to invade Iran once Iraq and its oil are 'liberated.' They hope civil war will erupt in Iran, which is driven by bitterly hostile factions, after which a pro-U.S. regime will take power. If this does not occur, then Iraq-based U.S. forces will be ideally positioned to attack Iran. Or, they could just as well move west and invade Syria, another of Israel's most bitter enemies" (E. Margolis, "After Iraq, Bush Will Attack His Real Target," *Toronto Sun* [November 10, 2002]).

38. D. Harvey, *A Brief History of Neoliberalism* (New York: Oxford University Press, 2007), 7.

39. A. Juhasz, "Ambitions of Empire: The Bush Administration Economic

Plan for Iraq (and Beyond)," *Left Turn* 12 (February/March 2004): 27–32. N. Klein has explained in detail the economic impositions on Iraq in *The Shock Doctrine*, 342–354.

40. J. E. Stiglitz and L. J. Bilmes, *The Three-Trillion-Dollar War: The True Cost of the Iraq Conflict* (New York: Norton, 2008), 141.

41. Although the official number of casualties is very difficult to ascertain considering the amount of interest there has been in promoting the war, in an article entitled "What Is the Real Death Toll in Iraq?" J. Steele and S. Goldenberg (*Guardian*, March 19, 2008), explained that "five years after Bush and Tony Blair launched the invasion of Iraq against the wishes of a majority of UN members, no one knows how many Iraqis have died. We do know that more than two million have fled abroad. Another 1.5 million have sought safety elsewhere in Iraq. We know that the combined horror of car bombs, suicide attacks, sectarian killing and disproportionate US counter-insurgency tactics and air strikes have produced the worst humanitarian catastrophe in today's world. But the exact death toll remains a mystery. . . . An independent UK-based research group, calling itself the Iraq Body Count (IBC), collates all fatality reports in the media where there are two or more sources as well as figures from hospitals and other official sources. At least four household surveys have been done asking Iraqis to list the family members they have lost. The results have then been extrapolated to Iraq's total population to give a nationwide estimate. The results range from just under 100,000 dead to well over a million. Inevitably, the issue has become a political football, with the Bush administration, the British government and other supporters of the US-led occupation seizing on the lowest estimates and opponents on the highest."

Also, according to Amnesty International, "the latest and largest survey of civilian deaths in Iraq, published in early January 2008, [indicate that] 151,000 people were killed between March 2003 and June 2006. The survey was carried out by the World Health Organization (WHO) and Iraq's Health Ministry. The Iraqi government, led by Prime Minister Nuri al- Maliki, apparently accepts this estimate. Until the end of 2007, figures published on civilian casualties had ranged from 601,027 deaths, reported by US researchers in 2006 in the medical *Lancet* publication, to 47,668 by the Iraq Body Count" ("Iraq: Carnage and Despair. Five Years On," Amnesty International, Index Number: MDE 14/001/2008, http://www.amnesty .org/en/library/info/MDE14/001/2008/en).

42. During the release of the 2009 International Narcotics Control Strategy Report, David T. Johnson, assistant secretary of state for international narcotics and law enforcement affairs, stated that regardless of the NATO invasion, "Afghanistan remains, by far, the world's largest producer of opium poppy" (http://www.state.gov/p/inl/rls/rm/119890.htm).

43. This operation, called "Strike of the Sword," was launched into southern Afghanistan at the beginning of July 2009.

44. President Obama, "Remarks by the President on a New Strategy for Afghanistan and Pakistan," March 27, 2009, Office of the Press Secretary, http://www.whitehouse.gov/the_press_office/Remarks-by-the-President -on-a-New-Strategy-for-Afghanistan-and-Pakistan/.

45. Ibid. Obama used similar vocabulary and rhetoric in his speech at his Nobel Prize ceremony in December 2009. Unfortunately, Obama has pursued Bush's presupposition that those responsible for 9/11 were known. But, as Chomsky reminds us, "they were not[,] as the government quietly informed us eight months after the bombings. . . . In June 2002, FBI director Robert Mueller testified before a Senate committee, delivering what the press described as some of 'his most detailed public comments on the origins of the attacks' of 9-11. Mueller informed the Senate that 'investigations believe the idea of Sept. 11 attacks on the World Trade Center and Pentagon came from al Qaeda leaders in Afghanistan,' though the plotting and

financing may trace to Germany and the United Arab Emirates. 'We think the masterminds of it were in Afghanistan, high in the al Qaeda leadership,' Mueller said. If the indirect responsibility of Afghanistan could only be surmised in June 2002, it evidently could not have been known eight months before, when President Bush ordered the bombing of Afghanistan" (N. Chomsky, *Hegemony or Survival* [London: Penguin, 2003], 202).

46. R. Fisk, "Democracy Will Not Bring Freedom," *Independent* (August 21, 2009). For a full analysis of the different "networks" that characterize Afghani tribes, see L. Dupree, *Afghanistan* (London: Oxford University Press, 1998).

47. J. Metzl and C. Fair, "Let Afghans Lead Afghan Reform," *Khaleej Times Online* (September 3, 2009).

48. As Chomsky explained, Washington will support anyone who accords with U.S policies, including Saddam Hussein. "Long after the war was over and more than a year after Saddam's gassing of the Kurds, President Bush I issued a national security directive declaring that 'normal relations between the United States and Iraq would serve our longer-term interest and promote stability in both the Gulf and the Middle East.' . . . The US offered subsidized food supplies that Saddam's regime badly needed after its destruction of Kurdish agricultural production, along with advanced technology and biological agents adaptable to WMD" (Chomsky, *Hegemony or Survival*, 111–112).

49. According to the Pew Research Center for the People and the Press, although support for Bush drastically decreased during his second term in office, right after 9/11 support for his policy increased enormously. In its recent survey report, the Pew Center explains how his "first few months as president were largely unremarkable, despite the contentious 2000 election. But the horrific terror attacks of Sept. 11, 2001 greatly altered the course forward. The attacks transformed American public opinion and fundamen-

tally reshaped Bush's image. His job approval rating reached 86% by late September. The public expressed broad willingness to use military force to combat terrorism" ("Bush and Public Opinion: Reviewing the Bush Years and the Public's Final Verdict," December 18, 2008, http://people-press .org/report/478/bush-legacy-public-opinion).

50. Stiglitz, "Global Crisis—Made in America," *Spiegel Online* (December 11, 2008).

51. It is not only the retention of the Bush-appointed Robert Gates as defense secretary that alarmed most Democrats hoping for change but also the appointment of Timothy Geithner as U.S. secretary of the treasury. Geithner was the president of the Federal Reserve Bank of New York before directing the recent allocation of $350 billion in Wall Street bailout funds. The appointment of both secretaries is an indication of the will to conserve the established military and financial systems. Other dubious appointments by Obama include Robert Rubin and Larry Summers, who were major advocates of the one-sided deregulation of the financial industry.

52. P. Wintour and A. Clark, "G20 Leaders Map out New Economic Order at Pittsburgh Summit," *Guardian* (September 26, 2009). Against these protesters the police also used a new urban-warfare weapon, the Long Range Acoustic Device, which "concentrates voice commands and a car alarm–like sound in a 30- or 60-degree cone that can be heard nearly two miles away. It is about two feet square and mounted on a swivel such that one person can point it where it's needed. The volume measures 140–150 decibels three feet away—louder than a jet engine—but dissipates with distance." (J. Mandak, "Police Use Acoustic Warfare to Disperse G20 Crowds," *Associated Press* [October 1, 2009]). We must note that this summit was preceded by other two meetings: one in Washington in November 2008 and the other in London in 2009.

53. During this summit, Chris Ramirez reported the following declarations

by Stiglitz: "Having 20 nations is better than eight or nine . . . but there's still about 170 others who aren't being represented. It's important that the voices of the poorest nations are heard" (C. Ramirez, "Top Economist Stiglitz Calls for Expanded G-20," *Pittsburgh Tribune-Review* [September 24, 2009]).

54. Krugman, "How Did Economists Get It So Wrong?" *New York Times* (September 6, 2009).

55. Ibid.

56. R. Rorty, *Philosophy and the Mirror of Nature* (Princeton, N.J.: Princeton University Press, 1979), 384.

57. Krugman, "How Did Economists Get It So Wrong?" D. Rodrik notes how the public benefits when "economists disagree," that is, when the metaphysical nature of economics is put aside because "the world gets exposed to legitimate differences of views on how the economy operates. It is when they agree too much that the public should beware" (D. Rodrik, "Blame the Economist, Not Economics," *Guatemala Times* [March, 11, 2009]).

58. According to H. De Soto, much of the poverty in the Third World is caused by the lack of "formal property rights" over their own assets (homes, plots of land, or informal businesses), which could become productive financial assets if formalized, by blocking, for example, their use as collateral for needed borrowing. The Peruvian economist is convinced that as long as poor citizens of the Third World consider their own property a "thing" instead of a "value" to be used within the market, they are forced remain within the "grubby basement of the pre-capitalist world" (*The Mystery of Capital: Why Capitalism Triumphs in the West and Fails Everywhere Else* [New York: Basic Books, 2000], 55). Recently, Searle's main follower, B. Smith, together with D. M. Mark and I. Ehrlich, edited a book that analyzed and endorsed (with a contribution by Searle) de Soto's application of Searle's social ontology: *The Mystery of Capital and the Construction of Social Re-*

ality (Chicago: Open Court, 2008). A critical assessment of de Soto's thesis is available in *Demystifying the Mystery of Capital: Land Tenure and Poverty in Africa and the Caribbean*, ed. R. Home and H. Lim (London: Glasshouse Press, 2004).

59. Krugman, "How Did Economists Get It So Wrong?"

60. Ibid. Krugman also points out that neither of the two major macroeconomics models that prevailed for years predicted this crisis—that is, "freshwater" (propounded by economists such as Milton Friedman, who insist that free markets never go off track) and "saltwater" (espoused by economists such as John Maynard Keynes who, though they admit the possibilities of certain deviations, are certain these would eventually be corrected by national policy).

61. For an explanation of the Internet bubble, see E. Ofek and M. Richardson, "DotComMania: The Rise and Fall of Internet Stock Prices," *Journal of Finance* 68, no. 3 (June 2003): 1113–1137. The cost of the war is analyzed clearly in Stiglitz and Bilmes, *The Three-Trillion-Dollar War*. It is Stiglitz's belief that there is not one single responsible actor in this crisis: "any discussion of 'who is to blame' conjures up names like Robert Rubin, co-conspirator in deregulation and a senior official in one of the two financial institutions into which the American government has poured the most money. Then there is Alan Greenspan, who also pushed the deregulatory philosophy; who failed to use the regulatory authority that he had; who encouraged homeowners to take out highly risky adjustable mortgages; and who supported President Bush's tax cut for the rich, making lower interest rates, which fed the bubble, necessary to stimulate the economy. But these people hadn't been there, others would have occupied their seats, arguably doing similar things. There were others equally willing and able to perpetrate the crimes. Moreover, the fact that similar problems arose in other countries—with different people playing the parts of the protagonist—suggests that there were

more fundamental economic forces at play. The list of institutions that must assume considerable responsibility for the crisis includes the investment banks and the investors; the credit-rating agencies; the regulators, including the SEC and the Federal Reserve; the mortgage brokers; and a string of administrations, from Bush to Reagan, that pushed a financial sector deregulation" (J. Stiglitz, "The Anatomy of a Murder: Who Killed America's Economy?" *Critical Review* 21, no. 2–3 [2009]: 33). D. Baker predicted and analyzed this housing bubble in "The Menace of an Unchecked Housing Bubble," in *The Economist's Voice*, ed. J. Stiglitz, A. Edlin, and J. Bradford De-Long (New York: Columbia University Press, 2008), 288–295, and in his recent text *Plunder and Blunder*.

62. Stiglitz, "The Anatomy of a Murder," 334.

63. Ibid., 338.

64. Ibid., 336.

65. It should be pointed out that 9/11 was also used in this way, that is, to intensify and conserve the political domination in the Middle East.

66. Stiglitz, "Too Big to Fail or Too Big to Save? Examining the Systemic Threats of Large Financial Institutions," Testimony for the Joint Economic Committee hearing, April 21, 2009, Washington, D.C., http://www2.gsb.columbia .edu/faculty/jstiglitz/download/papers/2009_JEC_TooBigToFail.pdf. In this paper, Stiglitz specifies how the "Congressional Oversight Panel has made it clear that some of the too-large-to-fail banks have been the recipients of huge subsidies [$700 billion] under TARP [Troubled Asset Relief Program]. . . . In the first set of TARP transactions, the largest subsidies, both in amounts and in percentage, went to Citigroup, Inc. and AIG."

67. Ibid.

68. As Stiglitz reminds us, "The IMF is a public institution, established with money provided by taxpayers around the world. This is important to remember because it does not report directly to either the citizens who fi-

nance it or those whose lives it affects. Rather, it reports to the ministers of finance and the central banks of the governments of the world. They assert their control through a complicated voting arrangement based largely on the economic power of the countries at the end of World War II. There have been some minor adjustments since, but the major developed countries run the show, with only one country, the United States, having effective veto" (Stiglitz, *Globalization and Its Discontents*, 12).

69. Stiglitz, "A Global Recovery for a Global Recession," *The Nation* (July 13, 2009).

70. J. Stiglitz, *Making Globalization Work* (New York: Norton, 2007), 18.

71. Richard Wray of the *Guardian* noted that the limitations of the reforms that the draft communiqué of the G20 summit in Pittsburgh were directed to giving more voting power to developing countries: "Voting power on the 24-person IMF board reflects the loans that each member makes to the fund, calculated based on their share of the global economy. That model owes a lot to the fund's foundation in the wake of the second world war and is skewed towards Europe and the US. As a result emerging markets are under-represented—just two directors speak for 43 African countries. The US wants the number of directors reduced. France and the UK in particular are worried they could lose their individual seats, and want to see an end to the effective veto that the US has because of its voting weight in decision-making. Under plans being discussed at the G20 today, the world's rich nations would surrender up to 5% of their voting rights to emerging economies such as China—which currently has only 3.7% of the vote in the IMF" (R. Wray, "G20 Summit: What It Will Decide," *Guardian* [September 25, 2009]).

72. D. Baker, "G20: Why Support the IMF?" *Guardian* (April 2, 2009). In this article, Baker also emphasizes the conservative nature of the G20: "Unfortunately, the G20 agreement seems to reaffirm the leading role of the IMF

and to at least imply a position of official hostility to innovation." We should also indicate the Grameen Bank, which is having a lot of success through its microcredits to the impoverished without requiring collateral. In a later chapter, we explore the constitution of the Bank of the South.

73. Davis, *Planet of Slums*, 205.

74. Iraq suffered under international sanctions from 1990 to 2003, and more than 1 million people died for lack of food, water, and medicine.

75. We are referring here primarily to South America and other "Third World developing countries."

76. "Growth," says Stiglitz, "must be sustainable. . . . You can get GPD up by despoiling the environment, by depleting scarce natural resources, by borrowing from abroad—but this kind of growth is not sustainable" (Stiglitz, *Making Globalization Work*, 45).

77. Stiglitz, "GDP Fetishism," *Turkish Weekly* (September 15, 2009).

78. J. Stiglitz, A. Sen, et al., "Report by the Commission on the Measurement of Economic Performance and Social Progress," http://www.stiglitz-sen-fitoussi.fr/en/index.htm, 21. Although this report was commissioned by President Nicolas Sarkozy of France, one of the first states to follow its recommendations, as we will see in chapter 4, was Venezuela.

79. This has also been pointed out by the recent United Nations Human Settlements Programme report of 2008 in relation to Iraq before and after the 2003 invasion: "Despite an upturn in economic indicators that show a doubling of gross domestic product (GDP) from $15 billion in 2003 to $32.3 billion in 2005, Iraqis remain reliant on social assistance, rations and subsidies. The pre-2003 political regime used urban social goods and opportunities as a way of bestowing or withholding patronage, resulting in exclusion of a large proportion of the urban population from the benefits of urban life. An estimated 35 per cent of Baghdad's working population still lives in poverty. Some households are particularly vulnerable to poverty, including those

headed by women or youth. Iraq's future remains uncertain. A recent survey shows that the country's urban population is deeply concerned with the security situation, which has worsened in the last five years. Perceived or real levels of vulnerability to violence and murder were greater in 2006 than they were in 2002" (UN-HABITAT, *State of the World's Cities 2008/2009: Harmonious Cities* [London, 2008], 117).

80. L. Gallino, *Con i soldi degli altri: Il capitalismo per procura contro l'economia* (Torino: Einaudi: 2009), 9.

81. The "working poor" are people unable to earn enough to lift themselves and their families above the poverty line of US$2 per person per day. "Vulnerable employees" are contributing workers who are unable to benefit from the safety nets that guard against loss of income during economic crisis. "Service" in this context should be not interpreted in the same sense as we diagnosed in the term "servants of the dominant establishment" in Fukuyama and Kagan; while the latter are voluntary, the former are forced. Global Employment Trends reported that in "2007, the service sector pulled further ahead of agriculture in contributing to employment in the world. The service sector now provides 42.7 per cent of jobs in the world, whereas agriculture accounts for only 34.9 per cent. The industry sector, which had seen a slight downward trend between 1997 and 2003, has continued a rather slow upward trend in more recent years. In 2007, 22.4 per cent of jobs were found in this sector" (*Global Employment Trends* [January 2008]: 11).

82. This report also specifies that many workers with these types of "employment status, particularly in developing economies but at times in developed economies as well, do not benefit from a social safety net if they lose their livelihoods or face challenges such as personal or family member illnesses. These workers are also less likely than more formal wage and salary employees to receive an adequate income and have their fundamental labour rights respected" (*Global Employment Trends, Update* [May 2009], ILO, 13).

83. S. Zizek, "The Free World . . . of Slums," *In These Times* (September 23, 2004).

84. J. Gugler, "Overurbanization Reconsidered," in *Cities in the Developing World: Issues, Theory, and Policy*, ed. J. Gugler (Oxford: Oxford University Press, 1997), 114–123; Davis, *Planet of Slums*, 16.

85. A. K. Tibaijuka, *Global Employment Trends, Update* (May 2009), iv.

86. UN-HABITAT, "Sounding the Alarm on Forced Evictions," press release, 20th session of the Governing Council, Nairobi, April 4–8, 2005.

87. *Planet of Slums* is the title of Mike Davis's groundbreaking study, which further developed the UN-HABITAT report *The Challenge of Slums: Global Report on Human Settlements 2003* (London, 2003). In an interview with "Tomdispatch," Davies specified: "By its conservative accounting, a billion people currently live in slums and more than a billion people are informal workers, struggling for survival. They range from street vendors to day laborers to nannies to prostitutes to people who sell their organs [for transplant]. These are staggering figures, even more so since our children and grandchildren will witness the final build-out of the human race. Sometime around 2050 or 2060, the human population will achieve its maximum growth, probably at around 10 to 10.5 billion people. Nothing as large as some of the earlier apocalyptic predictions, but fully 95% of this growth will occur in the cities of the south. . . . The entire future growth of humanity will occur in cities, overwhelmingly in poor cities, and the majority of it in slums" (Davis, "Humanity's Ground Zero," a Tomdispatch interview [May 9, 2006]).

88. Davis, *Planet of Slums*, 201–202.

89. These walls are not only semantic but also real, considering the oppressive function they play in Tijuana, Baghdad, and Jerusalem. As the journalist Bernd Debusmann reports, some of these walls are "reinforced by motion

detectors, heat-sensing cameras, X-ray systems, night-vision equipment, helicopters, drones and blimps. Some are still under construction, some in the planning stage. When completed, the barriers will run thousands of miles, in places as far apart as Mexico and India, Afghanistan and Spain, Morocco and Thailand, Malaysia and Saudi Arabia, and Iraq. They are meant to keep job-hungry immigrants, terrorists and smugglers out, thwart invaders, and keep antagonists apart. . . . By an irony of history, the United States—the country that hastened the fall of the Berlin Wall in 1989—has emerged as a champion wall builder. . . . The latest wall to divide city neighborhoods went up in Baghdad in April [2007], built by American soldiers using 12-foot (3.7-metre) high grey concrete slabs weighing more than six metric tons each. The 3-mile-long construction separates a Sunni Muslim district from a Shi'ite area. It provoked protests from both communities and Shi'ite cleric Moqtada al-Sadr termed it 'racist.' The wall that snakes through Jerusalem to seal off the eastern (Arab) part of the ancient city from the West Bank is of similar construction and inspires similar charges. In contrast, the people of the Mexican border city of Tijuana have become resigned to the wall of thick, rusty corrugated metal that runs from the surf of the Pacific beach up and down the California hills, separating them from the U.S. city of San Diego. (The official border crossing is the world's busiest—around 17 million cars and 50 million people a year). Further inland, the wall turns into a 17-foot (5-meter) fence, with metal mesh so fine prospective climbers cannot get their fingers through, and an overhanging portion to make scaling even more difficult. It stretches east for 14 miles" (B. Debusmann, "Around Globe, Walls Spring up to Divide Neighbors," *Reuters* [April 30, 2007]). A systematic analysis of the various examples of resistance taking place is available in G. Curran, *Twenty-First-Century Dissent: Anarchism, Anti-Globalization, and Environmentalism* (New York: Palgrave, 2006).

90. Davis, *Planet of Slums*, 205.

91. "The contrast with the 1960s is dramatic: forty years ago ideological warfare between the two great Cold War blocs generated competing visions of abolishing world poverty and rehousing slum-dwellers. With its triumphant Sputniks and ICBMs, the Soviet Union was still a plausible model of breakneck industrialization via heavy industries and five-year plans. On the other side, the Kennedy administration officially diagnosed Third World revolutions as 'diseases of modernization,' and prescribed—in addition to Green Berets and B-52s—ambitious land reforms and housing programs. . . . But the promised lands of the 1960s no longer appear on neoliberal maps of the future." Ibid., 200.

92. On the new urban warfare weapons, see note 52.

93. Major R. Peters, "Our Soldiers, Their Cities," *Parameters* (Spring 1996): 43–50. On the future wars in cities, see Alice Hills, *Future War in Cities: Rethinking a Liberal Dilemma* (London: Frank Cass, 2004); and on its environmental cost, see Barry Sanders, *The Green Zone: The Environmental Cost of Militarism* (Oakland, Calif.: AK Press, 2009).

94. Nick Turse, in his compelling study of the way the military invades our everyday lives, shows, among many other examples, how "technologies used in war zones like occupied Iraq have also found their way back to the homeland. In 2006, for instance, it was revealed that the Los Angeles County Sheriff's Department had begun testing the use of remote-controlled surveillance drones. Later that year, according to the Associated Press, Air Force Secretary Michal Wynne decided to invert the normal weapons testing order, professing his belief that futuristic pain-producing weapons 'such as high-power microwave devices should be used on American citizens in crowd-control situations before they are used on the battlefield'" (N. Turse, *The Complex* [New York: Metropolitan Books, 2008], 253).

95. Rear Admiral C. J. Parry, *The DCDC Global Strategic Trends Programme: 2007–2036*, 3.

3. INTERPRETATION AS ANARCHY

1. This understanding of interpretation in Kant, Hobbes, and Weber has been pointed out by H. White, in "The Politics of Historical Interpretation: Discipline and De-Sublimation," *Critical Inquiry* (September 1982): 114.

2. R. R. Sullivan, *Political Hermeneutics* (Philadelphia: Pennsylvania State University Press, 1989); R. Alejandro, *Hermeneutics, Citizenship, and the Public Sphere* (Cambridge, Mass.: The MIT Press, 1993), T. Carver and M. Hyvärinen, eds., *Interpreting the Political: New Methodologies* (London: Routledge, 1997). G. Burns, M. Ferraris, J. Grondin, P. Lanceros, A. Ortiz-Osés, L. Ormiston, R. Palmer, J. Risser, A.D. Schrift, J. Weinsheimer, and others have written extensive histories, introductions, and dictionaries of hermeneutics that are listed in the bibliography.

3. On the revolutionary political outcome of hermeneutics since its main formulation in Gadamer's *Truth and Method*, see G. Vattimo, "The Political Outcome of Hermeneutics," in *Consequences of Hermeneutics*, ed. J. Malpas and S. Zabala (Chicago: Northwestern University Press, 2010), 281–87.

4. M. Ferraris, *History of Hermeneutics*, trans. L. Somigli (Englewood Cliffs, N.J.: Humanities Press, 1996), 4.

5. Ferraris, *History of Hermeneutics*, 28.

6. M. Luther, *Dr. Martin Luthers Tischreden (1531–1546)* (Weimar: Hermann Böhlaus, 1914), 3:170.

7. S. Freud, *The Interpretation of Dreams*, trans. James Strachey (New York: Basic Books, 2010), 604.

8. We must point out that M. Ferraris has dedicated several pages to Freud's hermeneutics in his *History of Hermeneutics*, 134–39.

9. J. Habermas, *Knowledge and Human Interest*, trans. J. J. Shapiro (Boston: Beacon Press, 1971), 220.

10. R. J Bernstein, *Beyond Objectivism and Relativism: Sciences, Hermeneutics, and Praxis* (Philadelphia: University of Pennsylvania Press, 1983), 31.

11. Heidegger specified how "the fundamental event of modernity is the conquest of the world as picture. From now on the word 'picture' means: the collective image of representing production [*das Gebild des vorstellenden Herstellens*]. Within this, man fights for the position in which he can be that being who gives to every being the measure and draws up the guidelines. Because this position secures, organizes, and articulates itself as world view, the decisive unfolding of the modern relationship to beings becomes a confrontation of world views; not, indeed, any old set of world views, but only those which have already taken hold of man's most fundamental stance with the utmost decisiveness. For the sake of this battle of world views, and according to its meaning, humanity sets in motion, with respect to everything, the unlimited process of calculation, planning, and breeding. Science as research is the indispensable form taken by this self-establishment in the world; it is one of the pathways along which, with a speed unrecognized by those who are involved, modernity races towards the fulfillment of its essence. With this battle of world views modernity first enters the decisive period of its history, and probably the one most capable of enduring" (M. Heidegger, "The Age of the World Picture," in *Off the Beaten Track*, ed. and trans. J. Young and K. Haynes [Cambridge University Press, 2002], 71).

12. F. Nietzsche, *The Will to Power*, trans. Walter Kaufmann and R. J. Hollingdale (London: Weidenfeld and Nicolson, 1968), section 481, 267.

13. In this work, Nietzsche posits the two fundamental impulses of life as the Dionysian, the impulse of the creation of the new at the cost of the old, and the Apollonian, the impulse for the stable and definite form.

14. "And whoever must be a creator in good and evil: verily, he must first be an annihilator and shatter values" (F. Nietzsche, *Thus Spoke Zarathustra* [1885], trans. G. Parkes [New York: Oxford University Press, 2005], 100).

15. In *Ecce Homo*, Nietzsche would go on to state, "I am the anti-donkey par excellence."

16. In *The Essence of Philosophy* (1907), Dilthey states that Nietzsche, Carlyle, Emerson, Ruskin, Tolstoy, and Maeterlinck "have some relation to systematic philosophy, and yet still more consciously, more firmly than Montaigne they turn away from it, still more consistently they have broken every bond with philosophy as a science" (W. Dilthey, *The Essence of Philosophy*, trans. S. A. Emery and W. T. Emery [Chapel Hill: University of North Carolina Press, 1954], 31). See also G. Vattimo, "Nietzsche, Heidegger's Interpreter," in G. Vattimo, *Dialogue with Nietzsche*, trans. W. McCuaig (New York: Columbia University Press, 2008), 181–189.

17. Heidegger used the theory of the "ontological difference" in *Being and Time* as a starting point for philosophy after metaphysics, that is, after the permanent nominal presence of Being determined as objectness. This is why "the distinction between the Being of existing Dasein and the being of beings unlike Dasein (for example, reality) may seem to be illuminating, but it is only the point of departure for the ontological problematic; it is not something with which philosophy can rest and be satisfied" (*Being and Time* [1927], trans. Joan Stambaugh [New York: SUNY Press, 2010], 397).

18. While natural sciences pretend to "explain" events according to laws established experimentally, human sciences do not describe and measure but try to "understand."

19. See chapter 1, note 63.

20. L. Pareyson, *Esistenza e interpretazione* (1950; Genoa: Il Melangolo, 1985), 218. Pareyson's hermeneutics is analyzed in G. Vattimo, *Art's Claim to Truth*,

ed. S. Zabala, trans. L. D'Isanto (New York: Columbia University Press, 2008); and also in R. Valgenti, "The Primacy of Interpretation in Luigi Pareyson's Hermeneutics of Common Sense," *Philosophy Today* 49, no. 4 (Winter 2005).

21. R. Rorty, *Take Care of Freedom and Truth Will Take Care of Itself*, ed. E. Mendieta (Stanford, Calif.: Stanford University Press, 2006), 58.

22. Here is Nietzsche's passage:

The History of an Error

1. The real world, attainable to the wise, the pious, the virtuous man—he dwells in it, *he is it*. (Oldest form of the idea, relatively sensible, simple, convincing. Transcription of the proposition "I, Plato, *am* the truth").

2. The real world, unattainable for the moment, but promised to the wise, pious, the virtuous man ("to the sinner who repents"). (Progress of the idea: it grows more refined, more enticing, more incomprehensible—it becomes a woman, it becomes Christian . . .)

3. The real world, unattainable, undemonstrable, cannot be promised, but even when merely thought of, a consolation, a duty, an imperative. (Fundamentally the same old sun, but shining through mist and skepticism; the idea grown sublime, pale, northerly, Königsbergian.)

4. The real world,—unattainable? Unattained, at any rate. And if unattained, also *unknown*. Consequently also no consolation, no redemption, no duty: how could we have a duty towards something unknown? (The grey of dawn. First yawning of reason. Cockcrow of positivism).

5. The "real world"—an idea no longer of any use, not even a duty any longer—an idea grown useless, superfluous, *consequently* a refuted idea: let us abolish it! (Broad daylight; breakfast; return of cheerfulness and *bon sens*; Plato blushes for shame; all free spirits run riot).

6. We have abolished the real world: what world is left? the apparent world perhaps? . . . But no! *with the real world we have also abolished the apparent world!* (Mid-day; moment of the shortest shadow; end of the longest error; zenith of mankind; *Incipit Zarathustra*).

F. Nietzsche, *Twilight of the Idols*, trans. R. J. Hollingdale (Harmondsworth: Penguin, 1968), 50–51.

23. Reconstructions of the history of weak thought can be found in: P. A. Rovatti, "Weak Thought 2004," in *Weakening Philosophy*, ed. S. Zabala (Montreal: McGill-Queen's University Press, 2007), 131–145; S. Zabala, "Gianni Vattimo and Weak thought," in *Weakening Philosophy*, ed. S. Zabala (Montreal: McGill-Queen's University Press, 2007), 3–34; and G. Giorgio, *Il pensiero di Gianni Vattimo* (Milan: Franco Angeli, 2007).

24. With such results as the end of Eurocentrism, the triumph of cultural pluralism, and universal communication that dismisses violent dogmatism, established traditions, and ancient taboos.

25. While facing the problem of overcoming metaphysics, Heidegger, in the second period of his thought, individuated the appropriate term in order to surpass metaphysics without falling back into it: instead of overcoming "*überwinden,*" he called for a "*verwindung,*" a getting over, of metaphysics. While the first term designates a complete abandonment of metaphysics, which leads toward its substitution with just another thought, the second instead alludes to the way one surpasses a major disappointment not by overlooking it but rather by coming to terms with it, like "when, in the human realm, one works through grief or pain" (M. Heidegger, *The Question Concerning Technology*, trans. W. Lovitt [New York: Harper & Row, 1977], 39).

26. C. Taylor, "Modern Moral Rationalism," in *Weakening Philosophy*, ed. S. Zabala (Montreal: McGill-Queen's University Press, 2007), 75.

27. R. Schürmann, *Heidegger on Being and Acting: From Principles to Anarchy* (Bloomington: Indiana University Press, 1990), 57.

28. Note that in the first edition (in French), the title and subtitles are reversed from the English translation: *Le Principe d'Anarchie: Heidegger et la question de l'agir*.

29. R. Schürmann, "'What Must I Do' at the End of Metaphysics," in *Phenomenology in a Pluralistic Context*, eds. William Leon McBride and Calvin O. Schrag (Albany, N.Y.: SUNY Press, 1983), 57.

30. J-F. Lyotard, *The Postmodern Condition: A Report on Knowledge*, trans. Geoff Bennington and Brian Massumi (Minneapolis: University of Minnesota Press, 1999), 10.

31. R. Rorty, *Philosophy and the Mirror of Nature* (Princeton, N.J.: Princeton University Press, 1979), 315.

32. R. Rorty, "Hermeneutics, General Studies, and Teaching," 14.

33. Rorty, *Philosophy and the Mirror of Nature*, 389.

34. Ibid., 378.

35. R. Rorty, "Heideggerianism and Leftist Politics," in *Weakening Philosophy*, ed. S. Zabala (Montreal: McGill-Queen's University Press, 2007), 157.

36. R. Rorty, "Persuasion Is a Good Thing," in *Take Care of Freedom and Truth Will Take Care of Itself*, ed. E. Mendieta (Stanford, Calif.: Stanford University Press, 2006), 81.

4. HERMENEUTIC COMMUNISM

1. V. I. Lenin, "Our Foreign and Domestic Position and Party Tasks," speech delivered to the Moscow Gubernia Conference of the R.C.P. (B.), November 21, 1920. In V. I. Lenin, *Collected Works*, trans. J. Katzer (Moscow: Progress Publishers, 1965), 31:408–426.

2. Here is the whole passage of Heidegger's original response to the *Spiegel* journalists (Rudolf Augstein, Georg Wolff, Schriftsteller Heinrich, and

Wiegand Petzet): "*Spiegel*: Good. Now the question naturally comes up: can the individual in any way influence this network of inevitabilities, or could philosophy influence it, or could both together influence it inasmuch as philosophy could guide the individual or several individuals toward a specific action? Heidegger: Let me respond briefly and somewhat ponderously, but from long reflections: philosophy will not be able to effect an immediate transformation of the present condition of the world. This is not only true of philosophy, but of all merely human thought and endeavor. Only a god can save us. The sole possibility that is left for us is to prepare a sort of readiness, through thinking and poetizing, for the appearance of the god or for the absence of the god in the time of foundering (*Untergang*); for in the face of the god who is absent, we founder. . . . The preparation of a readiness may be the first step. The world cannot be what it is or the way it is through man, but neither can it be without man. According to my view this is connected with the fact that what I name with the word Being, a word which is of long standing, traditional, multifaceted and worn out, needs man for its revelation, preservation and formation. I see the essence of technology in what I call the frame (*das Ge-Stell*), an expression which has often been laughed at and is perhaps somewhat clumsy. The frame holding sway means: the essence of man is framed, claimed and challenged by a power which manifests itself in the essence of technology, a power which man himself does not control. To help with this realization is all that one can expect of thought. Philosophy is at an end" (M. Heidegger, "Only a God Can Save Us: *Der Spiegel*'s Interview," in M. Heidegger, *Philosophical and Political Writings*, ed. Manfred Stassen and trans. M. P. Alter and J. D. Caputo [New York: Continuum, 2003], 38. The original German version of this interview is now also available on the site of *Der Spiegel*: http://wissen.spiegel.de/wissen/dokument/59/03 /dokument.html?id=9273095&top=SPIEGEL).

3. Recently, Fidel Castro (together with Chomsky, Obama, and other international figures) has insisted that the human species is facing a "serious extinction threat," owing to the fruits of science, which appear limitless and whose capacity for destruction is beyond reason. This concern was also exposed in one of Castro's responses to I. Ramonet when he stated that "saving the species will be a titanic undertaking, but it will never be possible through economic and social systems in which the only things that count are profit and advertising" (F. Castro, *My Life*, ed. I. Ramonet, trans. A. Hurley [London: Penguin, 2006], 356).

4. This argument is sustained with the pretext of the necessary dysfunctional collective economics, because "only capitalism," as Thatcher used to say, can produce and distribute wealth and happiness; the architect of neoliberal economics was M. Friedman, whose *Capitalism and Freedom* (1962) significantly influenced Thatcher's macroeconomic advisers. See P. Minford, "Inflation, Unemployment, and the Pound," in *Margaret Thatcher's Revolution: How It Happened and What It Meant*, ed. S. Roy and J. Clarke (London: Continuum, 2005), 50–66; and M. Friedman, "Comment," in *Margaret Thatcher's Revolution: How It Happened and What It Meant*, ed. S. Roy and J. Clarke (London: Continuum, 2005), 66.

5. J. Derrida, *Specters of Marx*, trans. P. Kamuf (New York: Routledge, 1994).

6. As we mention in chapter 1, among the goals of Heidegger's destruction of metaphysics was the concern to recover the forgotten history of Being, that is, of the oppressed. Perhaps this is also why he dedicated a whole essay to a saying of Anaximander ("Whence things have their coming into being there they must also perish according to necessity; for they must pay a penalty and be judged for their injustice, according to the ordinance of time"), where the injustice of imposition is at the essence of the nature of things, that is, Being. See M. Heidegger, "Anaximander's Saying," in *Off the Beaten*

Track, ed. and trans. J. Young and K. Haynes (Cambridge: Cambridge University Press 2002), 242–281.

7. It seems appropriate to quote again Rorty's comment about the significance of "representative democratic government" because "it gives the poor and weak a tool they can use against the rich and powerful, especially against the unconscious cruelty of the institutions the powerful have imposed upon the weak" (Rorty, "Persuasion Is a Good Thing," in *Take Care of Freedom and Truth will Take Care of Itself*, ed. E. Mendieta [Stanford, Calif.: Stanford University Press, 2006], 81).

8. J. Derrida, *Specters of Marx*, 85. As we have seen, Bush's and Obama's political programs are both founded not only on liberal self-certainty but also on the conservation of capitalism regardless of its flaws.

9. The historian D. Losurdo, in his recent *Stalin: Storia e critica di una leggenda nera*, managed to demonstrate, through a variety of documents and historical reconstructions, why these violent connotations were necessary not only because of the danger that Nazi Germany posed but also because of the industrialization all nations were competing for. While we will quote a significant passage of the text, we suggest his text be consulted for a complete exposition of this complex historical reconstruction. "In Soviet Russia, terror emerges in the period which starts with the First World War, which opens the second period of disorders, and the Second World War, which threatens to inflict to the country and nation in its totality an ever greater catastrophe: those clearly announced decimated and slavery letters of *Mein Kampf*. The terror emerges over the course of a forced industrialization aimed to save the country and nation, during which the horror of the ferocious repression on all sides is interwoven with processes of real emancipation (the massive diffusion of instruction and culture, vertical miraculous mobility, the emergence of the social state, the turbulent and

contradictory leading role of social classes until that moment when they were sentenced to a total subordination)" (D. Losurdo, *Stalin: Storia e critica di una leggenda nera* [Rome: Carocci, 2008], 156).

10. K. Marx, *Theories of Surplus Value* (New York: Prometheus Books, 2000), 6.

11. An outline of the "hermeneutic" turn in contemporary political thought is available in G. Warnke, "The Hermeneutic Turn in Recent Political Philosophy," in *Justice and Interpretation* (Cambridge, Mass.: The MIT Press, 1994): 1–12. Analyses by Habermas, Ricoeur, Gadamer, Rorty, and others of this turn are listed in the bibliography.

12. P. Krugman, "How Did Economists Get It So Wrong?" *New York Times* (September 6, 2009).

13. As we argued earlier, "dialogues," contrary to "conversations," are framed within a truth imposed by global organization and used to "moralize politics." An exposition of this difference is available in S. Zabala, "Being Is Conversation," in *Consequences of Hermeneutics*, ed. J. Malpas and S. Zabala (Evanston, Ill.: Northwestern University Press, 2010), 161–176.

14. "What does nihilism mean? *That the highest values devaluate themselves.* The aim is lacking; 'why?' finds no answer. . . . *Radical nihilism* is the conviction of an absolute untenability of existence when it comes to the highest values one recognizes" (F. Nietzsche, *The Will To Power*, trans. Walter Kaufmann and R. J. Hollingdale [London: Weidenfeld and Nicolson, 1968], 3).

15. G. Therborn has reconstructed the historical perspective of the development of Marxism in his recent study *From Marxism to Post-Marxism?* (London: Verso, 2008).

16. W. Benjamin, "On the Concept of History" (1939), in *Selected Writings: 1938–1940*, ed. H. Eiland and M. W. Jennings (Cambridge, Mass.: The Belknap Press of Harvard University Press, 2003), 4:390.

17. Sami Naïr recently emphasized the "extremely deep crisis" that European socialist parties are going through. According to Naïr, if "we set aside the ex-

ception of Northern countries (where the socialist tradition is very particular and social conflicts less acute) or also the socialist countries of Eastern Europe (too recent to be judged), it is obvious, with the exception of Spain, that in all the other places—France, Great Britain, Germany, Italy—socialist parties are falling apart. . . . First, the Western socialist parties accepted in the 1990s adopting liberal globalization (baptized as *third way* or *culture of government*) not only without offering an alternative project to its voters (middle and popular classes), but also refusing to acknowledge the ideological consequences of this decision. With this option they have certainly won efficacy to govern, but have also ruined their own identity. Here is the current paradox: socialists have been dragged down by liberalism's crisis while the liberal right has no problem with applying traditional welfare prescriptions to the current crisis. In other words, the right is much more pragmatic than the left which, after having lost its socialist identity, fully believed in the virtues of socialist liberalism" (Sami Naïr, "El dilema del socialismo europeo," *El País* [October 13, 2009]).

18. It should be emphasized how most framed democracies' governments have been at the service of these corporations rather than served by them. A detailed analysis of this situation can be found in David C. Korten, *When Corporations Rule the World* (Bloomfield: Kumarian Press, 2001); and N. Klein, *No Logo* (New York: Picador: 2000).

19. Derrida, *Specters of Marx*, 85.

20. G. Curran, in his *Twenty-first Century Dissent: Anarchism, Anti-Globalization, and Environmentalism* (New York: Palgrave, 2006), not only exposes the elements that constitute these Western social movements but also concludes by emphasizing how "it is a resurgent 'traditional' socialism that appears to be capturing both governments and world attention, especially in Latin America. The socialist Venezuelan president Chávez has made a compelling case for a new kind of 'socialism for the 21st century,' and it seems

that many other socialist leaders in other Latin American countries are following suit" (229–230). Although Chávez is missing from their analysis, the political significance of ecology has recently been developed by A. Negri and M. Hardt in their *Commonwealth* (Cambridge, Mass.: Harvard University Press, 2009).

21. Among the first to discuss the economic implications of degrowth was N. Georgescu-Roegen, *Demain, la décroissance. Entropie, écologie, économie* (Paris: Éditions Sang de la terre, 1995). Recent developments of societies, economics, and culture without growth can be found in S. Latouche, *In the Wake of the Affluent Society: An Exploration of Post-Development*, trans. M. O'Connor and R. Arnoux (London: Zed Books, 1993).

22. M. Naím is the editor in chief of *Foreign Policy*; among his many articles against South American politics, see "Hugo Chávez's Criminal Paradise," *Los Angeles Times* (November 10, 2007). M. Vargas Llosa is a novelist who not only openly criticized the Spanish prime minister Zapatero for endorsing Evo Morales (in *El País* [November 15, 2009]) but also often alarms the West over the region's socialist governments. A collection of his articles is now available in *Sables y Utopías. Visiones de América Latina* (Madrid: Aguilar, 2009). T. L. Friedman, a *New York Times* columnist, attacked Chávez's address at the U.N. General Assembly (referring to President Bush, Chávez said, "The devil came here yesterday, right here. It smells of sulfur still today") in his article "Fill 'Er up with Dictators," *New York Times* (September 27, 2006). Because U.S. and world media tend to emphasize such attacks (for example, Pat Robertson on Fox News, who suggested Chávez's assassination), Oliver Stone recently felt compelled to released a documentary against these media distortions. Entitled *South of the Border* (with the collaboration of Tariq Ali), it includes interviews with Chávez, Morales, and other South American democratically elected leaders.

23. It should not come as a surprise that F. Fukuyama also expressed his obsession about these democracies in the following articles: "A Quiet Revolution," *Foreign Policy* (November/December 2007); and "History's Against Him," *Washington Post* (August 6, 2006). A recent issue on Latin America of the distinguished journal *Current History* (February 2009) is predominantly critical of the whole region's political shift to the left.

24. Analysis of the democratic procedures in Western democracies can be found in G. Vattimo, *Nihilism and Emancipation*, ed. S. Zabala (New York: Columbia University Press, 2005); R. Rorty, *Achieving Our Country* (Cambridge, Mass.: Harvard University Press, 1997); and L. M. Bartels, *Unequal Democracy: The Political Economy of the New Gilded Age* (Princeton, N.J.: Princeton University Press, 2008).

25. N. Chomsky, *What We Say Goes* (London: Penguin, 2007), 65.

26. As Chomsky said, if "you don't think countries should influence other countries' elections, then shut down the National Endowment for Democracy and shut down the State Department, which is right now [2006], for example, intervening massively in the Nicaraguan election" (ibid., 47). For a clear reconstruction of how the National Endowment for Democracy has influenced other nations, see Colin S. Cavell, *Exporting "Made-in-America" Democracy: The National Endowment for Democracy and U.S. Foreign Policy* (Washington, D.C.: University Press of America, 2002).

27. A reconstruction of President Morales's rise to power and partnership with Chávez is available in F. Hylton and S. Thomson, *Revolutionary Horizons: Past and Present in Bolivian Politics* (London: Verso, 2007).

28. N. Kozloff explained that "Chávez himself came up through poverty. The son of schoolteachers, he grew up in a small village on the Venezuelan Plain in the west of the country. Chávez, who had formed his own party, the MVR or Fifth Republic Movement, blew apart Venezuela's corrupt

two-party system and won the election with 56 percent of the vote. Like other South American regimes that would later seek to reconfigure politics and the relationship between state and society, Chávez quickly convened a new National Constituent Assembly. The Venezuelan president hoped that the new body would end the isolation between the political system and the Venezuelan masses. Venezuelans voted to give all but six seats in the new assembly to legislators associated with Chávez movement" (Kozloff, *Revolution! South America and the Rise of the New Left* [New York: Palgrave: MacMillan, 2008], 3).

29. In 1998, Chávez received 56 percent; Römer 39 percent. In 2000, Chávez received 59 percent; Cárdenas 37 percent. The 2004 referendum confirmed Chávez with 58 percent in favor and 42 percent against. Former U.S. president Jimmy Carter declared that these were the freest elections he had ever seen. In 2006, Chávez beat the opposition candidate Manuel Rosales by 62 percent to 37 percent. As stated, "Chávez's 26 percentage point margin of victory was the largest in Venezuela's post-dictatorship history" (G. Wilpert, *Changing Venezuela by Taking Power* [London: Verso: 2007], 27). The second constitutional referendum, held in 2009 to decide whether to abolish term limits for the offices of president, state governors, mayors, and National Assembly deputies, was held on February 15, 2009; 54 percent voted in favor and 45 against.

30. As the *Washington Post* reported, Chávez can run for office in 2012 and beyond only "if he continues winning elections" (J. Forero, "Chávez Wins Removal of Term Limits," [February 16, 2009]).

31. This coup is now known as the "media coup," because RCTV played a central part: "After Chávez was elected in 1998, RCTV, under the direction of the country's wealthy oligarchy and the likes of Station Chief Marcel Granier, came out strongly against Chávez. For two days prior to the April 11, 2002 coup RCTV preempted normal programming and provided wall-to-

wall coverage of a general strike that sought to topple Chávez. A series of commentators voiced vitriolic attacks against the president, and the station allowed no time for a response from the regime, instead airing nonstop ads encouraging Venezuelans to participate in an April 11 march designed to oust Chávez. RCTV provided blanket coverage of the event. When the march ended in tragedy and violence, RCTV ran manipulated video blaming Chavistas for scores of deaths and injuries. 'After military rebels overthrew Chávez and he disappeared from public view for two days,' remarks *The Los Angeles Times*, 'RCTV's biased coverage edged fully into sedition.' When thousands of Chavistas poured into the streets to demand the president's return, RCTV refused to cover the protests, instead choosing to run cartoons, soap operas, and old movies. To top it off, Granier personally went to Miraflores, the presidential palace, on April 13 to pledge support to Dictator-For-a-Day Pedro Carmora, who had abolished the nation's Supreme Court, Constitution, and National Assembly. [Andrés] Izarra [the news director at RCTV at the time] resigned from RCTV during the coup and later testified before the National Assembly that he had received an order from his superiors at RCTV: 'Zero pro-Chávez, nothing related to Chávez or his supporters. . . . The idea was to create a climate of transition and to start to promote the dawn of a new country.' . . . 'RCTV practiced a form of media terrorism,' Izarra has remarked. 'The families that own RCTV hate my guts for saying that, but the oligarchy that once controlled Venezuela is finally coming apart' " (Kozloff, *Revolution!*, 195–196). T. Ali has reported how, despite the 2002 coup, "not a single Venezuelan newspaper or TV station has been taken over or punished by the Chávez administration" (T. Ali, *Pirates of the Caribbean* [London: Verso 2006], 17). Other very clear reconstructions of this media coup can be found in E. Golinger, "The Media War Against the People: A Case Study of Media Concentration and Power in Venezuela," in *The Venezuela Reader: The Building of a People's Democracy,* ed. Olivia Burlingame Goumbri (Washington, D.C.: Epica, 2005); Brian A. Nelson, *The Silence and the Scorpion: The Coup Against Chávez and the Making of Modern Venezuela* (New York: Nation Books, 2009); and N. Klein, "Venezuela's Media Coup," *The Nation* (February 13, 2003).

32. In 2004 "in Venezuela, five major private television networks control at least 90% of the market and smaller private stations control another 5%. This 95% of the broadcast market began to outwardly express its opposition to President Chávez's administration as early as 1999, soon after Chávez began his first term in office. After President Chávez came to power in 1998, the five main privately owned television channels—Venevisión, Radio Caracas Televisión (RCTV), Globovisión, Televen and CMT—and nine out of the ten major national newspapers, including *El Universal, El Nacional, Tal Cual, El Impulso, El Nuevo País,* and *El Mundo,* took over the role of the traditional political parties, Acción Demcrática (AD) and COPEI, which had lost power after Chávez won the presidential election. The investigations, interviews, reports and commentaries of these mass media have all pursued the same objective for the past four years: to undermine the legitimacy of the government and to severely damage the president's popular support" (E. Golinger, "A Case Study of Media Concentration and Power in Venezuela," Venezuelanalysis.com [September 25, 2004]).

33. The *Los Angeles Times* journalist Bart Jones was among the few to report this media coup, and he also asked the essential question: how long would "a network that aided and abetted a coup against the government be allowed to operate in the United States? The U.S. government probably would have shut down RCTV within five minutes after a failed coup attempt—and thrown its owners in jail. Chavez's government allowed it to continue operating for five years, and then declined to renew its 20-year license to use the public airwaves. It can still broadcast on cable or via satellite dish" (Bart Jones, "Hugo Chavez Versus RCTV," *Los Angeles Times* [May 30, 2007]).

In 2010, RCTV was forced off the air again because it refused to transmit the president's January 23 speech. Again, one must ask: what would happen in the United States if Fox refused to transmit one of Obama's speeches? The *New York Times* report ("Cable TV Station Critical of Chávez Is Shut Down" [January 24, 2010]) did not ask this question.

34. President Lula of Brazil refers to Chávez as a "progressive soldier" (R. Gott, "Southern Comfort," *Guardian* [February 1, 2009]).

35. Kozloff, *Revolution!*, 5. A complete history of Chávez is available in the outstanding study by Wilpert, *Changing Venezuela by Taking Power*.

36. R. Gott, in his study *Hugo Chávez and the Bolívarian Revolution* (London: Verso, 2005), explains that Chávez could have obtained power immediately if he had joined the national oligarchy, as it would have come with the support of the global financial press.

37. Kozloff points out how oil plays a huge economic role in Venezuela: "Oil accounted for 90 percent of the country's export earnings and about half the government's revenue in 2005. Venezuela is the fourth-largest exporter of crude to the US. For years, US oil companies such as Standard Oil and Gulf had dominated the local industry, setting up a massive petroleum infrastructure in the Lake Maracaibo region" (*Revolution!*, 4).

38. The detailed "Oil Sowing Plan (2005–2030)" is revealed on the PDVSA site: http://www.pdvsa.com/index.php?tpl=interface.en/design/readmenu princ.tpl.html&newsid_temas=32.

39. Ali, *Pirates of the Caribbean*, 70. It should be pointed out, as M. Davies explains, that Chavez was forced to request Cuban doctors because of the degree of "political polarization" that still exists in Venezuela, where "the ferocity of middle-class resistance to the demands of the poor" is still very large (M. Davies, "Humanity's Ground Zero: A Tomdispatch Interview with Mike Davis" Tomdispatch [May 9, 2006]). Also, it should be emphasized that Chávez, following Stiglitz's recommendations, changed the

instrument traditionally used to measure the GDP in order to incorporate the benefits that the "population receives through the various free Socialist missions or programs" (Patrick J. O'Donoghue, "Chavez to Change GDP Measuring to Stiglitz Report Recommendations," VHeadline.com [September 22, 2009], http://www.vheadline.com/readnews.asp?id=84197).

40. These data can be found in a report published by the Center for Economic and Policy Research, a Washington-based think tank, now available online at http://www.cepr.net/documents/publications/venezuela-2009–02.pdf.

41. The enormous social progress that Chávez managed to bring about for the weak population of Venezuela is remarkable, as C. Boudin of *The Nation* reminds us: "Chávez's sustained popularity is based on concrete changes he has delivered to Venezuela's poor majority. According to a report published by the Center for Economic and Policy Research, a Washington-based think tank, since 2003 the poverty rate has been cut by more than half, from 54 percent of households to 26 percent at the end of 2008. Extreme poverty has fallen by even more, down 72 percent. These poverty rates measure only cash income and do not take into account increased access to healthcare or education—areas where the government has substantially expanded free service provision. In the past five years, fueled by an oil boom, Venezuela's real (inflation-adjusted) GDP has nearly doubled, growing by 94.7 percent in 5.25 years, or 13.5 percent annually, making it one of the strongest economies in the hemisphere. Over the entire decade of Chávez's presidency, infant mortality fell by more than one-third and the number of primary-care physicians in the public sector increased twelvefold. Few countries can boast such remarkable gains in just a decade" (C. Boudin, "Chavez for Life?" *The Nation* [February 20, 2009]).

42. Wilpert, *Changing Venezuela by Taking Power*, 162.

43. Correa of Ecuador is one of the few politicians, together with Chávez and Morales, who has been under heavy attack from the world media. Among

the few journalists who tried to set the story right is M. Weisbrot, who recently explained why Correa got reelected: "There are a number of reasons that most Ecuadorians might stick with their president, despite what they hear on the TV news. Some 1.3 million of Ecuador's poor households (in a country of 14 million) now get a stipend of $30 a month, which is a significant improvement. Social spending as a share of the economy has increased by more than 50% in Correa's two years in office. Last year the government also invested heavily in public works, with capital spending more than doubling. Correa has delivered on other promises that were important to his constituents, not least of which was a referendum allowing for a constituent assembly to draft a new constitution, which voters approved by a nearly two-thirds majority. It is seen as one of the most progressive constitutions in the world, with advances in the rights of indigenous people, civil unions for gay couples and a novel provision of rights for nature. The latter would apparently allow for lawsuits on the basis of damage to an ecosystem. Many thought Correa was joking when he said during his presidential campaign that he would be willing to keep the US military base at Manta if Washington would allow Ecuadorian troops to be stationed in Florida. But he wasn't, and the base is scheduled to close later this year. He also resisted pressure from the US Congress and others in a multi-billion-dollar lawsuit that Ecuadorian courts will decide, in which Chevron is accused of dumping billions of gallons of toxic oil waste that polluted rivers and streams. And in an unprecedented move last November, Correa stopped payment on $4bn of foreign debt when an independent Public Debt Audit Commission, long demanded by civil society organizations in Ecuador, determined that this debt was illegally and illegitimately contracted" (M. Weisbrot, "Why Latin America's Left Keeps Winning," *Guardian* [May 1, 2009]).

44. Morales, F. Hylton and S. Thomson state, "was born in Oruro in 1959." As a child: "he migrated to Chapare with his family and has been involved in

cocalero organizing since his early teens. In 1998, six coca-grower federations in rural Chapare set up the Movimiento al Socialismo to fight for electoral representation. Morales was elected MAS senator for the Cochabamba department, and MAS took several mayoralties in the region. It was not until the general election of 2002 that MAS would break out of its regional and sectoral base" (F. Hylton and S. Thomson, "The Chequered Rainbow," *New Left Review* 35 [September/October 2005]: 47).

45. M. Weisbrot, "Latin America Economic Rebels," *Guardian* (October 28, 2009).

46. Hylton and Sinclair, "The Chequered Rainbow," 41. Together with Kozloff's *Revolution!*, two other works provide a solid panorama of both U.S. and IMF influence over the region: G. Grandin, *Empire's Workshop: Latin America, the United States, and the Rise of the New Imperialism* (New York: Owl Books, 2007); and N. Chomsky, *Latin America: From Colonization to Globalization* (Melbourne: Ocean Press, 1999).

47. S. Romero of the *New York Times* reported that representatives of Mitsubishi, General Motors, Nissan, Ford, and BMW, among other carmakers, all "in the rush to build the next generation of hybrid or electric cars," were sent to La Paz "to meet with Mr. Morales's government about gaining access to the lithium," which is a critical component for the "batteries that power cars and other electronics" (S. Romero, "In Bolivia, Untapped Bounty Meets Nationalism," *New York Times* [February 3, 2009]). Among these foreign exploiters, a major role was played by the consortium that controlled Bolivia's water, which "was dominated by well-known US companies, Bechtel and (prior to its demise) Enron." They, explains Ali, "had made it illegal for the poor to collect rainwater, giving the exclusive rights to do so to Bechtel's local proxy, Aguas del Tanari. . . . By the turn of the millennium, the Andean struggles against privatization (water in Cochabamba, electricity in Cuzco) were far more advanced than anywhere else in the world. *La Guerra*

del Agua (the War For Water) erupted after the killing of seventeen-year-old Victor Hugo Diaz, who was shot dead by the Army in April 2000 for joining a protest in Cochabamba against the increase in water rates. . . . Anguish turned to anger. The government had declared martial law, but Cochabamba, suffering from chronic water shortages, would not be silenced. A million people inhabited this old Andean town and most of them appeared to be on the streets. . . . Their leaders had been arrested and taken to remote prisons in the Amazon, but the movement carried on. . . . Bechtel was run out of town and the city government once again took charge of its water supply and a new water law prioritizing the needs of the people against the 'rights' of the corporations, a law from 'written from below,' was passed. . . . Morales could not have won without the support of social movements of this type" (Ali, *Pirates of the Caribbean*, 91–92).

48. R. Gott, "A Landmark for Bolivia," *Guardian* (January 26, 2009).

49. Ibid.

50. This referendum was observed by a group deployed by the European Union. See http://europa.eu/rapid/pressReleasesAction.do?reference=IP/08/20 10&format=HTML&aged=0&language=EN&guiLanguage=en.

51. Morales, in D. Estrada, "South America: Leaders Express Full Support for Bolivia's Morales," Inter Press Service Agency (September 16, 2008), http://ipsnews.net/news.asp?idnews=43887.

52. Among the social consequences of Chávez's politics it is important to point out how just "under a million Venezuelan children from the shanty towns and the poorest villages now obtain a free education; 1.2 million illiterate adults have been taught to read and write; secondary education has been made available to 250,000 children whose social status excluded them from this privilege during the ancien régime; three new university campuses were functioning by 2003 and six more are due to be completed by 2006" (Ali, *Pirates of the Caribbean*, 69). Among Morales's many reforms,

the obligation that, along with Spanish, schools also teach indigenous languages such as Aymara, Guaraní, and Quechua has managed to increase the proportion of the population who can be offered service by the educational system. Government employees are now also requested to take indigenous language training. R. Carroll of the *Guardian* reports how in Bolivia the "president has also championed elements of indigenous culture that were under attack. Previous governments targeted the coca leaf in US-backed crackdowns on cocaine trafficking. Morales, in contrast, has embraced the leaf as a national symbol. For indigenous movements in Chile, Ecuador, Venezuela and Central America, Bolivia has become a beacon. The pace of change has been startling. As recently as the 1950s, indigenous people were not allowed to vote or even cross the plaza in front of the presidential palace" (R. Carroll, "Bolivia's 'Little Indians' Find Voice," *Guardian* [April 26, 2009]). Chomsky has recently commented on these indigenous politics in N. Chomsky, Lois Meyer, and Benjamín Maldonado Alvarado, *New World of Indigenous Resistance: Voices from the Americas* (San Francisco: City Lights Publishers, 2010).

53. Kozloff, *Revolution!*, 2.

54. The other major organizations are the Comunidad Andina (Andean Community of Nations), PetroCaribe (Caribbean oil alliance), Asociación Latinoamericana de Integración (Latin American Integration Association), and the recent Comunidad de Estados Latinoamericanos y Caribeños (Community of Latin American and Caribbean States). It should be pointed out that Telesur, the new pan–Latin America TV channel, is also contributing to integration within the region to oppose the Western media monopoly.

55. Kozloff, *Revolution!*, 2, rightly explains how today "South America is a potent symbol to many in the Third World because it has managed to challenge the capitalist system."

56. On Stiglitz, see R. Carroll, "Nobel Economist Endorses Chávez Regional Bank Plan," *Guardian* (October 12, 2007). N. Chomsky has emphasized the factor of choice in South American politics in "South America: Toward an Alternative Future," *International Herald Tribune* (January 5, 2007).

57. Kozloff, *Revolution!*, 3.

58. Gott, "Southern Comfort."

59. N. Chomsky, "Historical Perspectives on Latin American and East Asian Regional Development," *Asian-Pacific Journal. Japan Focus* (December 20, 2006).

60. Weisbrot, "Why Latin America's Left Keeps Winning."

61. There are other U.S. bases in Peru, Paraguay, and probably, before Morales was elected, in Bolivia. Although the Pentagon's annual Base Structure Report (www.acq.osd.mil/ie/download/bsr/BSR2009Baseline.pdf) gives updates on the (official) military presence in the region, for a detailed analysis of the situation, see the essays collected in Catherine Lutz, ed., *The Bases of Empire: The Global Struggle Against U.S. Military Posts* (New York: New York University Press, 2009); David Vine, *Island of Shame: The Secret History of the U.S. Military Base on Diego Garcia* (Princeton, N.J.: Princeton University Press, 2009); and Greg Grandin, "Muscling Latin America," *The Nation* (February 8, 2010).

62. H. O'Shaughnessy of the *Independent* has reported how "the United States is massively building up its potential for nuclear and non-nuclear strikes in Latin America and the Caribbean by acquiring unprecedented freedom of action in seven new military, naval and air bases in Colombia. . . . The country has received military aid worth $4.6bn (£2.8bn) from the US since 2000, despite its poor human rights record. Colombian forces regularly kill the country's indigenous people and other civilians, and last year raided the territory of its southern neighbor, Ecuador, causing at least 17 deaths. . . .

Much of the new US strategy was clearly set out in May in an enthusiastic US Air Force (USAF) proposal for its military construction programme for the fiscal year 2010. One Colombian air base, Palanquero, was, the proposal said, unique 'in a critical sub region of our hemisphere where security and stability is under constant threat from . . . anti-US governments.' The proposal sets out a scheme to develop Palanquero which, the USAF says, offers an opportunity for conducting 'full-spectrum operations throughout South America. . . . It also supports mobility missions by providing access to the entire continent, except the Cape Horn region, if fuel is available, and over half the continent if un-refueled'" (H. O'Shaughnessy, "US Builds Up Its Bases in Oil-Rich South America," *Independent* [November 22, 2009]). "Full-spectrum operations" is the Pentagon's jargon for its long-established goal of securing crushing military superiority with atomic and conventional weapons across the globe and in space.

63. On June 28, 2009, the democratically elected president of Honduras, M. Zelaya, "was taken from his home at gunpoint by soldiers and flown into exile . . . after months of pushing for a constitutional referendum that Honduras's courts and Congress had called illegal. Many suspected the referendum was an attempt to remain in power after his term ends in January, although Zelaya denies this. . . . The new regime [guided by Roberto Micheletti] has meanwhile rebuffed demands by the international community to reinstate Zelaya and now faces the prospect of economic sanctions if the Organization of American States decides to suspend its membership" (B. Quinn, "Honduran Military Regime Threatens Reprisals as President Plans Return," *Guardian* [July 5, 2009]). M. Weisbrot explains the U.S. involvement and support for the coup in "Who's in Charge of US Foreign Policy?" *Guardian* (July 16, 2009).

64. M. Weisbrot, "Restoring Democracy in Honduras," *Guardian* (July 30, 2009). Also, Greg Grandin has reported that "just a month before his over-

throw, Zelaya . . . introduced a law that would have required community approval before new mining concessions were granted; it also banned open-pit mines and the use of cyanide and mercury. That legislation died with his ouster. Zelaya also tried to break the dependent relationship whereby the region exports oil to US refineries only to buy back gasoline and diesel at monopolistic prices; he joined Petrocaribe—the alliance that provides cheap Venezuelan oil to member countries—and signed a competitive contract with Conoco Phillips. This move earned him the ire of Exxon and Chevron, which dominate Central America's fuel market" (Greg Grandin, "Muscling Latin America," *Nation* [February 8, 2010]).

65. O'Shaughnessy, "US Builds Up Its Bases."

66. N. Chomsky, "Militarizing Latin America," *In These Times* (September 9, 2009).

67. "Nuestra America—the Spectre Haunting Washington," by G. Lievesley and S. Lundam, is the last chapter of their edited volume on Latin American communism: *Reclaiming Latin America: Experiments in Radical Social Democracy* (London: Zed Books, 2009), 217–229. On the future of Latin American communism, see *La nueva izquierda en America Latina*, ed. C. A. Rodríguez Garavito, P. S. Barrett, and D. Chávez (Bogotá: Norma, 2004).

68. F. Fukuyama, "A Quiet Revolution," *Foreign Affairs* (November/December 2007): http://www.foreignaffairs.com/articles/63039/francis-fukuyama/a-quietrevolution?page=show. Fukuyama has also expressed his critical views on Chávez in "History's Against Him," *Washington Post* (August 6, 2006).

69. Grandin, "Muscling Latin America."

70. After Obama's first year in office, the distinguished historian Howard Zinn, in his last editorial for *The Nation*, explained that "on foreign policy, [Obama's is] hardly any different from a Republican—as nationalist, expansionist, imperial and warlike. . . . On domestic policy, traditionally

Democratic presidents are more reformist, closer to the labor movement, more willing to pass legislation on behalf of ordinary people—and that's been true of Obama. But Democratic reforms have also been limited, cautious. Obama's no exception. On healthcare, for example, he starts out with a compromise, and when you start out with a compromise, you end with a compromise of a compromise, which is where we are now. I thought that in the area of constitutional rights he would be better than he has been. That's the greatest disappointment, because Obama went to Harvard Law School and is presumably dedicated to constitutional rights. But he becomes president, and he's not making any significant step away from Bush policies. Sure, he keeps talking about closing Guantánamo, but he still treats the prisoners there as 'suspected terrorists.' They have not been tried and have not been found guilty. So when Obama proposes taking people out of Guantánamo and putting them into other prisons, he's not advancing the cause of constitutional rights very far. And then he's gone into court arguing for preventive detention, and he's continued the policy of sending suspects to countries where they very well may be tortured. I think people are dazzled by Obama's rhetoric, and that people ought to begin to understand that Obama is going to be a mediocre president—which means, in our time, a dangerous president—unless there is some national movement to push him in a better direction" (H. Zinn, "Obama at One: A Nation Forum," *The Nation* [February 1, 2010]: 21).

71. A complete account of these criminal operations is available in J. Dinges, *The Condor Years: How Pinochet and His Allies Brought Terrorism to Three Continents* (New York: The New Press, 2004); and J. Patrice McSherry, *Predatory States: Operation Condor and Covert War in Latin America* (London: Rowman & Littlefield, 2005).

72. A recent example of Lula's capacity to maintain an alternative voice, that is, a voice against the United States, took place in 2009, when he became the

first Western leader to recognize the victory of President Mahmoud Ahma-dinejad and his right to enrich uranium. As M. Weisbrot reported, "Brazil is on the same page with Venezuela regarding Iran, as is most of the world. Brazil's foreign minister went to Iran last December, where he publicly de-fended Iran's right to enrich uranium, and announced that expanding com-mercial and other ties to Iran were 'a foreign policy priority' for Brazil. And President Lula himself also defended Iran" (M. Weisbrot, "Morgen-thau's Axis Debunked," http://www.huffingtonpost.com/mark-weisbrot /morgenthaus-axis-debunked_b_283871.html). Regardless of the legiti-macy of the 2009 Iran election, the fact that the United States contested the result implies that it was not convenient. After all, the United States has always rejected Iran's right to develop a nuclear program. The recent "Twit-ter revolution" in Iran must also be read with a certain caution, considering the great possibilities of technological manipulation, that is, of "manufac-turing consent" (as Walter Lippmann, Noam Chomsky, and E. H. Herman would say). After all, Lt. Gen. Robert J. Elder Jr., who heads the Air Force's cyberoperations command, recently explained that as "the U.S. Air Force is planning to establish by October [2008] a Cyber Command for waging a future war that is fought not only by land, sea and air but also in cyber-space" (Anick Jesdanun, "U.S. Military Prepares Cyberwarfare Offensive," *USA Today* [April 7, 2008]). This is probably why an editorial "in the *Peo-ple's Daily* accused the US of launching a 'hacker brigade' and said it had used social media such as Twitter to spread rumours and create trouble" (Tania Branigan, "China Accuses US of Online Warfare in Iran," *Guardian* [January 24, 2010]).

73. A reconstruction of the history of U.S. terrorist attacks on Cuba is avail-able in Lars Schoultz, *That Infernal Little Cuban Republic: The United States and the Cuban Revolution* (Chapel Hill: University of North Carolina Press, 2009), 170–212.

74. N. Chomsky, "Cuba's Fifty Years of Defiance: An Interview with Noam Chomsky," by Bernie Dwyer, *Counterpunch* (November 3, 2003).

75. Although we do not have space to expose the whole history of this exploitation, it is worthwhile to mention, as the historian Louis A. Pérez Jr., explains, how Arthur M. Schlesinger recalled a visit before the revolution: "I was enchanted by Havana—and appalled by the way that lovely city was being debased into a great casino and brothel for American businessmen over for a big week-end from Miami. My fellow countrymen reeled through the streets, picking up fourteen-year-old girls and tossing coins to make men scramble in the gutter. One wondered how any Cuban—on the basis of this evidence—could regard the United States with anything but hatred" (Louis A. Pérez Jr., *Cuba and the United States: Ties of Singular Intimacy* [Athens: University of Georgia Press, 1990], 225).

76. Mao Tse-Tung, *Quotations from Chairman Mao Tse-Tung* (Hong Kong: China Books & Periodicals Inc., 1990), 11–12.

77. As Luis Bilbao reported, on "the evening of November 20, 2009, the day before the opening of the first extraordinary PSUV congress, a feeling of vertigo swept over tens of thousands of people who heard Hugo Chávez, either on TV or on the internet, speak before delegates of parties from 30 or so countries, and launch a proposal that was as long desired as it was unexpected: to set to work to build the Fifth Socialist International" (Luis Bilbao, "Fifth Socialist International—Time for Definitions," *Links International Journal of Socialist Renewal*, http://links.org.au/node/1491).

78. Direct documentation of these masses' participation in Venezuela and Honduras can be found in C. Martinez, J. Farrell, and F. Michael, eds., *Venezuela Speaks! Voices from the Grassroots* (Oakland, Calif.: PM Press, 2010); and Dana Frank, "Hondurans' Great Awakening," *The Nation* (March 18, 2010).

BIBLIOGRAPHY

Achcar, Gilbert, and Noam Chomsky. *Perilous Power: The Middle East and U.S. Foreign Policy Dialogues on Terror, Democracy, War, and Justice.* Boulder, Colo.: Paradigm, 2007.

Alejandro, Roberto. *Hermeneutics, Citizenship, and the Public Sphere.* Cambridge, Mass.: The MIT Press, 1993.

Alexander, Werner. *Hermeneutica Generalis: Zur Konzeption und Entwicklung der allgemeinen Verstehenslehre im 17. und 18. Jahrhundert.* Stuttgart: M&P Verlag für Wissenschaft und Forschung, 1993.

Ali, T. *Pirates of the Caribbean.* London: Verso, 2006.

Allen, Barry. *Knowledge and Civilization.* Boulder, Colo.: Westview Press, 2002.

——. *Truth in Philosophy.* Cambridge, Mass.: Harvard University Press, 1993.

Amnesty International. "Iraq: Carnage and Despair. Five Years On." Amnesty International, Index Number: MDE 14/001/2008. http://www.amnesty .org/en/library/info/MDE14/001/2008/en.

Apel, Karl-Otto. "Regulative Ideas or Truth Happening? An Attempt to An-swer the Question of the Conditions of the Possibility of Valid Understand-ing." In *From a Transcendental-Semiotic Point of View*. Manchester: Man-chester University Press, 1998.

———. "The Self-Recuperative Principle of a Critical-Hermeneutic Reconstruc-tion of History." In *From a Transcendental-Semiotic Point of View*. Manches-ter: Manchester University Press, 1998.

Apel, Karl-Otto, and Jürgen Habermas, eds. *Hermeneutik und Ideologiekritik*. Frankfurt am Main: Suhrkamp, 1971.

Aristotle. *The Complete Works of Aristotle*. Revised Oxford translation. Ed. J. Barnes. Princeton, N.J.: Princeton University Press, 1971, 1984.

Austin, J. L. *How to Do Things with Words: The William James Lectures Delivered at Harvard University in 1955*. Oxford: Clarendon, 1962.

Babich, Babette. "Nietzsche and the Condition of Post-Modern Thought: Post-Nietzschean Post-Modernism." In *Nietzsche as Postmodernist: Essays Pro and Contra*, ed. Clayton Koelb, 249–266. Albany: State University of New York Press, 1990.

Badiou, Alain, and Slavoj Žižek. *Philosophy in the Present*. Ed. P. Engelmann. Trans. Peter Thomas and Alberto Toscano. London: Polity Press: 2009.

Baker, Dean. "G20: Why Support the IMF?" *Guardian* (April 2, 2009).

———. "The Menace of an Unchecked Housing Bubble." In *The Economist's Voice*, ed. J. Stiglitz, A. Edlin, and J. Bradford DeLong. New York: Columbia University Press, 2008.

———. *Plunder and Blunder: The Rise and Fall of the Bubble Economy*. Foreword by T. Frank. Sausalito, Calif.: PoliPoint Press, 2009.

Bartels, L. M. *Unequal Democracy: The Political Economy of the New Gilded Age.* Princeton, N.J.: Princeton University Press, 2008.

Barthold, Lauren Swayne. *Gadamer's Dialectical Hermeneutics.* Lanham, Md.: Lexington Books, 2009.

Baudrillard, Jean. *Selected Writings.* Ed. Mark Poster. London: Polity Press, 2001.

Beaumont, Peter. "History's Man." *Guardian* (August 15, 2004).

Benso, Silvia, and Brian Schroeder. *Between Nihilism and Politics: The Hermeneutics of Gianni Vattimo.* Albany, N.Y.: SUNY Press, 2010.

Benjamin, Walter. *Gesammelte Schriften.* Vol. 1. Ed. R. Tiedemann and H. Schweppenhäser. Frankfurt: Surhkamp, 1972.

——. *Illuminations: Essays and Reflections.* New York: Schocken Books, 1969.

——. *Selected Writings: 1938–1940.* Vol. 4. Ed. H. Eiland and M. W. Jennings. Cambridge, Mass.: Belknap Press of Harvard University Press, 2003.

——. *The Work of Art in the Age of Its Technological Reproducibility, and Other Writings on Media.* Cambridge, Mass.: Belknap Press of Harvard University Press, 2008.

Bennis, P. *Before and After: U.S. Foreign Policy and the War on Terrorism.* New York: Olive Branch Press, 2003.

Berlin, Isaiah. *The Proper Study of Mankind.* Ed. H. Hardy and R. Hausheer. New York: Farrar, Strauss and Giroux, 2000.

Bernstein, Richard. *Beyond Objectivism and Relativism: Science, Hermeneutics, and Praxis.* Philadelphia: University of Pennsylvania Press, 1983.

Bertman, Martin. "Hermeneutic in Nietzsche." *Journal of Value Inquiry* 7 (1973): 254–260.

Betti, Emilio. *Allgemeine Auslegungslehre als Methodik der Geisteswissenschaften.* Tübingen: J. C. B. Mohr/Paul Siebeck, 1962, 1967.

——. *Teoria generale della interpretazione.* 2 vols. Milan: Giuffre, 1955.

Bilbao, Luis. "Fifth Socialist International—Time for Definitions." Trans. Janet Duckworth. *Links International Journal of Socialist Renewal.* http://links .org.au/node/1491.

Blattner, William D. *Heidegger's Temporal Idealism.* Cambridge: Cambridge University Press, 1999.

Bloch, Ernst. *The Spirit of Utopia.* Trans. Anthony A. Nassar. Stanford, Calif.: Stanford University Press, 2000.

Blum, W. *Killing Hope: U.S. Military and CIA Interventions Since World War II.* Monroe, Maine: Common Courage Press, 2008.

Bobbitt, P. *The Shield of Achilles.* London: Allen Lane Penguin, 2002.

Boron, Atilio, *Siglo XXI. ¿Hay vida después del neoliberalismo?* Buenos Aires: Ediciones Luxemburg, 2009.

Boudin, C. "Chavez for Life?" *The Nation* (February 20, 2009).

Branigan, Tania. "China Accuses US of Online Warfare in Iran." *Guardian* (January 24, 2010).

Brogan, Walter, and James Risser, eds. *American Continental Philosophy.* Bloomington: Indiana University Press, 2000.

Bruns, Gerald L. *Hermeneutics: Ancient and Modern.* New Haven, Conn.: Yale University Press, 1992.

Bubner, Rüdiger. *Essays in Hermeneutics and Critical Theory.* Translated by Eric Matthews. New York: Columbia University Press, 1988.

——. "On the Ground of Understanding." In *Hermeneutics and Truth*, ed. Brice Wachterhauser, 68–82. Evanston, Ill.: Northwestern University Press, 1994.

Bubner, Rüdiger, K. Cramer, and R. Weihl, eds. *Hermeneutik und Dialektik.* 2 vols. Tübingen: J. C. B. Mohr, 1970.

Bubner, Rüdiger, et al. *"Sein, das verstanden werden kann, ist Sprache": Hommage an Hans-Georg Gadamer.* Frankfurt: Suhrkamp, 2001.

Burke, J. *Al-Qaeda: The True Story of Radical Islam.* London: Penguin, 2007.

Butler, J., E. Laclau, and S. Žižek. *Contingency, Hegemony, Universality: Contemporary Dialogues on the Left*. London: Verso, 2000.

Caputo, John. *More Radical Hermeneutics: On Not Knowing Who We Are*. Bloomington: Indiana University Press, 2000.

——. *Radical Hermeneutics: Repetition, Deconstruction and the Hermeneutic Project*. Bloomington: Indiana University Press, 1987.

Caputo, John, and M. J. Scanlon, eds. *God, the Gift, and Postmodernism*. Bloomington: Indiana University Press, 1999.

Carroll, R. "Bolivia's 'Little Indians' Find Voice." *Guardian* (April 26, 2009).

——. "Nobel Economist Endorses Chávez Regional Bank Plan." *Guardian* (October 12, 2007).

Carver, T., and M. Hyvärinen, eds. *Interpreting the Political: New Methodologies*. London: Routledge, 1997.

Castro, Fidel. *My Life*. Ed. I. Ramonet. Trans. A. Hurley. London: Penguin, 2006.

Cavell, Colin S. *Exporting 'Made-In-America' Democracy: The National Endowment for Democracy & U.S. Foreign Policy*. Washington, D.C.: University Press of America, 2002.

Chomsky, Noam. "Barak Obama and the 'Unipolar Moment.'" *In These Times* (October 6, 2009).

——. "Cuba's Fifty Years of Defiance: An Interview with Noam Chomsky by Bernie Dwyer." *Counterpunch* (November 3, 2003).

——. "Elections 2008 & Obama's Vision." *Z Magazine* 22, no. 2 (February 2009).

——. *Failed States*. London: Penguin, 2006.

——. *Hegemony or Survival*. London: Penguin, 2003.

——. "Historical Perspectives on Latin American and East Asian Regional Development." *Asian-Pacific Journal. Japan Focus* (December 20, 2006).

——. *Language and Politics.* Edited by C. P. Otero. Oakland, Calif.: AK Press, 2004.

—— *Latin America: From Colonization to Globalization.* Melbourne: Ocean Press, 1999.

——. "Militarizing Latin America." *In these Times* (September 9, 2009).

——. "South America: Toward an Alternative Future." *International Herald Tribune* (January 5, 2007).

——. *What We Say Goes: Conversations on U.S. Power in a Changing World: Interviews with David Barsamian.* New York: Metropolitan Books, 2007.

Chomsky, N., Lois Meyer, and Benjamín Maldonado Alvarado. *New World of Indigenous Resistance: Voices from the Americas.* San Francisco: City Lights, 2010.

Cockburn, P. *The Occupation: War and Resistance in Iraq.* London: Verso, 2007.

Code, Lorraine, ed. *The Feminist Interpretations of Hans-Georg Gadamer.* University Park: Pennsylvania State University Press, 2003.

Coltman, Rod. *The Language of Hermeneutics: Gadamer and Heidegger in Dialogue.* Albany, N.Y.: SUNY Press, 1998.

Critchley, Simon. *Infinitely Demanding: Ethics of Commitment, Politics of Resistance.* London: Verso, 2008.

Critchley, Simon, and Reiner Schürmann. *On Heidegger's* Being and Time. Ed. S. Levine. London: Routledge, 2008.

Crowell, Steven, and J. Malpas, eds. *Transcendental Heidegger.* Stanford, Calif.: Stanford University Press, 2007.

Culler, Jonathan. *On Deconstruction: Theory and Criticism After Structuralism.* Abingdon: Routledge, 2008.

Curran, Giorel. *Twenty-first Century Dissent: Anarchism, Anti-Globalization, and Environmentalism.* New York: Palgrave, 2006.

Dahlstrom, Daniel, O. *Heidegger's Concept of Truth.* Cambridge, Mass.: Cambridge University Press, 2001.

Davidson, Donald. *Inquiries into Truth and Interpretation*. Oxford: Clarendon, 2001.

——. *Truth and Predication*. Cambridge, Mass.: Harvard University Press, 2005.

Davis, Mike. "Humanity's Ground Zero [Interview]." *Tomdispatch* (May 9, 2006).

——. *Planet of Slums*. London: Verso: 2006.

Debusmann, Bernd. "Around Globe, Walls Spring up to Divide Neighbors." *Reuters* (April 30, 2007).

Derrida, Jacques. *Aporias*. Trans. T. Dutoit. Stanford, Calif.: Stanford University Press, 1993.

——. *The Beast and the Sovereign*. Ed. Geoffrey Bennington. Chicago: University of Chicago Press, 2009.

——. "Circumfession." In *Jacques Derrida*, by Jacques Derrida and Geoffrey Bennington. Trans. Geoffrey Bennington. Chicago: University of Chicago Press, 1993.

——. *Deconstruction in a Nutshell*. Ed. John D. Caputo. New York: Fordham University Press, 1997.

——. *Dissemination*. Trans. B. Johnson. Chicago: University of Chicago Press, 1981.

——. *The Ear of the Other: Otobiography, Transference, Translation*. Ed. Christie McDonald. Lincoln: University of Nebraska Press, 1985.

——. *Edmund Husserl's* Origin of Geometry: *An Introduction*. Trans. John P. Leavey Jr. Lincoln: University of Nebraska Press, 1989.

——. "Geschlect II: Heidegger's Hand." In *Deconstruction and Philosophy*, ed. John Sallis, trans. John P. Leavey Jr., 161–196. Chicago: University of Chicago Press, 1987.

——. *The Gift of Death*. Trans. David Willis. Chicago: University of Chicago Press, 1995.

———. *Ethics, Institutions, and the Right to Philosophy*. Ed. P. Pericles Trifonas. Lanham, Md.: Rowman & Littlefield, 2002.

———. *Limited Inc*. Trans. Samuel Weber. Evanston, Ill.: Northwestern University Press, 1988.

———. *Margins of Philosophy*. Trans. Alan Bass. Chicago: University of Chicago Press, 1982.

———. *Of Grammatology*. Trans. G. Chakravorty Spivak. Baltimore, Md.: The Johns Hopkins University Press, 1997.

———. *Of Hospitality*. Trans. Rachel Bowlby. Stanford, Calif.: Stanford University Press, 2000.

———. *Of Spirit: Heidegger and the Question*. Trans. Geoffrey Bennington and Rachael Bowlby. Chicago: University of Chicago Press, 1989.

———. *Paper Machine*. Trans. Rachel Bowlby. Stanford, Calif.: Stanford University Press, 2005.

———. *Philosophy in a Time of Terror*. Ed. Giovanna Borradori. Chicago: University of Chicago Press, 2003.

———. *Points . . . Interviews 1974–1994*. Ed. Elisabeth Weber. Trans. Peggy Kamuf and others. Stanford, Calif.: Stanford University Press, 1995.

———. *Politics of Friendship*. Trans. George Collins. London: Verso, 1997.

———. *Positions*. Trans. Alan Bass. London: Continuum, 2002.

———. *Specters of Marx*. Trans. Peggy Kamuf. London: Routledge, 1996.

———. *Speech and Phenomena, and Other Essays on Husserl's Theory of Signs*. Trans. David Allison. Evanston, Ill.: Northwestern University Press, 1973.

———. *A Taste for the Secret*. Ed. M. Ferraris. London: Blackwell, 2001.

———. "The Time of a Thesis: Punctuations." In *Philosophy in France Today*, ed. A. Montefiore, trans. K. McLaughlin, 34–50. Cambridge: Cambridge University Press, 1983.

———. *The Work of Mourning*. Ed. Pascale-Anne Brault and Michael Nass. Chicago: University of Chicago Press, 2001.

——. *Writing and Difference*. Trans. Alan Bass. Chicago: University of Chicago Press, 1978.

Derrida, Jacques, Terry Eagleton, Fredric Jameson, Antonio Negri, et al. *Ghostly Demarcations: A Symposium on Jacques Derrida's Specters of Marx.* Ed. Michael Sprinker. London: Verso, 1999.

Derrida, Jacques, and Gianni Vattimo, eds. *Religion.* Stanford, Calif.: Stanford University Press, 1998.

Dilthey, Wilhelm. *The Construction of History in the Human Sciences.* Princeton, N.J.: Princeton University Press, 2004.

——. *The Essence of Philosophy.* Trans. S. A. Emery and W. T. Emery. Chapel Hill: University of North Carolina Press, 1954.

——. *The Formation of the Historical World in the Human Sciences.* Ed. Rudolf A. Makkreel and Frithjof Rodi. Princeton, N.J.: Princeton University Press, 2002.

——. *Gesammelte Schriften.* Göttingen: Vanderhoeck & Ruprecht, 1961–2001.

——. *Hermeneutics and the Study of History.* Ed. Rudolf A. Makkreel and Frithjof Rodi. Princeton, N.J.: Princeton University Press, 1996.

——. *Introduction to the Human Sciences.* Trans. R. J. Betanzos. Detroit, Mich.: Wayne State University Press, 1989.

Dinges, John. *The Condor Years: How Pinochet and His Allies Brought Terrorism to Three Continents.* New York: The New Press, 2004.

Dostal, Robert. *The Cambridge Companion to Gadamer.* Cambridge: Cambridge University Press, 2002.

——. "The Development of Gadamer's Thought." *Journal of the British Society for Phenomenology* 34 (2003): 247–264.

Drew, C., and E. Bumiller. "Military Budget Reflects a Shift in U.S. Strategy." *New York Times,* April 6, 2009.

Dummett, Michael. *The Nature and Future of Philosophy.* New York: Columbia University Press, 2010.

Dupree, L. *Afghanistan*. London: Oxford University Press, 1998.

Ebeling, Gerhard. "Die Anfange von Luthers Hermeneutik." *Zeitschrift für Theologie und Kirche* 48 (1951): 174–230.

Egginton, William. *Perversity and Ethics*. Stanford, Calif.: Stanford University Press, 2005.

——. *The Philosopher's Desire: Psychoanalysis, Interpretation, and Truth*. Stanford, Calif.: Stanford University Press, 2007.

Escobar, Pepe. *Red Zone Blues: A Snapshot of Baghdad During the Surge*. Ann Arbor, Mich.: Nimble Books, 2007.

——. "Get Osama! Now! Or Else . . . " *Asia Times Online* (August 30, 2001).

Estrada, D. "South America: Leaders Express Full Support for Bolivia's Morales." *Inter Press Service Agency* (September 16, 2008). http://ipsnews.net /news.asp?idnews=43887.

Faulconer, James E., and Mark A. Wrathall, eds. *Appropriating Heidegger*. Cambridge: Cambridge University Press, 2000.

Ferraris, Maurizio. *History of Hermeneutics*. Trans. L. Somigli. Englewood Cliffs, N.J.: Humanities Press, 1996.

Fisk, Robert. "Democracy Will Not Bring Freedom." *The Independent* (August 21, 2009).

Fleischman, Luis. "Brazil's Tilt Towards Chavez and Iran." *The Americas Report* (October 8, 2009). http://www.centerforsecuritypolicy.org/p18195 .xml?cat_id=252.

Forero, J. "Chávez Wins Removal of Term Limits." *Washington Post* (February 16, 2009).

Foucault, Michel, *The Archeology of Knowledge and the Discourse on Language*. New York: Pantheon, 1971.

——. "Nietzsche, Freud, Marx." In *Nietzsche: Cahiers de Royaumont*, ed. Martial Gueroult, 183–192. Paris: Gallimard, 1966.

Frank, Dana. "Honduras' Great Awakening." *The Nation* (April 5, 2010).

Frank, Manfred. *The Boundaries of Agreement*. Aurora, Colo.: Davies Group, 2008.

———. *Das Sagbare und das Unsagbare: Studien zur neuesten französischen Herme-neutik und Texttheorie*. Frankfurt: Suhrkamp, 1980.

Freud, Sigmund. *The Interpretation of Dreams* [1900]. Trans. James Strachey. New York: Basic Books, 2010.

Friedman, M. *Capitalism and Freedom*. Chicago: University of Chicago Press, 1962.

———. "Comment." In *Margaret Thatcher's Revolution: How It Happened and What It Meant*, ed. S. Roy and J. Clarke. London: Continuum, 2005.

Friedman, T. L. "Fill 'Er up with Dictators." *New York Times*, September 27, 2006.

Fukuyama, Francis. "Back to the End of History: Interview with M. Phillips." *Newsweek* (September 29, 2008).

———. *The End of History and the Last Man*. New York: Free Press, 1992, 2006.

———. "History's Against Him." *Washington Post* (August 6, 2006).

———. "A Quiet Revolution." *Foreign Policy* (November/December 2007). http://www.foreignaffairs.com/articles/63039/francis-fukuyama/a-quiet -revolution?page=show.

Fusaro, Diego. *Bentonato Marx: Il ritorno di un pensiero rivoluzionario*. Milan: Bompiani, 2009.

Gadamer, Hans-Georg. *The Beginning of Philosophy*. Trans. Rod Coltman. New York: Continuum, 2001.

———. "Boundaries of Language [1985]." In *Language and Linguisticality in Ga-damer's Hermeneutics*, ed. Lawrence K. Schmidt, 9–17. Lanham, Md.: Lex-ington Books, 2000.

———. *A Century of Philosophy: A Conversation with Ricardo Dottori*. Trans. Rod Coltman and Sigrid Koepke. New York: Continuum, 2004.

———. "Conversation with Gadamer [by Michael Baur]." *Method* 8 (1990): 1–13.

———. *Gadamer in Conversation: Reflections and Commentary.* Ed. Richard Palmer. New Haven, Conn.: Yale University Press, 2003.

——— . *The Gadamer Reader: A Bouquet of the Later Writings.* Ed. and trans. Richard E. Palmer. Evanston, Ill.: Northwestern University Press, 2007.

———. *Gesammelte Werke.* Tübingen: J. B.C. Mohr, 1986–1995.

———. *Hans-Georg Gadamer on Education, Poetry, and History: Applied Hermeneutics.* Ed. D. Misgeld and G. Nicholson. Trans. L. Schmidt and M. Reuss. Albany, N.Y.: SUNY Press, 1992.

———. *Hegel's Dialectic: Five Hermeneutical Studies.* Trans. P. Christopher Smith. New Haven, Conn.: Yale University Press, 1976.

———. *Heidegger's Ways.* Trans. John W. Staley. Albany, N.Y.: SUNY Press, 1994.

———. "Hermeneutics and Logocentrism." In *Dialogue and Deconstruction: The Gadamer-Derrida Encounter,* ed. D. P. Michelfelder and R. E. Palmer, 114–125. Albany, N.Y.: SUNY Press, 1989.

———. *Hermeneutics, Religion, and Ethics.* Trans. Joel Weinsheimer. New Haven, Conn.: Yale University Press, 1999.

———. *Philosophical Hermeneutics.* Trans. David E. Linge. Berkeley: University of California Press, 1976.

———. *The Philosophy of Hans-Georg Gadamer.* Ed. Lewis Edwin Hahn. Library of Living Philosophers 24. Chicago: Open Court Press, 1997.

———. *Plato's Dialectical Ethics: Phenomenological Interpretations Relating to the Philebus.* Trans. R. M. Wallace. New Haven, Conn.: Yale University Press, 1991.

———. *Praise of Theory.* Trans. Chris Dawson. New Haven, Conn.: Yale University Press, 1998.

———. "Reply to My Critics." In *Hermeneutic Tradition: From Ast to Ricoeur,* ed. G. L. Ormiston and A. D. Schrift, trans. G. H. Leiner, 273–297. Albany, N.Y.: SUNY Press, 1990.

——. *Truth and Method* [1960]. Trans. J. Weinsheimer and D. G. Marshall. London: Continuum, 2004.

——."The Universality of the Hermeneutical Problem." In *Philosophical Hermeneutics*, ed. David E. Linge, 3–17. Berkeley: University of California Press, 1976.

Galeano, Eduardo. "Obama at One: A Nation Forum." *The Nation* (February 1, 2010): 20.

——. *Open Veins of Latin America: Five Centuries of the Pillage of a Continent.* New York: Monthly Review Press, 1997.

Gallino, Luciano. *Con i soldi degli altri: Il capitalismo per procura contro l'economia.* Torino: Einaudi, 2009.

Gasché, Rodolphe. *The Tain of the Mirror: Derrida and the Philosophy of Reflection.* Cambridge, Mass.: Harvard University Press, 1986.

——. *Views and Interviews: On 'Deconstruction' in America.* Aurora, Colo.: Davies Group, 2007.

Georgescu-Roegen, N. *Demain, la décroissance. Entropie, écologie, économie.* Paris: Éditions Sang de la terre, 1995.

Gilles, C. "Poll Reveals Backlash in Wealthy Countries Against Globalization." *Financial Times* (July 23, 2007).

Gilly, Adolfo. *Chiapas: la razon ardiente. Ensayo sobre la rebelion del mundo encantado.* Mexico City: Ediciones ERA, 2006.

Giorgio, Giovanni. *Il pensiero di Gianni Vattimo.* Milan: Franco Angeli, 2007.

Golinger, Eva. "A Case Study of Media Concentration and Power in Venezuela." *Venezuelanalysis.com* (September 25, 2004).

——. "The Media War Against the People: A Case Study of Media Concentration and Power in Venezuela." In *The Venezuela Reader: The Building of a People's Democracy*, ed. Olivia Burlingame Goumbri. Washington, D.C.: Epica, 2005.

Gott, Richard. *Hugo Chávez and the Bolívarian Revolution*. London: Verso, 2005.

———. "A Landmark for Bolivia." *Guardian* (January 26, 2009).

———. "Southern Comfort." *Guardian* (February 1, 2009).

Grandin, Greg. *Empire's Workshop: Latin America, the United States, and the Rise of the New Imperialism*. New York: Owl Books, 2007.

———. *The Last Colonial Massacre: Latin America in the Cold War*. Chicago: University of Chicago Press, 2004.

———. "Muscling Latin America." *The Nation* (February 8, 2010).

Greisch, Jean. *Paul Ricoeur: L'itinérance du sens*. Paris: Millon, 2001.

Grondin, Jean. "Continental or Hermeneutical Philosophy: The Tragedies of Understanding in the Analytic and Continental Perspectives." In *Interrogating the Tradition: Hermeneutics and the History of Philosophy*, ed. J. Sallis and J. Scott, 75–83. Albany, N.Y.: SUNY Press, 2000.

———. *Der Sinn der Hermeneutik*. Darmstadt: Wissenschaftliche Buchgesellschaft, 1994.

———. *Hans-Georg Gadamer. A Biography*. Trans. Joel Weinsheimer. New Haven, Conn.: Yale University Press, 2003.

———. "Hermeneutical Truth and Its Historical Presuppositions. A Possible Bridge Between Analysis and Hermeneutics." In *Anti-Foundationalism and Practical Reasoning*, ed. Evan Simpson, 45–58. Edmonton: Academic Printing and Publishing, 1987.

———. *Herméneutique*, Paris: PUF, 2009.

———. *"Hermeneutische Wahrheit?" Zum Wahrheitsbegriff Hans-Georg Gadamers*. Weinheim: Athenäum, 1994.

———. *L'horizon herméneutique de la pensée contemporaine*. Paris: Vrin, 1993.

———. *Introduction to Philosophical Hermeneutics*. Trans. Joel Weinsheimer. New Haven, Conn.: Yale University Press, 1994.

———. "La contribution silencieuse de Husserl à l'herméneutique." *Philosophiques* 22 (1993): 383–393.

———. *Le tournant dans la pensée de Martin Heidegger*. Paris: PUF, 1987.

———. *Le tournant herméneutique de la phénoménologie*. Paris: PUF, 2003.

———. "La thèse de l'herméneutique sur l'être." *Revue de métaphysique et de morale* 52 (2006): 469–481.

———. *The Philosophy of Gadamer*. Montreal: McGill-Queen's University Press, 2003.

———. *Sources of Hermeneutics*. Albany, N.Y.: SUNY Press, 1995.

Guéhenno, M. *The End of the Nation-State*. Trans. V. Elliott. Minneapolis: University of Minnesota Press, 1995.

Gugler, J. "Overurbanization Reconsidered." In *Cities in the Developing World: Issues, Theory, and Policy*, ed. J. Gugler. Oxford: Oxford University Press: 1997.

Gusdorf, G. *Les origines de l'herméneutique*. Paris: Payot, 1988.

Habermas, Jürgen. "After Historicism, Is Metaphysics Still Possible? On Hans-Georg Gadamer's 100th Birthday." In *Gadamer's Repercussions: Reconsidering Philosophical Hermeneutics*, ed. B. Krajewski, 15–20. Berkeley: University of California Press, 2004.

———. "Hans-Georg Gadamer: Urbanizing the Heideggerian Province." In *Philosophical-Political Profiles*, trans. Frederick Lawrence. Cambridge, Mass.: The MIT Press, 1983.

———. *The Inclusion of the Other: Studies in Political Theory*. Cambridge, Mass.: The MIT Press, 1998.

———. *Knowledge and Human Interest*. Cambridge, Mass.: The MIT Press, 1983.

———. *Knowledge and Human Interests*. Boston: Beacon Press, 1971.

———. *Moral Consciousness and Communicative Action*. Trans. C. Lenhardt and S. W. Nicholsen. Cambridge, Mass.: The MIT Press, 1990.

———. *Moral Consciousness and Communicative Action*. Trans. Thomas McCarthy. Cambridge: Polity Press, 1992.

———. *On the Logic of the Social Sciences*. Cambridge, Mass.: The MIT Press, 1988.

——. *The Philosophical Discourse of Modernity: Twelve Lectures.* Trans. Frederick G. Lawrence. Cambridge, Mass.: The MIT Press, 1987.

——. *Postmetaphysical Thinking.* Trans. W. M. Hohengarten. Cambridge, Mass.: The MIT Press, 1994.

——. *Pragmatics of Social Interaction.* Cambridge, Mass.: The MIT Press, 2002.

——. "A Review of Gadamer's Truth and Method." In *The Hermeneutic Tradition: From Ast to Ricoeur,* ed. G. Ormiston and A. Schrift, 213–245. Albany, N.Y.: SUNY Press, 1990.

——. *The Theory of Communicative Action.* Vol. 2, *Lifeword and System: A Critique of Functionalist Reason.* Trans. Thomas McCarthy. Boston: Beacon Press, 1985.

Hardt, Michael, and Antonio Negri. *Commonwealth.* Cambridge, Mass.: The Belknap Press of Harvard University Press, 2009.

——. *Empire.* Cambridge, Mass.: Harvard University Press, 2000.

——. *Multitude: War and Democracy in the Age of Empire.* London: Penguin, 2004.

Harvey, David. *A Brief History of Neoliberalism.* New York: Oxford University Press, 2007.

Hegel, G. W. F. *Phenomenology of the Sprit.* Trans. Terry Pinkard. Cambridge: Cambridge University Press, forthcoming.

Heidegger, Martin. *Basic Concepts.* Trans. G. E. Aylesworth. Bloomington: Indiana University Press, 1993.

——. *The Basic Problems of Phenomenology.* Trans. Albert Hofstadter. Bloomington: Indiana University Press, 1982.

——. *Being and Time* [1927]. Trans. Joan Stambaugh. New York: SUNY Press, 2010.

——. *Contributions to Philosophy (From Enowning).* Trans. P. Emad and K. Maly. Bloomington: Indiana University Press, 1999.

———. *The Essence of Truth: Plato's Cave Allegory and Theaetetus*. Trans. Ted Sadler. New York: Continuum, 2002.

———. *The Fundamental Concepts of Metaphysics: World, Finitude, Solitude*. Trans. Will McNeill and Nicholas Walker. Bloomington: Indiana University Press, 1995.

———. *Gesamtausgabe*. Frankfurt am Main: Vittorio Klostermann, 1978-.

———. *Identity and Difference* [1957]. Translated by Joan Stambaugh. Chicago: University of Chicago Press, 2002.

———. *Introduction to Metaphysics* [1953]. Trans. Gregory Fried and Richard Polt. New Haven, Conn.: Yale University Press, 2000.

———. *Logic: The Question of Truth*. Trans. Thomas Sheehan. Bloomington: Indiana University Press, 2010.

———. *Off the Beaten Track* [1950]. Trans. Julian Young and Kenneth Haynes. Cambridge: Cambridge University Press, 2002.

———. *On the Way to Language* [1959]. Trans. Peter D. Hertz. New York: Harper and Row, 1982.

———. *On Time and Being* [1969]. Translated by B. Johnson. Chicago: University of Chicago Press, 2002.

———. *Ontology—the Hermeneutics of Facticity*. Trans. J. van Buren. Bloomington: Indiana University Press, 1999.

———. "Overcoming Metaphysics." In *The End of Philosophy*, trans. J. Stambaugh. New York: Harper and Row, 1973.

———. *Pathmarks* [1967]. Ed. William McNeill. Cambridge, Mass.: The MIT Press, 2002.

———. *Philosophical and Political Writings*. Ed. Manfred Stassen. Trans. M. P. Alter and J. D. Caputo. New York: Continuum, 2003.

———. "Preface [1962]." In *Heidegger: Through Phenomenology to Thought*, ed. William Richardson, xiii–xxiii. New York: Fordham University Press, 2003.

——. *The Principle of Reason.* Trans. Reginald Lilly. Bloomington: Indiana University Press, 1991.

——. *The Question Concerning Technology.* Trans. W. Lovitt. New York: Harper & Row, 1977.

——. "Time and Being." In *On Time and Being*, trans. Joan Stambaugh. Chicago: University of Chicago Press, 2002.

——. *What Is Called Thinking?* Trans. J. Glenn Gray. New York: Harper & Row, 1968.

Herman, Edward S., and Noam Chomsky. *Manufacturing Consent: The Political Economy of the Mass Media* [1988]. New York: Pantheon, 2008.

Hills, Alice. *Future War in Cities: Rethinking a Liberal Dilemma.* London: Frank Cass, 2004.

Hobsbawm, Eric. "El comunismo continúa vigente como motivación y como utopía [Interview by Aurora Intxausti]." *El País* (April 12, 2003).

——. *The New Century: In Conversation with A. Polito*, trans. A. Cameron. London: Abacus, 2000.

Hollinger, Robert, ed. *Hermeneutics and Praxis.* South Bend, Ind.: University of Notre Dame Press, 1985.

Home, R., and H. Lim, eds. *Demystifying the Mystery of Capital: Land Tenure and Poverty in Africa and the Caribbean.* London: Glasshouse Press, 2004.

Hoy, David. *The Critical Circle: Literature, History, and Philosophical Hermeneutics.* Berkeley: University of California Press, 1978.

Husserl, Edmund. *The Crisis of European Sciences and Transcendental Phenomenology.* Evanston, Ill.: Northwestern University Press, 1970.

——. *Psychological and Transcendental Phenomenology and the Confrontation with Heidegger (1927–1931).* Ed. and trans. T. Sheehan and R. Palmer. Dordrecht: Kluwer Academic Publishers, 1997.

Hylton, F., and S. Thomson. "The Chequered Rainbow." *New Left Review* 35 (September–October 2005): 47.

——. *Revolutionary Horizons: Past and Present in Bolivian Politics*. London: Verso, 2007.

International Labour Organization. *Global Employment Trends, Update, May 2009*.

Jesdanun, Anick. "U.S. Military Prepares Cyberwarfare Offensive." *USA Today* (April 7, 2008).

Johnson, David T. "Afghanistan Remains, by Far, the World's Largest Producer of Opium Poppy." http://www.state.gov/p/inl/rls/rm/119890.htm.

Jones, Bart. "Hugo Chavez Versus RCTV." *Los Angeles Times* (May 30, 2007).

Juhasz, A. "Ambitions of Empire: The Bush Administration Economic Plan for Iraq (and Beyond)." *Left Turn* 12 (February/March 2004): 27–32.

Kagan, Robert. *The Return of History and the End of Dreams*. New York: Random House, 2008.

Kearney, Richard, ed. *Paul Ricoeur: The Hermeneutics of Action*. London: Sage, 1996.

Klein, Naomi. "A New Climate Movement in Bolivia." *The Nation*, April 21, 2010.

——. *No Logo*. New York: Picador: 2000.

——. *The Shock Doctrine*. London: Penguin, 2007.

——. "Venezuela's Media Coup." *The Nation*, February 13, 2003.

Kögler, Hans-Herbert. *The Power of Dialogue: Critical Hermeneutics After Gadamer and Foucault*. Cambridge, Mass.: The MIT Press, 1999.

Korten, David C. *When Corporations Rule the World*. West Hartford, Conn.: Kumarian Press, 2001.

Kozloff, N. *Revolution! South America and the Rise of the New Left*. New York: Palgrave, MacMillan, 2008.

Krajewski, Bruce, ed. *Gadamer's Repercussions: Reconsidering Philosophical Hermeneutics*. Berkeley: University of California Press, 2004.

Krugman, Paul. *The Conscience of a Liberal*. New York: Norton, 2009.

——. "How Did Economists Get It So Wrong?" *New York Times,* September 6, 2009.

——. *The Return of Depression Economics and the Crisis of 2008.* New York: Norton, 2009.

Kuhn, Thomas. *The Essential Tension: Selected Studies in Scientific Tradition and Change.* Chicago: University of Chicago Press, 1977.

——. *The Road Since Structure: Philosophical Essays, 1970–1993, with an Autobiographical Interview.* Chicago: University of Chicago Press, 2002.

——. *The Structure of Scientific Revolutions.* Chicago: University of Chicago Press, 1996.

Laclau, E., and C. Mouffe. *Hegemony and Socialist Strategy: Towards a Radical Democratic Politics.* London: Verso, 2001.

Latouche, Serge. *In the Wake of the Affluent Society: An Exploration of Post-Development.* Trans. M. O'Connor and R. Arnoux. London: Zed Books, 1993.

Lenin, V. I. *Collected Works.* Trans. J. Katzer. Moscow: Progress Publishers, 1965.

Lewis, Michael. *Heidegger Beyond Deconstruction: On Nature.* London: Continuum, 2007.

Lievesley, G., and S. Lundam. "Nuestra America: the Spectre Haunting Washington." In *Reclaiming Latin America: Experiments in Radical Social Democracy,* ed. G. Lievesley and S. Lundam, 217–229. London: Zed Books, 2009.

Lippmann, Walter. *Public Opinion* [1922]. New York: The Free Press, 1997.

Livingstone, Grace. *America's Backyard: The United States and Latin America from the Monroe Doctrine to the War on Terror.* London: Zed Books, 2009.

Losurdo, Domenico. *Controstoria del liberalismo.* Rome: Laterza, 2006.

——. *La non-violenza. Una storia fuori dal mito.* Rome: Laterza, 2010.

——. *Stalin: Storia e critica di una leggenda nera.* Rome: Carocci, 2008.

Lyotard, Jean-François. *The Inhuman: Reflections on Time.* Trans. Geoff Bennington and Rachel Bowlby. Stanford, Calif.: Stanford University Press, 1991.

———. "Notes sur le retour et le capital." in *Nietzsche aujourd'hui: 1: Intensités*, ed. Pierre Boudot et al., 141–57. In English translation as "Notes on the Return and Kapital," in *Semiotext(e)* 3 (1978): 44–53.

———. *The Postmodern Condition. A Report on Knowledge*. Trans. Geoff Bennington and Brian Massumi. Minneapolis: University of Minnesota Press, 1999.

Luther, Martin. *Dr. Martin Luthers Tischreden (1531–46)*. Weimar: Hermann Böhlaus, 1914.

Lutz, Catherine, ed. *The Bases of Empire: The Global Struggle Against U.S. Military Posts*. New York: New York University Press, 2009.

Maclean, Ian. "Un dialogue de sourds? Some Implications of the Austin-Searle-Derrida Debate [1985]." In *Jacques Derrida: Critical Thought*, ed. I. Maclachlan, 49–66. London: Ashgate, 2004.

Malpas, Jeff. *Heidegger's Topology: Being, Place, World*. Cambridge, Mass.: The MIT Press, 2007.

Malpas, Jeff, U. Arnswald, and J. Kertscher, eds. *Gadamer's Century*. Cambridge, Mass.: The MIT Press, 2002.

Makita, Etsura. *Gadamer-Bibliographie (1922–1994)*. New York: Peter Lang, 1995.

Mandak, J. "Police Use Acoustic Warfare to Disperse G20 Crowds." *Associated Press* (October 1, 2009).

Mao Tse-Tung. *Quotations from Chairman Mao Tse-Tung*. Hong Kong: China Books & Periodicals Inc., 1990.

Marcuse, Herbert. *Heideggerian Marxism*. Ed. R. Wolin and J. Abromeit. Lincoln: University of Nebraska Press, 2005.

Marder, Michael. "Carl Schmitt and the Event." *Telos* 147 (Summer 2009).

———. "Carl Schmitt and the Risk of the Political." *Telos* 132 (Fall 2005): 5–24.

———. "Carl Schmitt's 'Cosmopolitan Restaurant': Culture, Multiculturalism, and the *Complexio Oppositorum*." *Telos* 142 (Spring 2008): 29–47.

——. "From the Concept of the Political to the Event of Politics." *Telos* 147 (Summer 2009): 55–76.

——. "Given the Right—Of Giving (in Hegel's *Grundlinien der Philosophie des Rechts*)." *Epoché* 12, no. 1 (Fall 2007): 93–108.

——. *Groundless Existence: The Political Ontology of Carl Schmitt.* London: Continuum, 2010.

——. "On Lenin's 'Usability'; or, How to Stay on the Edge?" *Rethinking Marxism* 19, no. 1 (January 2007): 110–127.

——. "Political Hermeneutics; or, Why Schmitt Is Not the Enemy of Gadamer." In *Consequences of Hermeneutics*, ed. Jeff Malpas and Santiago Zabala. Evanston: Northwestern University Press, 2010.

——. "Taming the Beast: The Other Tradition in Political Theory." *Mosaic* 39, no. 4 (December 2006): 47–60.

Margolis, E. "After Iraq, Bush Will Attack His Real Target." *Toronto Sun* (November 10, 2002).

Marion, Jean-Luc. "The 'End of Metaphysics' as a Possibility." In *Religion After Metaphysics*, ed. Mark A. Wrathall, 166–189. Cambridge: Cambridge University Press, 2003.

Martinengo, Alberto. *Introduzione a Reiner Schürmann.* Rome: Meltemi, 2008.

Martinez, Carlos, Michael Fox, and JoJo Farrell, eds. *Venezuela Speaks! Voices from the Grassroots.* Oakland, Calif.: PM Press, 2010.

Marx, Karl. *Capital.* 3 vols. Penguin: London, 1992–1993.

——. *Grundrisse: Foundations of the Critique of Political Economy.* Penguin: London, 1993.

——. *Selected Writings.* Ed. David McLellan. Oxford: Oxford University Press, 2000.

——. *Theories of Surplus Value.* New York: Prometheus Books, 2000.

Marx, Karl, and Friedrich Engels. *The Communist Manifesto*. Oxford: Oxford University Press, 2008.

McDowell, John. *Mind and World*. Cambridge, Mass.: Harvard University Press, 1994.

McKeon, Richard. "Imitation and Poetry." In *Thought, Action, and Passion*, 102–221. Chicago: University of Chicago Press, 1954.

McNeill, William. "The First Principle of Hermeneutics." In *Reading Heidegger from the Start*, ed. T. Kiesel and J. van Buren, 393–408. Albany, N.Y.: SUNY Press, 1994.

McSherry, J. Patrice. *Predatory States: Operation Condor and Covert War in Latin America*. London: Rowman & Littlefield, 2005.

Mealla, Luis Tapia. *La invención del núcleo común. Ciudadanía y gobierno multi-societal*. La Paz: Autodeterminación-Muela del Diablo Editores, 2006.

Messuti, Ana. *La justicia decostruida*. Foreword by G. Vattimo and S. Zabala. Barcelona: Bellatera, 2009.

Metzl, J., and C. Fair. "Let Afghans Lead Afghan Reform." *Khaleej Times Online* (September 3, 2009).

Minà, Gianni. *Il continente desaparecido è ricomparso*. Milan: Sperling & Kupfer, 2005.

——. "Cyberwar a Cuba." *Il Manifesto*, December 6, 2009, 16.

——. *An Encounter with Fidel: An Interview by Gianni Mina*. Trans. Mary Todd. Melbourne: Ocean Press, 1992.

——. *Politicamente scorretto*. Milan: Sperling & Kupfer, 2007.

Minford, P. "Inflation, Unemployment, and the Pound." In *Margaret Thatcher's Revolution: How It Happened and What It Meant*, ed. S. Roy and J. Clarke, 50–66. London: Continuum, 2005.

Moati, Raoul. *Derrida/Searle: Déconstruction et langage ordinaire*. Paris: PUF, 2009.

Moisi, D. "Barack Obama's American Revolution." *Japan Times Online*, December 29, 2007.

Naím, M. "Hugo Chávez's Criminal Paradise." *Los Angeles Times*, November 10, 2007).

Nair, Naïr. "El dilema del socialismo europeo." *El País* (October 13, 2009).

Nancy, Jean-Luc. *The Inoperative Community.* Ed. Peter Connor. Minneapolis: University of Minnesota Press, 1991.

Nash, Gary B. *The Unknown American Revolution: The Unruly Birth of Democracy and the Struggle to Create America.* New York: Viking, 2005.

Nelson, Brian A. *The Silence and the Scorpion: The Coup Against Chávez and the Making of Modern Venezuela.* New York: Nation Books, 2009.

Nietzsche, Friedrich. *Complete Works.* Vol. 2: *Unfashionable Observations.* Trans. Richard T. Gray. Stanford, Calif.: Stanford University Press, 1995.

——. *Complete Works.* Vol. 3: *Human, All Too Human (I): A Book for Free Spirits.* Trans. Gary Handwerk. Stanford, Calif.: Stanford University Press, 1997.

——. *Complete Works.* Vol. 11: *Unpublished Writings from the Period of* Unfashionable Observations. Trans. Richard T. Gray. Stanford, Calif.: Stanford University Press, 1999.

——. *Ecce Homo.* Trans. Anthony. M. Ludovici. New York: Dover, 2004.

——. *On the Advantage and Disadvantage of History for Life.* Trans. Peter Preuss. Indianapolis, Ind.: Hackett, 1980.

——. *Philosophy and Truth: Selections from Nietzsche's Notebooks of the Early 1870s.* Ed. Daniel Breazeale. Amherst, N.Y.: Prometheus Books, 1990.

——. *Thus Spoke Zarathustra.* Trans. G. Parkes. New York: Oxford University Press, 2005.

——. *Twilight of the Idols.* Trans. R. J. Hollingdale. Harmondsworth: Penguin, 1968.

——. *The Will To Power.* Trans. Walter Kaufmann and R. J. Hollingdale. London: Weidenfeld and Nicolson, 1968.

Nozick, Robert. *Anarchy, State, and Utopia*. Malden: Blackwell, 1974.

Obama, Barak. "Remarks by the President on a New Strategy for Afghanistan and Pakistan, March 27, 2009." Office of Press Secretary. http://www.whitehouse.gov/the_press_office/Remarks-by-the-President-on-a-New-Strategy-for-Afghanistan-and-Pakistan/.

O'Donoghue, Patrick J. "Chavez to Change GDP Measuring to Stiglitz Report Recommendations." *VHeadline.com* (September 22, 2009). http://www.vheadline.com/readnews.asp?id=84197.

Ofek, E., and M. Richardson. "DotComMania: The Rise and Fall of Internet Stock Prices." *Journal of Finance* 58, no. 3 (June 2003): 1113–1137.

Ohmae, O. *The End of the Nation State*. New York: The Free Press, 1995.

Ormiston, Gayle L., and Alan D. Schrift, eds. *The Hermeneutic Tradition: From Ast to Ricoeur*. Albany, N.Y.: SUNY Press, 1990.

——. *Transforming the Hermeneutic Context: From Nietzsche to Nancy*. Albany, N.Y.: SUNY Press, 1990.

Ortiz-Osés, Andres, and Patxi Lanceros, eds. *Diccionario de hermenéutica*. Bilbao: Deusto, 1997.

O'Shaughnessy, H. "US Builds up Its Bases in Oil-Rich South America." *Independent* (November 22, 2009).

Palmer, Richard. "Gadamer and Confucius: Some Possible Affinities." *Journal of Chinese Philosophy* 33 (2006): 81–94.

——. *Hermeneutics: Interpretation Theory in Schleiermacher, Dilthey, Heidegger, and Gadamer*. Evanston, Ill.: Northwestern University Press, 1969.

——. "A Response to Richard Wolin on Gadamer and the Nazis." *International Journal of Philosophical Studies* 10 (2002): 467–482.

Palmer, Richard, and Diane Michelfelder, eds. *Dialogue and Deconstruction: The Gadamer-Derrida Encounter*. Albany, N.Y.: SUNY Press, 1989.

Pareyson, Luigi. *Esistenza e persona*. Genoa: Il Melangolo, 1985.

——. *Opere complete*. 20 vols. Ed. Centro Study Pareyson. Milan: Mursia, 1998–.

——. *Verità e interpretazione*. Milan: Mursia, 1971.

Parry, Rear Admiral C. J. *The DCDC Global Strategic Trends Programme: 2007–2036.* http://www.cuttingthroughthematrix.com/articles/strat_trends_23 jan07.pdf.

Pérez, Louis A. *Cuba and the United States: Ties of Singular Intimacy.* Athens: University of Georgia Press, 1990.

Peries, Sharmini. "Venezuela's Chavez Triumphant: History Making Democracy in Latin America." *Venezuelanalysis.com* (August 16, 2004).

Peters, Ralph. "Our Soldiers, Their Cities." *Parameters* (Spring 1996): 43–50.

Pew Research Center for the People and the Press. "Bush and Public Opinion: Reviewing the Bush Years and the Public's Final Verdict." December 18, 2008. http://people-press.org/report/478/bush-legacy-public-opinion.

Pippin, Robert P. *Modernism as a Philosophical Problem: On the Dissatisfactions of European High Culture.* Cambridge, Mass.: Blackwell, 1991.

Polt, Richard. *The Emergency of Being.* Ithaca, N.Y.: Cornell University Press, 2006.

——. "Metaphysical Liberalism in Heidegger's *Beiträge Zur Philosophie*." *Political Theory* 25, no. 5 (October 1997): 663.

Pöggeler, Otto. *Heidegger und die hermeneutische Philosophie.* Freiburg: Alber, 1983.

——. "Heideggers logische Untersuchungen." In *Martin Heidegger: Innen-und Aussenansichten: Forum für Philosophie Bad Hamburg*, 75–100. Frankfurt: Suhrkamp, 1989.

Popper, Karl. *The Logic of Scientific Discovery.* London: Routledge, 1959.

Prado, C. G. "A Conversation with Richard Rorty." *Symposium* 7 (2003): 227–231.

——. *A House Divided: Comparing Analytic and Continental Philosophy.* Amherst, N.Y.: Humanity Books, 2003.

——. *Searle and Foucault on Truth*. Cambridge: Cambridge University Press, 2006.

Psillos, Stathis, and Martin Curd, eds. *The Routledge Companion to Philosophy of Science*. London: Routledge, 2008.

Quine, W. V. O. *The Ways of Paradox and Other Essays*. Cambridge, Mass.: Harvard University Press, 1976.

Quinn, B. "Honduran Military Regime Threatens Reprisals as President Plans Return." *Guardian* (July 5, 2009).

Ramirez, C. "Top Economist Stiglitz Calls for Expanded G-20." *Pittsburgh Tribune-Review* (September 24, 2009).

Reinach, Adolf. *A Priori Foundations of the Civil Law* [1913]. Trans. J. Crosby. *Aletheia* 3 (1983): 1–142.

Ricoeur, Paul. *The Conflict of Interpretations*. Ed. Don Ihde. Trans. Kathleen McLaughlin. London: Continuum, 2004.

——. *Freud and Philosophy: An Essay on Interpretation*. Trans. Denis Savage. New Haven, Conn.: Yale University Press, 1970.

——. *From Text to Action: Essays in Hermeneutics II*. Trans. Kathleen Blamey and John B. Thompson. Evanston, Ill.: Northwestern University Press, 1991.

——. *Hermeneutics and the Human Sciences: Essays on Language, Action, and Interpretation*. Trans. John B. Thompson. Cambridge: Cambridge University Press, 1981.

——. *Interpretation Theory: Discourse and the Surplus of Meaning*. Fort Worth: Texas Christian University Press, 1976.

——. *Memory, History, Forgetting*. Trans. Kathleen Blamey and David Pellauer. Chicago: University of Chicago Press, 2006.

——. *Oneself as Another*. Trans. Kathleen Blamey. Chicago: University of Chicago Press, 1992.

Ricoeur, Paul, and Hans-Georg Gadamer. "The Conflict of Interpretations."

In *Phenomenology: Dialogues and Bridges*, ed. Ronald Bruzina and Bruce Wilshire, 299–320. Albany, N.Y.: SUNY Press, 1982.

Rieger, Reinhold. *Interpretation und Wissen. Zur philosophische Begründung der Hermeneutik bei Friedrich Schleiermacher und ihrem geschichtliche Hintergrund. Schleiermacher-Archiv.* Vol. 6. Ed. H. Fischer, H.-J. Birkner, G. Ebeling, and K.-V. Segle. Berlin: Walter de Gruyter, 1988.

Risser, James. "Gadamer's Hidden Doctrine: On the Simplicity and Humility of Philosophy." In *Consequences of Hermeneutics*, ed. Jeff Malpas and Santiago Zabala. Evanston, Ill.: Northwestern University Press, 2010.

——, ed. *Heidegger Toward the Turn: Essays on the Work of the 1930s.* Albany, N.Y.: SUNY Press, 1999.

——. *Hermeneutics and the Voice of the Other: Rereading Gadamer's* Philosophical Hermeneutics. Albany, N.Y.: SUNY Press, 1997.

——. "Interpreting Tradition." *Journal of the British Society for Phenomenology* 34, no. 3 (2003): 297–308.

——. "On the Continuation of Philosophy: Hermeneutics as Convalescence." In *Weakening Philosophy: Festschrift in Honor of Gianni Vattimo*, ed. Santiago Zabala, 184–202. Montreal: McGill-Queen's University Press, 2007.

——. "Philosophy and Politics at the End of Metaphysics." In *Between Nihilism and Politics: The Hermeneutics of Gianni Vattimo*, ed. S. Benso and B. Schroeder. Albany, N.Y.: SUNY Press, 2010.

Robbins, Jeffrey. *Radical Democracy and Political Theology.* New York: Columbia University Press, 2011.

Rodrik, Dani. "Blame the Economist, Not Economics." *Guatemala Times* (March 11, 2009).

Rodríguez Garavito, C. A, P. S. Barrett, and D. Chávez, *La nueva izquierda en America Latina.* Bogotá: Norma, 2004.

Romero, S. "In Bolivia, Untapped Bounty Meets Nationalism." *New York Times,* February 3, 2009.

Rorty, Richard. *Achieving Our Country: Leftist Thought in Twentieth-Century America*. Cambridge, Mass.: Harvard University Press, 1997.

——. "Being That Can Be Understood Is Language." In *Gadamer's Repercussions: Reconsidering Philosophical Hermeneutics*, ed. Bruce Krajewski, 21–29. Berkeley: University of California Press, 2004.

——. *Consequences of Pragmatism*. Minneapolis: University of Minnesota Press, 1982.

——. *Essays on Heidegger and Others*. Cambridge, Mass.: Cambridge University Press, 1991.

——. "Heideggerianism and Leftist Politics." In *Weakening Philosophy*, ed. Santiago Zabala. Montreal: McGill-Queen's University Press, 2007.

——. "Hermeneutics, General Studies, and Teaching." In *Richard Rorty on Hermeneutics, General Studies, and Teaching*, by Richard Rorty and C. Barry Chabot, 1–15. Fairfax, Va.: George Mason University Press, 1982.

——, ed. *The Linguistic Turn*. Chicago: University of Chicago Press, 1967.

——. *Objectivity, Relativism, and Truth*. Cambridge, Mass.: Cambridge University Press, 1991.

——. *Philosophy and Social Hope*. London: Penguin, 1999.

——. *Philosophy and the Mirror of Nature*. Princeton, N.J.: Princeton University Press, 1979.

——. *Philosophy as Cultural Politics*. Cambridge, Mass.: Cambridge University Press, 2007.

——. "Rorty on Hermeneutics, General Studies, and Teaching." *Synergos Seminars* 2 (1982): 1–15.

——. *Take Care of Freedom, Truth Will Take Care of Itself*. Ed. E. Mendieta. Stanford, Calif.: Stanford University Press, 2006.

——. *Truth and Progress*. Cambridge, Mass.: Cambridge University Press, 1998.

Rorty, Richard, with C. Barry Chabot. *Richard Rorty on Hermeneutics, General*

Studies, and Teaching: With Replies and Applications, Selected Papers from the Synergos Seminars. Vol. 2. Fairfax, Va.: George Mason University Press, 1982.

Rorty, Richard, and Pascal Engel. *What's the Use of Truth?* Ed. P. Savidan. Trans. W. McCuaig. New York: Columbia University Press, 2007.

Rovatti, Pier Aldo. "Weak Thought 2004." In *Weakening Philosophy*, ed. Santiago Zabala, 131–145. Montreal: McGill-Queen's University Press, 2007.

Sachs, Jeffrey D. "Obama's Military Conundrum." *Guardian* (May 22, 2009).

Sader, Emir. "Beyond Civil Society: The Left After Porto Alegre." *New Left Review* 17 (September–October 2002): 87–99.

Sanders, Barry. *The Green Zone: The Environmental Cost of Militarism.* Oakland, Calif.: AK Press, 2009.

Sartre, Jean-Paul. *Critique of Dialectical Reason* [1960]. Trans. Quentin Hoare. London: Verso, 2006.

Schleiermacher, Friedrich. *Hermeneutics: The Handwritten Manuscripts.* Trans. James Duke and Jack Forstman. Atlanta, Ga.: Scholars Press, 1986.

——. *"Hermeneutics and Criticism" and Other Writings.* Trans. Andrew Bowie. Cambridge: Cambridge University Press, 1998.

Schmidt, Lawrence K. *The Epistemology of Hans-Georg Gadamer.* Frankfurt: Peter Lang, 1985.

Schmitt, Carl. *The Concept of the Political.* Trans. G. Schwab. Chicago: University of Chicago Press, 2007.

——. *Die Geistesgeschichtliche Lage des Heutigen Parlamentarismus.* Berlin: Dunker and Humblot, 1926.

——. *Legality and Legitimacy.* Durham, N.C.: Duke University Press, 2004.

——. *Political Theology II: The Myth of the Closure of Any Political Theology.* Trans. Michael Hoeltzl and Graham Ward. London: Polity, 2008.

Scholtz, Gunter. *Ethik und Hermeneutik. Schleiermachers Grundlegung der Geisteswissenschaften.* Frankfurt am Main: Suhrkamp, 1995.

Schoultz, Lars. *That Infernal Little Cuban Republic: The United States and the Cuban Revolution*. Chapel Hill: University of North Carolina Press, 2009.

Schrift, Alan Douglas. *Nietzsche and the Question of Interpretation: Between Hermeneutics and Deconstruction*. New York: Routledge, 1990.

——. *Twentieth-Century French Philosophy: Key Themes and Thinkers*. New York: Wiley, 2004.

Schürmann, Reiner. *Broken Hegemonies*. Trans. R. Lilly. Bloomington: Indiana University Press, 2003.

——. *Heidegger on Being and Acting: From Principles to Anarchy*. Bloomington: University of Indiana Press, 1990.

——. "'What Must I Do' at the End of Metaphysics." In *Phenomenology in a Pluralistic Context*, ed. William L. McBride and C. O. Schrag. Albany, N.Y.: SUNY Press, 1983.

Schwartz, Peter, and Doug Randall. *An Abrupt Climate Change Scenario and Its Implications for United States National Security*. http://www.environmental defense.org/documents/3566_AbruptClimateChange.pdf.

Searle, John. *The Construction of Social Reality*. New York: The Free Press, 1995.

——. *Conversations with John Searle*. Ed. G. Faigenbaum. Montevideo: Libros en Red, 2001.

——. *Freedom and Neurobiology*. New York: Columbia University Press, 2007.

——. "Interview with Searle [Z. Sachs-Arellano]." *Harvard Review of Philosophy* 12 (2004): 132–133.

——. "La libertà è figlia del linguaggio." Interview by Alberto Papuzzi. *La Stampa*, 19 May 2008.

——. *Making the Social World: The Structure of Human Civilization*. Oxford: Oxford University Press, 2010.

——. *Philosophy in a New Century*. Oxford: Oxford University Press, 2008.

——. "Reiterating the Differences: A Reply to Derrida." *Glyph* 1 (1977): 198–208.

Seebohm, Thomas. "The New Hermeneutics." In *Continental Philosophy in America*, ed. H. J. Silverman, J. Sallis, and T. M. Seebohm, 64–89. Pittsburgh: Duquesne University Press, 1983.

Sennett, Richard. *The Corrosion of Character: The Personal Consequences of Work in the New Capitalism*. New York: W. W. Norton, 1998

——. *The Culture of the New Capitalism*. New Haven, Conn.: Yale University Press, 2005.

Sharp, Travis. "The Worst Kind of Stimulus." *Foreign Policy* (March 2009).

Sim, Stuart. *The End of Modernity: What the Financial and Environmental Crisis Is Really Telling Us*. Edinburgh: Edinburgh University Press, 2010.

Smith, Ashley. "Imperialism with a Human Face: Haiti After the Quake." *International Socialist Review* 70 (March–April 2010): 9–20.

Smith, Barry, ed. *John Searle*. Cambridge: Cambridge University Press, 2003.

Smith, Barry, et al. "Derrida Degree: A Question of Honour." *Times* (London) (May 9, 1992).

Smith, Barry, D. M. Mark, and I. Ehrlich, eds. *The Mystery of Capital and the Construction of Social Reality*. Chicago: Open Court, 2008.

Soto, H. de. *The Mystery of Capital: Why Capitalism Triumphs in the West and Fails Everywhere Else*. New York: Basic Books, 2000.

Spiegelberg, Herbert. *The Phenomenological Movement: A Historical Introduction*. Berlin: Springer, 2007.

Steele, J., and S. Goldenberg. "What Is the Real Death Toll in Iraq?" *Guardian*, March 19, 2008.

Stiglitz, Joseph. "The Anatomy of a Murder: Who Killed America's Economy?" *Critical Review* 21, nos. 2–3 (June 2009): 329–39.

——. *Freefall: America, Free Markets, and the Sinking of the World Economy*. New York: Norton, 2010.

——. "GDP Fetishism." *Turkish Weekly* (September 15, 2009).

——. "Global Crisis—Made in America." *Spiegel Online* (November 12, 2008).

——. *Globalization and Its Discontents*. New York: Norton, 2002.

——. "A Global Recovery for a Global Recession." *The Nation* (July 13, 2009).

——. *Making Globalization Work*. New York: Norton, 2006.

——. "Too Big to Fail or Too Big to Save? Examining the Systemic Threats of Large Financial Institutions." Testimony for the Joint Economic Committee hearing, April 21, 2009, Washington, D.C. http://www2.gsb.columbia .edu/faculty/jstiglitz/download/papers/2009_JEC_TooBigToFail.pdf.

Stiglitz, Joseph, and L. J. Bilmes. *The Three-Trillion-Dollar War: The True Cost of the Iraq Conflict*. New York: Norton, 2008.

Stiglitz, Joseph, Amartya Sen, Jean-Paul Fitoussi, et al. "Report by the Commission on the Measurement of Economic Performance and Social Progress." http://www.stiglitz-sen-fitoussi.fr/en/index.htm.

Strauss, Leo. "Notes on Carl Schmitt, *The Concept of the Political*." In *The Concept of the Political*, by Carl Schmitt, trans. G. Schwab, 81–108. Chicago: University of Chicago Press, 2007.

Sullivan, Robert. *Political Hermeneutics: The Early Thinking of Hans-Georg Gadamer*. University Park: Pennsylvania State University Press, 1990.

Tarski, Alfred, ed. *Introduction to Logic and to the Methodology of the Deductive Sciences*. New York: Oxford University Press, 1994.

——. "The Semantic Conception of Truth and the Foundations of Semantics." *Philosophy and Phenomenological Research* 4 (1944): 341–375.

Taylor, Charles. "Modern Moral Rationalism." In *Weakening Philosophy: Essays in Honour of Gianni Vattimo*, ed. Santiago Zabala. Montreal: McGill-Queen's University Press, 2007.

Therborn, Göran. *From Marxism to Post-Marxism*. London: Verso, 2008.

Thompson, John B. *Critical Hermeneutics: A Study in the Thought of Paul Ricoeur and Jürgen Habermas*. Cambridge: Cambridge University Press, 1981.

Tibaijuka, Anna K. *Global Employment Trends*. ILO Update, May 2009.

Tugendhat, Ernst. "Heidegger's Idea of Truth." In *Hermeneutics and Modern Philosophy*, ed. Brice Wachterhauser, 83–97. Albany, N.Y.: SUNY Press, 1986.

———. *Self-Consciousness and Self-Determination*. Trans. P. Stern. Cambridge, Mass.: The MIT Press, 1986.

Turse, Nick. *The Complex*. New York: Metropolitan Books: 2008.

UN-HABITAT. *The Challenge of Slums: Global Report on Human Settlements 2000*. London, 2003.

———. "Sounding the Alarm on Forced Evictions," press release, 20th Session of the Governing Council, Nairobi, 4–8 April 2005.

———. *State of the World's Cities 2008/2009: Harmonious Cities*. London, 2008.

Ugazio, Ugo. *Il problema della morte nella filosofia di Heidegger*. Milan: Mursia, 1976.

———. *Il ritorno del possible*. Torino: Silvio Zamorani, 1996.

Valgenti, Robert. "The Primacy of Interpretation in Luigi Pareyson's Hermeneutics of Common Sense." *Philosophy Today* 49, no. 4 (Winter 2005).

Vandevelde, Pol. *The Task of the Interpreter: Text, Meaning, and Negotiation*. Pittsburgh, Penn.: University of Pittsburgh Press, 2005.

Vattimo, Gianni. *The Adventure of Difference: Philosophy After Nietzsche and Heidegger*. Trans. C. P. Blamires and T. Harrison. Cambridge: Polity Press, 1993.

———. *After Christianity*. Trans. L. D'Isanto. New York: Columbia University Press, 2002.

———. *Art's Claim to Truth*. Ed. S. Zabala and Trans. L. D'Isanto. New York: Columbia University Press, 2008.

———. *Beyond Interpretation: The Meaning of Hermeneutics for Philosophy*. Trans. D. Webb. Cambridge: Polity Press, 1997.

———. "Communisme faible?" In *L'idée du communisme: Conférence de Londres, 2009*, ed. A. Badiou and S. Žižek, 287–89. Clamecy: Lignes, 2010.

——. *Dialogue with Nietzsche*. Trans. William McCuaig. New York: Columbia University Press, 2008.

——. *Ecce Comu. Come si ri-diventa ciò che si era*. Rome: Fazi, 2008.

——. *The End of Modernity: Nihilism and Hermeneutics in Postmodern Culture*. Trans. J. R. Snyder. Baltimore, Md.: The John Hopkins University Press, 1988.

——. *Essere, storia, e linguaggio in Heidegger*. Genoa: Marietti, 1989.

——. *Farewell to Truth*. Translated by William McCuaig. New York: Columbia University Press, 2011.

——. "Gadamer and the Problem of Ontology." In *Gadamer's Century*, ed. J. Malpas, U. Arnswald, and J. Kertscher, 299–306. Cambridge, Mass.: The MIT Press, 2002.

——. *Il soggetto e la maschera: Nietsche e il problema della liberazione*. Milan: Bompiani, 1974.

——. *Nietzsche: Philosophy as Cultural Criticism*. Trans. Nicholas Martin. Stanford, Calif.: Stanford University Press, 2002.

——. *Nihilism and Emancipation: Ethics, Politics, and Law*. Ed. Santiago Zabala. Trans. William McCuaig. New York: Columbia University Press, 2004.

——. "The Political Outcome of Hermeneutics: To Politics Through Art and Religion." In *Consequences of Hermeneutics*, ed. J. Malpas and S. Zabala, 281–87. Evanston, Ill.: Northwestern University Press, 2010.

——. *Responsibility of the Philosopher*. Ed. Franca D'Agostini. Trans. William McCuaig. New York: Columbia University Press, 2010.

——. *The Transparent Society*. Trans. David Webb. Baltimore, Md.: The Johns Hopkins University Press, 1992.

Vattimo, Gianni, and John Caputo. *After the Death of God*. Ed. J. Robbins. New York: Columbia University Press, 2009.

Vattimo, Gianni, and Carmelo Dotolo. *Dio: La possibilità buona*. Ed. Giovani Giorgio. Soveria Mannelli: Rubbettino, 2009.

Vattimo, Gianni, and René Girard. *Christianity, Truth, and Weakening Faith: A Dialogue.* Ed. P. Antonello. Trans. William McCuaig. New York: Columbia University Press, 2010.

Vattimo, Gianni, and Richard Rorty. *The Future of Religion.* Ed. Santiago Zabala. New York: Columbia University Press, 2005.

Vattimo, Gianni, and Pier Aldo Rovatti, eds. *Il pensiero debole.* Milan: Feltrinelli, 1983.

Vargas Llosa, M. *Sables y Utopías. Visiones de América Latina.* Madrid: Aguilar, 2009.

Vine, David. *Island of Shame: The Secret History of the U.S. Military Base on Diego Garcia.* Princeton, N.J.: Princeton University Press, 2009.

Wach, Joachim. *Das Verstehen: Grundzge einer Geschichte der hermeneutischen Theorie im 19. Jahrhundert.* 3 vols. Tübingen: J. C. B. Mohr, 1926–1933.

Wachterhauser, Brice R. *Beyond Being: Gadamer's Post-Platonic Hermeneutic Ontology.* Evanston, Ill.: Northwestern University Press, 1999.

——, ed. *Hermeneutics and Modern Philosophy.* Albany, N.Y.: SUNY Press, 1986.

——. *Hermeneutics and Truth.* Evanston, Ill.: Northwestern University Press, 1994.

Warnke, Georgia, *Gadamer: Hermeneutics, Tradition, and Reason.* Stanford, Calif.: Stanford University Press, 1987.

——. "Hermeneutics and the Social Sciences: A Gadamerian Critique of Rorty." In *Richard Rorty,* vol. 4, ed. Alan Malachowski. London: Sage, 2002.

——. *Justice and Interpretation.* Cambridge, Mass.: The MIT Press, 1994.

Weber, Max, *Economy and Society.* 2 vols. Berkeley: University of California Press, 1978.

——. *The Protestant Ethic and the Spirit of Capitalism* [1930]. London: Routledge, 2002.

Weinsheimer, Joel. *Eighteenth-Century Hermeneutics: Philosophy of Interpretation in England from Locke to Burke.* New Haven, Conn.: Yale University Press, 1993.

——. *Gadamer's Hermeneutics: A Reading of* Truth and Method. New Haven, Conn.: Yale University Press, 1985.

——. *Philosophical Hermeneutics and Literary Theory.* New Haven, Conn.: Yale University Press, 1991.

Weisbrot, M. "Latin America Economic Rebels." *Guardian* (October 28, 2009).

——. "Morgenthau's Axis Debunked." http://www.huffingtonpost.com/mark -weisbrot/morgenthaus-axis-debunked_b_283871.html.

——. "Restoring Democracy in Honduras." *Guardian* (July 30, 2009).

——. "Why Latin America's Left Keeps Winning." *Guardian* (May 1, 2009).

White, Hayden. "The Politics of Historical Interpretation: Discipline and De-Sublimation." *Critical Inquiry* (September 1982): 113–137.

Whitehouse, David. "Afghanistan Sinking Deeper." *International Socialist Review* 69 (January–February 2010): 23–29.

Wilpert, G. *Changing Venezuela by Taking Power: The History and Policies of the Chávez Government.* London: Verso, 2007.

Wintour, P., and A. Clark. "G20 Leaders Map out New Economic Order at Pittsburgh Summit." *Guardian* (September 26, 2009).

Wittgenstein, Ludwig. *Culture and Value.* Trans. Peter Winch. Oxford: Blackwell, 1980.

——. *Philosophical Investigations.* Trans. G. E. M. Anscombe. New York: Macmillan, 1953.

Wolf, A. *The Future of Liberalism.* New York: Knopf: 2009.

Wolf, Naomi. "The Bush in Obama." *Sunday Times* (August 2, 2009).

Wolin, Richard. "Richard Rorty in Retrospect." *Dissent* (Winter 2010): 73–79.

Wood, Ellen Meiksins. *Democracy Against Capitalism: Renewing Historical Materialism*. Cambridge: Cambridge University Press, 1995.

——. *Empire of Capital*. London: Verso, 2003.

——. *The Origin of Capitalism: A Longer View*. London: Verso, 2002.

Wray, Richard. "G20 Summit: What It Will Decide." *Guardian* (September 25, 2009).

Wright, Kathleen, ed. *Festivals of Interpretation: Essays on Hans-Georg Gadamer's Work*. Albany, N.Y.: SUNY Press, 1990.

Wujin, Yu. "Marx's Philosophy as Practical Hermeneutics." *Fudan Journal* (June 2009).

Zabala, Santiago. "Being Is Conversation." In *Consequences of Hermeneutics*, ed. J. Malpas and S. Zabala. Evanston, Ill.: Northwestern University Press, 2010.

——. "Financing Our Economics of Fear." In *Elements for an Economics of Fear: Institutions, Politics, and Policies*, ed. Mario Cedrini and M. Novarese. Andhra Pradesh: IFCAI University Press, 2010.

——. "Gianni Vattimo and Weak Thought." In *Weakening Philosophy: Essays in Honour of Gianni Vattimo*, ed. Santiago Zabala, 3–34. Montreal: McGill-Queen's University Press, 2007.

——. *The Hermeneutic Nature of Analytic Philosophy: A Study of Ernst Tugendhat*. New York: Columbia University Press, 2008.

——. *The Remains of Being: Hermeneutic Ontology After Metaphysics*. New York: Columbia University Press, 2009.

——. "Truth's Absence: The Hermeneutic Resistance to Phenomenology." In *Phenomenological Variations on Truths: The Hermeneutic Challenge*, ed. Kevin Hermberg and Pol Vandevelde. London: Continuum, 2011.

——, ed. *Weakening Philosophy: Essays in Honour of Gianni Vattimo*. Montreal: McGill-Queen's University Press, 2007.

Zabala, Santiago, and Jeff Malpas, eds. *Consequences of Hermeneutics: Fifty Years After Gadamer's* Truth and Method. Evanston, Ill.: Northwestern University Press, 2010.

Zabala, Santiago, and Michael Marder, eds. *Being Shaken: Ontology and the Event.* Forthcoming.

Zibechi, Raul. *Territorios en resistencia. Cartografía política de las periferias latinoamericanas.* Buenos Aires: Lavaca, 2008.

Zinn, H. "Obama at One: A Nation Forum." *The Nation* (February 1, 2010): 21.

——. *A People's History of the United States: 1492–Present.* New York: HarperCollins, 2005.

Žižek, Slavoj. *First as Tragedy, Then as Farce.* London: Verso, 2009.

——. "The Free World . . . of Slums." *In These Times* (September 23, 2004).

——. *In Defense of Lost Causes.* London: Verso, 2008.

——. *The Parallax View.* Cambridge, Mass.: The MIT Press, 2006.

——. *The Ticklish Subject: The Absent Centre of Political Ontology.* London: Verso, 2000.

Žižek, Slavoj, and C. Douzinas, eds. *The Idea of Communism.* London: Verso, 2010.

Zolo, Danilo. *Terrorismo umanitario: Dalla guerra del Golfo alla strage di Gaza.* Reggio Emilia: Diabasis, 2009.

——. *Victors' Justice: From Nuremberg to Baghdad.* Trans. M. W. Weir. London: Verso, 2009.

INDEX

absolute poverty, 50

accomplished nihilism, 137

Afghanistan: imposed liberalization of, 52, 54–58, 151n1, 159n45; oil reserves of, 157n34

age of divergence, 47

"Age of the World Picture, The" (Heidegger), 87

aggression, of humanitarian war, 143n10

al Qaeda, 56–58, 159n45

analytic philosophy, imperialistic approach of, 35–36, 149n61

anarchy through interpretation, 75–107; anarchic vein of hermeneutics, 78–87; existence as interpretation, 87–95; Freud's hermeneutic operation, 82–84; hermeneutics as weak thought, 95–107; Kuhn's hermeneutic operation, 84–86; Luther's hermeneutic operation, 80–82

antifoundationalism, 98–106

Arendt, Hannah, 15, 77

Argentina, weak communism in, 126, 129

Aristotle, 19, 79

armed capitalism, 45–71; conservation of financial recession in, 58–64; fighting against weak in, 64–71; impositions of liberal state in, 51–58; oppression in, 45–51

Austin, John L., 33

Badiou, Alain, 3

bailouts, 62, 164n66

Baker, D., 165n72

Banco del Sur (Bank of the South), 64, 128

Bank of the South. *See* Banco del Sur

banks: bailouts of, 62, 164n66; failure of, 61–62, 164n66

basic facts, 30–32

Being: as event, 89, 94; Heidegger's discussions of, 5, 13, 16, 20–22; hermeneutic conception of, 93; history and, 94, 178n6; lack of emergency and, 28; metaphysics neglect of, 16; oblivion of, 38; in politics of descriptions, 13–14; winners' beliefs toward, 37–38

Being and Time (Heidegger), 20–21, 92–93, 173n17

Benjamin, Walter, 117; on other oppressed history, 40–41; weak defined by, 7, 16

Berlin Wall, 113–14

Bible, interpretation of, 81–82

Bilmes, L. J., 56

Birth of Tragedy, The (Nietzsche), 88–89

Bolívar, Simón, 124

Bolivarian Revolution, 123–26

Bolivia: nationalization in, 126–27; natural resources in, 190n47; support for indigenous peoples of, 126–27, 191n52; weak communism in, 6, 123, 126–27

Bové, José, 142n7

Brazil, weak communism in, 126, 133

Bremer, Paul, 55–56

Broken Hegemonies (Schürmann), 98

Bush, George W.: economic policies of, 58–59, 62–63; in imposed liberalization of Iraq, 55–57; 9/11 attacks and, 160n49; philosophy endorsed by, 11–12

capitalism: communism as critique of, 5–6; communism dominated by, 109; current reign of, 7–8; as example of politics of descriptions, 16; inheritance and, 93; market laws and, 114; metaphysics and, 59–60, 113–14; oppression of, 48–49; overcoming of, 3–4; South American communism as alternative to, 5–8, 119–51, 142n6; the weak as discharge of, 6–7. *See also* armed capitalism

Castro, Fidel, 125–26, 178n3

Chávez, Hugo, 6, 119, 142n6; Bolivarian Revolution of, 123–26; as case for socialism, 181n20; education reforms of, 191n52; election of, 123–24, 183nn28–29; as example of weak communism, 127–28; Fifth International of, 138, 142n6, 198n77; media attacks on, 122–24, 142n7, 182n22; as model for Obama, 131–40; social progress of, 125, 188n41; 2002 media coup against, 123, 184nn31–33

Chile, weak communism in, 126

Chomsky, Noam: on Cuba as symbol of resistance, 133–34; on imposed liberalization of Iraq, 55; on influencing elections, 183n26; on multipolar world, 153n6; on 9/11 attackers, 159n45; on South American alternative, 122, 128; on U.S. support of Hussein, 160n48

classes, in communism, 116

Clavis scripturae sacrae (Flacius), 79

Cockburn, Alexander, 142n7

Colm Hogan, Patrick, 75–76

Columbia, U.S. military presence in, 129–32, 193n62

communication, Derrida and Searle debate over, 34–35

communism: as capitalism critique, 5–6; without classes, 116; domination of, by capitalism, 109; economic successes of, 128–29; Heidegger on, 4–5, 111, 176n2; hermeneutics brought together with, 3–4, 110–11; interpretative element in, 115; necessary dysfunction of, 112, 178n4; ownership in, 116–17; problem with complete realization of, 116–17; return to, 111–13; as social function, 5–6; spectral nature of, 109, 117–21; truth in, 116; of twenty-first century, 5–6, 142nn6–7; as utopia, 117; weakened, 113–21. *See also* hermeneutic communism; South American communism; Soviet communism

comparative disadvantage, 50

conservation: of financial recession, 58–64; of IMF, 59, 62–64, 165n72; by realism, 26–36

conversation: dialogue compared with, 25–26; as substitute for truth, 103–5

Correa, Rafael, 126, 188n43

creation, through destruction, 88–89

Critique of Dialectical Reason (Sartre), 140

Cuba: exploitation of, 134, 198n75; freedom in, 136; as symbol of resistance, 133–34

Cuban doctors, in Venezuela, 125, 187n39

culture, in hermeneutic communism, 137–38

Dannhauer, Johann, 79

Davis, Mike, 49, 68–69, 168n87

Debusmann, Bernd, 168n89

Decline of the West, The (Spengler), 15

deconstruction, meaning of, 33

defeated history, 40–41

degrowth, 121

democracy: communism domination by, 109; end of truth as beginning of, 23; freedom and, 57; lack of emergency as chief priority of, 51–52; metaphysics and, 27–28, 37–38; in South America, 131–33; in Western capitalist democracies, 136. *See also* framed democracy

democratic consensus, 79

Derrida, Jacques: on communism, 119–20; on Fukuyama's failure to

acknowledge oppression, 48–49; on hermeneutics, 6; iterability notion of, 34–35; on metaphysical nature of philosophy, 13; on return to communism, 112–13; Searle's debate with, 29, 33–36; on spectral communism, 109; the weak defined by, 6–7, 16

descriptions, 78–79. *See also* imposing descriptions; politics of descriptions

De Soto, Hernando, 60, 162n58

destruction, creation through, 88–89

Dialectic of Enlightenment (Adorno and Horkheimer), 15

dialogue: in conservation by realism, 26–29; conversation compared with, 25–26; in service of establishment, 26–29; silencing by, 19; transformation excluded by, 27–28; truth and, 19, 23–25, 27–28

difference, as principle to follow, 102–3

Dilthey, Wilhelm, 80, 89–90

disadvantage, as threat against framed democracy, 50

dominion: in communism, 116; metaphysics as consequence of, 12

Dussel, Enrique, 53

economic crisis of 2008: causes of, 163n61; conservation of, 58–64;

failed predictions of, 163n60; lack of change in response to, 45–46

economic oppression, 48–49

economic policies: of Bush, 58–59, 62–63; of IMF, 58–59, 62–64; of Obama, 58–59, 62–63

economics: metaphysics and, 59–60; rationality in, 59–61; of South American weak communism, 128–29

economists: disagreements among, 162n57; in economic crisis of 2008, 61–62

Ecuador, weak communism in, 126

elections: imposed, 57; influences on, 183n26; in Venezuela, 123–24, 183nn28–29

El Salvador, weak communism in, 126

emancipation: emergencies as effective conditions for, 41–43; through hermeneutics, 93–94; interpretation as call for, 77–78; from metaphysics, 4

emergency: as effective condition for emancipation, 41–43; lack of emergency as, 28, 64–65; South American communism as, 131–33; for the weak, 64–65; the weak as, 66, 69–70; WMD and al Qaeda as, 57–58. *See also* lack of emergency

Empire of Capital (Meiksins Wood), 45

empirical sciences: Freud and, 82–84; Kuhn and, 84–86; within power structures, 12–17; sane philosophy based on, 30–31, 33

End of History and the Last Man, The (Fukuyama), 37

Engel, Pascal, 17

Enlightenment, 13–15

epochs, changing principles of, 98–99

establishment: dialogue in service of, 26–29; philosophy's role in sustaining of, 25

Eurocentrism, hermeneutics and end of, 110–11

Europe, shift to right-wing governments in, 118–19, 180n17

event: Being as, 89, 94; ontology of, 89; of unconcealment, 22–23, 27, 42–43

existence: as interpretation, 87–95; thrown project of, 92–93

external realism, as precondition for having theories, 30–31

facts: dependence on, 30–32; interpretations compared with, 87–88

Fair, Christine, 57

Fifth International, 138, 142n6, 198n77

fighting. *See* war

financial recession: conservation of, 58–64. *See also* economic crisis of 2008

Fisk, Robert, 57

Flacius, Matthias, 79

foundations, antifoundational hermeneutics in place of, 98–106

Fourth Fleet, 130

"framed," Heidegger's use of, 145n9

framed democracy, 11–43, 45–71; coming threats against, 47–51; communism dominated by, 109; as completion of history, 39–40; conservation of financial recession in, 58–64; conservative nature of realism in, 26–36; emancipation from, 41–43; fighting against weak in, 64–71; imposing descriptions of, 11–43; impositions of liberal state in, 51–58; lack of emergency in, 28–29; as metanarrative, 38; oppression within, 45–51; poverty and, 50, 68, 167nn81–82; truth's violence in, 17–26; weak communism as political alternative to, 128; winner's history in, 37–43

freedom: in Cuba compared with United States, 136; democracy and, 57; institutional structures' limit of, 32; lack of emergency and, 28; liberal view of, 53; politics and, 77; via privatization, 56; realism and, 30; truth and, 94

Freedom and Neurobiology (Searle), 11

free market. *See* markets

Freud, Sigmund, 82–84

Friedman, Thomas L., 122, 182n22

Fukuyama, Francis, 37; on how science dictates history, 39, 150n68; on liberal democracy as only form of government, 46–49; on objective truth, 116; in situating politics outside of history, 38–39; on Venezuela, 131; as voice of winners, 7

Future of Religion, The (Rorty), 75

Gadamer, Hans-Georg, 76–77

Galeano, Eduardo, 142n7

Gallino, Luciano, 67

Gates, Robert, 161n51

Gay Science, The (Nietzsche), 95–96

GDP. *See* gross domestic product

Geithner, Timothy, 161n51

God, death of, 96, 111–12

Goldenberg, S., 158n41

Gott, Richard, 126–27

Grandin, Greg, 131–32

Granier, Marcel, 184n31

Greenspan, Alan, 163n61

Grondin, Jean, 142n8

gross domestic product (GDP), exclusion of the weak in, 66–67, 166n76, 166n79

growth, sustainable, 66, 166n76

G20 summit: protesters at, 59, 161n52; on reform of IMF voting power, 165n71; reinforcement of IMF by, 59, 62–64, 165n72; Stiglitz on, 161n53

Gugler, Josef, 68

Haiti earthquake (2010), military and aid response to, 143n10

Hegel, Georg Wilhelm Friedrich, 12, 26–27

Heidegger, Martin, 173n17; on Being, 5, 13, 16, 20–22; on changing thinking and world, 1; on communism, 4–5, 111, 176n2; conservativeness of, 76–77; in dispute over "Phenomenology" article for *Encyclopaedia Britannica*, 29–30; on end of metaphysics, 95–96; on event of uncealment, 42–43; on getting over metaphysics, 175n25; on I, 52–53, 156n25; on lack of emergency, 28–29; on liberalism, 52–53; Nietzsche and, 89–90; on purpose of hermeneutics, 146n19; on recovering forgotten history of Being, 178n6; on science as servant of dominant political class, 14–15; on theory of interpretation within Marx's philosophy, 4; on thrown project of human existence, 92–93; on truth, 20–23; use of "framed" by, 145n9; "weak" defined by, 6; on world picture, 87, 172n11

Heidegger on Being and Acting: From Principles to Anarchy (Schürmann), 98

hermeneutic communism, 109–40; Chávez as model for Obama, 131–40; South American alternative as, 5–8, 119–51, 142n6; weakened communism as, 113–21

hermeneutics, 6, 75–107; anarchic vein of, 78–87; communism brought together with, 3–4, 110–11; creation of, 79–80; emancipation through, 93–94; end of Eurocentrism and, 110–11; at end of metaphysics, 95–97; existence as interpretation, 87–95; Freud's hermeneutic operation, 82–84; Kuhn's hermeneutic operation, 84–86; Luther's hermeneutic operation, 80–82; in Marxism, 115;

Long Range Acoustic Device, 161n52

Losurdo, D., 179n9

love, necessity of, 111–12

Lula da Silva, Luiz Inácio, 126, 128, 133, 196n72

Luther, Martin, 80–82

Lyotard, Jean-François, 98, 100–103

Mao, on revolution, 136–37

Marcuse, Herbert, 15

Margolis, E., 157n37

Marion, J.-L., 147n27

market laws, capitalism and, 114

markets, rationality in, 59–61

Marx, Karl: contemporary interpretation of, 2–3, 141n2; interpretation in philosophy of, 4–5; on materialism, 114–15; metaphysical tradition contributing to Marxist failure, 1–3; totalitarianism of, 26–27

materialism, 114–15

media attacks: on Chávez, 122–24, 142n7, 182n22; on Correa, 188n43; on South American communism, 122–23, 182n22

media coup, against Chávez, 123, 184nn31–33

Meiksins Wood, Ellen, 7, 153n6; on capitalism, 51; on military excesses,

45; on reasons for attacking Afghanistan, 157n34

Meno (Plato), 24

metanarratives, 38, 101–3

metaphysics: alarms against, 11–17; Berlin Wall and, 113–14; capitalism and, 59–60, 113–14; communism and hermeneutics brought together by dissolution of, 3–4, 110–11; as consequence of dominion, 12; current reign of, 7–8; democracy and, 27–28, 37–38; in dream of philosophy as series of regional ontologies, 29–30; in economics, 59–60; emancipation from, 4; end of, 78–79, 95–100, 110–14; Eurocentrism and, 110–11; getting over, 175n25; Heidegger's need for overcoming, 4–5; Marxism failure within, 1–3; overcoming of, 1–2; realism's conservative nature and, 26–36; in return to realism, 27; as succession of epochal principles, 99; truth within, 17–24; winner's history in, 37–43

Metzl, Jamie, 57

military presence, U.S., 129–32, 143n10, 193n62

military spending, of Obama, 45–46, 151n1

objectivism (*continued*)

1–2; in politics of descriptions, 12–17; turning from solidarity to, 17–18; unjustness of, 15

oblivion of Being, 38

oil reserves, of Iraq and Afghanistan, 157n34

Oil Sowing Plan, 125, 187n37

ontologies: philosophy as series of, 29–30; of B. Smith, 150n63

ontology of event, 89

open society, 26–27

Open Society and Its Enemies, The (Popper), 15, 26–27

oppressed history, 40–41

oppression, in framed democracy, 45–51

"Origin of the Work of Art, The" (Heidegger), 42–43

Origins of Totalitarianism, The (Arendt), 15

other history, 40–41

overurbanization, 68, 168n87

ownership, in communism, 116–17

Pakistan, imposed liberalization of, 56–58

Paraguay, weak communism in, 126

Parry, C. J., 49–50

Parthenon, epochs dominating, 99

Pérez, C. A., 123–24

Peri hermeneias (De interpretatione) (Aristotle), 79

Peters, Ralph, 70

phenomenological theory, 19–20

"Phenomenology" article for *Encyclopaedia Britannica*, Husserl and Heidegger dispute over, 29–30

philosophy: conservation by, 28–29; fragmentation of, 142n8; imperialism within, 35–36, 149n61; loss of control by, 35; Plato's view of, 25; sane, 30–31, 33; science within, 11–14, 150n63; as series of regional ontologies, 29–30; as servant of dominant political class, 14; as suggesting alternative possibilities, 14

Philosophy and the Mirror of Nature (Rorty), 103

philosophy of language, Tarski's, 19–20

Pilger, John, 142n7

Planet of Slums (Davis), 49, 69, 168n87

Plato, 19, 23–25; on hermeneutics, 80; as servant of dominant political class, 12; totalitarianism of, 26–27

plurality of interpretations, 77–79, 101–3

political power, claims of truth as, 17–26

political project of hermeneutics, 76–79

politics: in economic crisis of 2008, 61–62; end of metaphysics and, 78–79; freedom and, 77; interpretation relationship with, 75–76; moralization of, 19, 23–24; outside of history, 38–39; truth and, 27, 78–79, 98–106; using basic structure for guidance of, 31–32

politics of descriptions, 11–43; Being in, 13–14; conservative nature of realism in, 26–36; dissolution of, 78–79; failure of American capitalist system as example of, 16; overcoming of, 3–4; in service of power, 12–17; truth's violence in, 17–26; unjustness of, 15; winner's history in, 37–43

politics of interpretation: transformation of politics of descriptions into, 78–79; truth within, 17, 22–23

Politics of Interpretation, The (Colm Hogan), 75–76

Polt, Richard, 53

Popper, Karl, 15, 26–27

Postmodern Condition, The (Lyotard), 98, 100

postmodernism: antifoundationalism and, 98–106; hermeneutics fit with, 77–79

poverty: causes of, 162n58; framed democracy and, 50, 68, 167nn81–82; in Iraq, 166n79

power: central role of empirical sciences in, 12–17; claims of truth as, 17–26; loss of challenge against, 46; politics of descriptions in service of, 12–17

practical action, of hermeneutics, 80

practico-inert, 140

principles, antifoundational hermeneutics in place of, 98–106

privatization, as guarantee of freedom, 56

property rights, poverty and, 162n58

psychology, Freud's revolution of, 82–84

Quine, W. V. O., 14

Radio Caracas Televisión (RCTV), coup against Chávez led by, 123, 184nn31–33

rationality, in economics, 59–61

realism, 14; alarms against, 11–17; conservative nature of, 26–36;

realism (*continued*)

in modern financial economics, 60; as precondition for having theories, 30–31; return to, 27; of Searle, 29–35; of B. Smith, 150n63; of truth, 17

real world, myth of, 95, 174n22

recession. *See* financial recession

reformism, of today, 118–19

Reinach, Adolf, 30

relativism, of hermeneutic weak thought, 106

representative democratic government, 107, 179n7

Return of History and the End of Dreams, The (Kagan), 37

revolution, 136–37; in hermeneutic communism, 3–4; through interpretation, 77–78; scientific, 84–86; world, 138–40

Rodrik, D., 162n57

Rorty, Richard: on freedom, 94; on hermeneutics, 6, 75; on interpreting Marx, 2–3, 141n2; on objective truth, 13; postmodern antifoundationalism of, 98, 103–6; on representative democratic government, 107, 179n7; on submitting philosophy to science, 14; on truth, 17–18

Rosen, Stanley, 75

Rubin, Robert, 161n51, 163n61

Sachs, Jeffrey D., 151n1

Sartre, Jean-Paul, 140

Schlesinger, Arthur M., 198n75

Schmitt, Carl, 52

Schürmann, Reiner, 78, 98–100

science: economics submission to, 60; Freud and, 82–84; history dictated by, 39, 150n68; human, 90–91, 173n18; Kuhn's view of, 84–86; within philosophy, 11–14, 150n63; within power structures, 12–17; sane philosophy based on, 30–31, 33; truth and, 42–43

scientific revolutions, Kuhn's view of, 84–86

Searle, John: on basic facts and structure, 30–32; debate with Derrida, 29, 33–36; on imperialistic nature of analytic philosophy, 149n61; National Humanities Medal awarded to, 11; on phenomenology, 30; realism of, 29–35; as servant of dominant political class, 12; on submitting philosophy to science, 11, 14; as voice of winners, 7 self-security, of liberalism, 51–58

Sennett, Richard, 53

September 11. *See* 9/11 attacks

silencing, by dialogue, 19

slums: as containers of indispensable specters for framed democracies, 69; growth of, 68, 168n87; reform of, 70, 170n91; as social community, 69; of Venezuela, 125; war against, 50–51, 64–71; weak in, 68–70; weakness of, 66

Smith, Ashley, 143n10

Smith, Barry, 36, 150n63

social function, communism as, 5–6

socialism, for twenty-first century, 181n20

socialist parties of Europe, 118–19, 180n17

social ontology, lack of emergency and, 29

social progress, of Chávez, 125, 188n41

solidarity, turning to objectivism from, 17–18

"Solidarity or Objectivity?" (Rorty), 17–18

South America: Cuba as symbol of resistance for, 133–34; democracy movement in, 131–33; U.S. military presence in, 129–32, 193n62

South American communism: as alternative to capitalism, 5–8, 119–51, 142n6; as emergency, 131–33; media attacks on, 122–23, 182n22; weakness of, 7

Soviet communism: crisis of, 115–16; end of metaphysics and, 111; ideal of development in, 4–5; ownership in, 116–17; scientific claims of, 114; violence of, 113–15, 179n9

specter, communism as, 109, 117–21

Specters of Marx (Derrida), 48–49, 109

speech acts, Austin's, 33

stability, myth of, 138

Stalin: Storia e critica di una leggenda nera (Losurdo), 179n9

state building, 52

status functions, 32, 35

Steele, J., 158n41

Stiglitz, Joseph, 7; Banco del Sur endorsement by, 128; on banks too big to fail, 164n66; on financial crisis of 2008, 58, 61–63, 163n61; on G20 summit, 161n53; on IMF, 164n68; on market change as increasing inequality, 66;

Uruguay, weak communism in, 126
useless shareholders, war against, 50–51
utopia, communism as, 117

Vargas Llosa, Mario, 122, 182n22
Venezuela: coup d'état (1992) in, 123–24; Cuban doctors in, 125, 187n39; elections in, 123–24, 183nn28–29; as emergency, 131–33; slums of, 125; social progress in, 125, 188n41; weak communism in, 6, 129, 142n6
violence: metaphysics end and, 111; of Soviet communism, 113–15, 179n9; of truth, 17–26
vulnerable employees, 68, 167nn81–82

wall building, 69, 168n89
war: humanitarian, 7, 143n10; metaphysics end and, 111; against slums, 50–51, 64–71; against weak, 64–71
War for Water. See La Guerra del Agua
Warnke, Georgia, 76
Washington Consensus, 63
weak, the, 6–7, 16; as emergency for framed democracies, 66, 69–70; fighting against, 64–71; hermeneutic weak thought as thought of, 107; history of, 40–41; Luther's defense

of, 80–82; as necessary workforce for framed democracies, 68–69; oblivion of, 38; philosophy favoring, 2; in Plato's cave allegory, 23–25; South American communism's defense of, 5–6; in urban slums, 68–70
weakened communism, 113–21; Chávez as example of, 127–28; Morales as example of, 127–28; as political alternative to framed democracy, 128
weakness: of communism, 3; of Iraq, 65–66; of slums, 66; of South American communism, 7; of weak thought, 97–98
weak thought: hermeneutics as, 95–107; in postmetaphysical condition, 3–4
wealth, disparities and inequalities in, 49–50, 66–68
weapons of mass destruction (WMD), 55–58
Weisbrot, Mark, 129, 188n43
Western capitalist democracies: dissatisfaction with, 49–50, 155n16; unchecked power of, 46; use of truth by, 24; value of democracy in, 136
"What Is the Real Death Toll in Iraq?" (Steele and Goldenberg), 158n41
Whitehouse, David, 151